Ve

Before It's Too Late

Dear General Goff:

Please accept my book "Before It's Too Late" as a small token of appreciation for participating in our SCVA Veteran's Day celebration.

It's an honor to have you as our guest speaker and thank you for your service to our country

Arnold Rosen

WWW. VETERANS PROFILES. US

Before It's Too Late

Our Aging Veterans Tell Their Stories

Arnold Rosen

To order additional copies of this book, contact:
Xlibris Corporation
1-888-795-4274
www.Xlibris.com
Orders@Xlibris.com
60933

Contents

World War II Era Veteran

Military Service Between The Wars

Korean War Era

Vietnam War Era

For my beloved Marylyn
And the joys of my life, Paul, Suzy, Cyrus and Gus

Also by Arnold Rosen

Machine Transcription, published by Media Systems, Inc. (a subsidiary of Harcourt Brace Jovanovich, Inc.), 1975.

Word Processing, published by Prentice-Hall, Inc., 1977, 1982.

Word Processing Keyboarding Applications & Exercises, published by John Wiley & Sons, Inc., 1981, 1985.

Language Skills for Transcription, published by Media systems, Inc. (a subsidiary of Harcourt Brace Jovanovich, Inc.), 1981.

Administrative Procedures for the Electronic Office, published by John Wiley & Sons, Inc., 1982, 1985.

Getting the Most out of Your Word Processor, published by Prentice-Hall, Inc., 1983.

Information Processing: Keyboarding Applications & Exercises, published by John Wiley & Sons, Inc., 1985.

Telecommunications, published by Harcourt Brace Jovanovich, Inc., 1987.

Office Automation and Information Systems, published by Merrill Publishing Co., 1987.

Desktop Publishing: Applications & Exercises, published by Harcourt Brace Jovanovich, Inc., 1989.

The Word Perfect Book, published by Harcourt Brace Jovanovich, Inc., 1989.

Using PFS: First Publisher (served as technical editor), published by Que Corporation, 1990.

Quick Reference Guide to Pagemaker 4.0—IBM Version, published by Wm. C. Brown, Publishers, 1992.

Quick Reference Guide to Coreldraw, 3.0, published by Wm. C. Brown, Publishers, 1993.

Quick Reference Guide to Word Perfect 5.1, published by Wm. C. Brown, Publishers, 1993.

Quick Reference Guide to Word Perfect for Windows, published by Wm. C. Brown, Publishers, 1993.

Quick Reference Guide to Lotus 1-2-3, Version 2.3, published by Wm. C. Brown, Publishers, 1993.

Quick Reference to Harvard Graphics, published by Wm. C. Brown, Publishers, 1993.

Quick Reference Guide to Pagemaker, Macintosh Version, published by Wm. C. Brown, Publishers, 1993.

Sea Gate Remembered: New York City's First Gated Community, published by Xlibris Corporation, 2004.

Keeping Memories Alive: Our Aging Veterans Tell Their Story, published by Xlibris Corporation, 2008.

Acknowledgements

The foundation of my success in preparing this book was the support and tolerance of someone closest to me—my beloved Marylyn. She has been incredibly supportive throughout this process. She offered me the love and encouragement I needed to carry me through the rigors of creating this book. To you, Marylyn, I say thank you.

I can't say enough about my childhood friend, writer and former editor of the *Potomac Review*, Eli Flam. We grew up together as childhood friends in our special community, Sea Gate, Brooklyn, New York. He read the entire manuscript (more than once), and I am indebted to him for his meticulous proofreading, guidance and suggestions throughout the writing and crafting of this book. I also express my gratitude to his wife, Lucy; a fine writer and editor in her own right, she weighed in cogently many times on many fronts.

I would also like to give a shout-out to Tom Schneck and Jim Quirk (Sun City Veterans Association officers), who connected me with many veterans who were willing to "tell their story." In addition, two talented Sun City friends—Brian Cripps and Roger Harrison—deserve special mention. Brian, a graphic artist genius, created the stunning cover and Roger, a photographic restoration expert, stepped up to fashion a website, www.veteransprofiles.us.

Finally, a special thanks to all the gracious veterans (plus their children and surviving spouses) who were willing to sit for an interview and shared their memories and some of their photos and memorabilia.

Introduction

My prior book—*Keeping Memories Alive: Our Aging Veterans Tell Their Story*—profiled 35 Sun City, South Carolina veterans, chiefly of World War II, the Korean War and the Vietnam War. It was published in 2008 and enthusiastically received by our local community and families of veterans across the country. Primed by articles and reviews in magazines and on the Internet, I was urged by many veterans and their families to do a follow-up edition. I couldn't refuse the challenge; the result is *Before It's Too Late: Our Aging Veterans Tell Their Stories*. Though the new book's profiles focus on the same three wars, they especially highlight the veterans of World War II because time is truly running out for our "greatest generation" to tell their stories.

Our World War II veterans are dying every day. For so many, this is a last chance to alert and remind current and future generations of a hard-won past epoch.

To the newcomers' children and grandchildren, this may present a chance to say "Thank you," and also, "We will remember, we will honor the freedom you have handed down to us." Some of the features in this new volume include:

- **Forty-seven profiles, featuring 30 from WW II, one from Korea War, one from between the wars and 15 from the Vietnam War;**
- **One hundred and eighty-eight photos and illustrations;**
- **First-hand descriptions of historic battles and events—the Battle of Iwo Jima, the Battle of the Bulge, the Battle of Leyte, the sinking of the USS Wasp, the liberation of the Dachau Concentration Camp,**

- **D-Day (June 6, 1944) and the India-China-Burma Theater, tied to "flying over the hump."**

The value of oral histories

The stories of long-past wars were largely left to historians and those in the upper echelons—civilian and military. Where are the oral histories for the veterans of the Civil War, the Spanish-American War, even World War I? Here we help to preserve this history related to our time. We want to get it in time to preserve it.

Recording the memories and oral histories of vets on a large scale these days does take place in Washington, D.C., by such organizations as the National World War II Museum and the Library of Congress. My efforts here are small scale, but I feel extraordinarily gratified and honored to interview the vets. The expression of thanks from the vets and their families are heartwarming and personally rewarding. In the interviews there is an immediate sense of personal connection. Eye-to-eye contact creates a comfort level for the veteran being interviewed and their stories pour forth without hesitation.

Oh, the stories they tell!

Their stories often are amazing, but always give a picture of what they went through—including taking part in major battles throughout the world. Some bailed out of burning bombers, abandoned large carriers when torpedoed and survived extended stays in open seas, were imprisoned in POW German stalags, participated in liberating Nazi concentration camps and braved the hardships of a death march during the coldest winter in European history.

Take **Charles Burton.** He served in the U.S. Navy aboard the USS Dixie—a destroyer tender that took part in 17 major battles in World War II as part of an armada of battleships, cruisers and carriers. Charles recalls: "We were the first American ship to go into the Philippine Islands. Our ship took a hit by a Japanese suicide bomber and sustained a six-foot hole below the water line. I was lucky to survive!"

During what was to be his last interview, Charles told me he never regretted his military service. "If I hadn't been married," he said, "I would have stayed in. I'm just thankful to be here. I served my country, survived the war and am happy to have these stories recorded." In 2008 he was diagnosed with congenital heart disease. Charles Earl Burton died on January 28, 2009—at his home in Sun City, two weeks after his interview.

Each story is revealing in an individual way. **Elaine Barlett** served in World War II as a Navy WAVE. Says she, "It was the best thing I could have ever done for myself." She is a courageous cancer survivor and her final impression of military service echoes that of other servicewomen I profiled. "I made the most of my opportunity to learn, grow and mature while enjoying the benefit of travel and meeting a diverse group of people and establishing long lasting friendships." Gwyneth Saunders and Rita Baker both retired Navy senior chiefs, express similar feelings. They, too, served with honor and distinction.

Not all of the profiles depict heroism, suffering or hardships. Some vets served in exotic places and never fired a shot or encountered danger. Their stories are worthy and deserving as they, too, put on the uniform and served their country in a patriotic way. They were the support that backed up the fighting force in every campaign and mission—from the cook, the clerk typist and the radio operator to the yellow- and red-shirters who served aboard aircraft carriers.

Humor and love in war

Bud Ledbetter installed and repaired radio and sonar equipment on the carrier USS Wasp before it was hit by three torpedoes from a Japanese sub. The captain ordered all crew to abandon ship. "There were 2,000 of us in the water," Bud recalled. "Approximately 300 were killed immediately. Some were in rafts; many others were floating aimlessly. While I was in the water I saw a sailor who was vomiting. He was really ill; his head was bobbing in the water. I grabbed hold of his life jacket and turned him on his back and pulled him along with me for the next hour-and-a-half. We were both finally loaded on a raft.

"I remember a little bitter humor in the midst of disaster. We had an executive officer who was a regulation guy, a stickler for proper uniform attire. White socks were a 'no-no' for him. Everyone had to wear black socks. There was a fireman in the water with us, an Olympic swimmer. The firemen (and the engineers) were the last ones to get off the ship. The Olympic swimmer swam near the raft where the executive officer was. Our stickler exec was on the life raft with 20 other guys who were all standing up. The raft was under water. They yelled to the swimmer, 'Come on aboard!' The fireman yelled back, 'I can't! I got white socks on!' And away he went."

John Guarneri and Lillian Billella had met and become best friends and sweethearts in early adolescence, and the way seemed clear to marriage—until Pearl Harbor. John left Brooklyn to enlist, but, determined to maintain the closeness of their relationship despite time and distance, wrote to Lillian almost every day from his duty station in the Pacific. These letters, endearing, affectionate and moving, also reflect the humor that was part of John's nature. Kept by John and Lillian's daughter, the letters are in their original hand-written envelopes with postage stamps that range from three to eight cents. The missives provide a different glimpse of the wide-ranging history of World War II.

New Caledonia
March 19, 1945

My dearest beloved sweetheart,

Hello darling: I love you. Writing you a few words dear, letting you know that I am well, and feeling in the best of health. I'm hoping to hear the same from you. Darling, I better hurry up and get home, for you may not want me anymore. Boy, I am slowly getting old. Today I am twenty-four years old.

Honey, if this damn war wasn't going on, we would be, by this time, the parents of at least three beautiful children. There is nothing slow about me, is there darling?

Oh well honey, some day them good old days will come for you and me. You know, dear, I was supposed to have bought a couple of cases of beer so we would have had a little party tonight. But the boys were one step ahead of me, and they bought it. It sure made me feel good in how they thought of me.

Incidentally dear, as I am writing, I feel as if I am sitting on air—ahem, I wonder why? I have had the blues all day long today, dear. Because I know that you must have been thinking of the times we were together. But honey, this war can't last forever, and some day we will be together again, just as we belong. I love you darling. I love you above all.

I still haven't received the package your mom sent me, but I hear that some boats came in so I hope they were on one of them. My darling, its one o'clock now, and the boys are still in bed. So I guess I will close now and put the light out.

My love and kisses to mom, pop and Salvatore and a million love kisses to you my beloved. I love you above all. Regards to all our mutual friends,

Affectionately as ever,
Your beloved,
I love you darling
Always and forever yours
Love,
Johnny

The coldest winter in Europe

Sixty-eight years later, **Earl Rogers** can still hear the machine guns. He was 21 when he parachuted into St. Mere Eglise, Normandy, France at 1:30 in the morning of June 6, 1944—six hours before the Normandy beach landing of D-Day. He watched in horror as some of his buddies drowned after they landed in fields flooded by the Germans. Many men in the 82nd Airborne unit were loaded down with their backpack, weapons and ammo and couldn't unstrap their parachute harness. Later Earl took part in liberating two concentration camps, at Dachau and Wobbelin. "Gosh, it was pitiful! The dead were lying everywhere. The ovens and everything were there, even skeletons of the people. Dysentery got others. The smell was awful."

During his tour of duty in WW II, Earl had many close encounters with death. "The worst battle I got into was during the Battle of the Bulge. I was about to freeze to death. It was 10 below zero—we didn't have a place to go. I was hoping and praying that a shell would hit and bust that frozen ground so that we could dig a hole to crawl into." Said he, "I'm glad I served my country and I am thankful I survived the war,"

Bob Holly also was in the Battle of the Bulge. The Ardennes Offensive (December 16, 1944-January 25, 1945) was a major German thrust launched towards the end of World War II through the forested Ardennes Mountains region of Belgium.

"My worst memories of combat were trying to survive from the cold. I was cold, cold, cold! We couldn't carry much equipment in our backpack for warmth. I didn't have a heavy coat, just a field jacket and I was freezing. The Army tried to ship us overcoats but they never arrived. We just had to huddle together to keep warm. I remember taking off my paratroop boots one night. My buddy told me, 'Don't do that, Bob, you'll freeze!' But my feet were so cold I took my boots off anyway to rub my feet. The next morning the boots were frozen solid and it took a long time to soften them up to get them back on. I'm still cold, after all these years! It's up here (Bob points to his head with his finger). Some guys were desperate. They were saying, 'Sometimes I wish I would shoot off a finger'—as they pointed a finger in the air—'so they could take me back to the States and get me out of here.'"

Fred Anderson was assigned to the 45th Infantry Division (the Thunderbirds) and the 179th Regiment. His company was walking on patrol during the big push toward Berlin.

"It was freezing cold. I wore long underwear top and bottom, an OD (olive drab) army shirt, a sweater, a field jacket and a parka with a wool knit cap under my helmet liner. (I didn't wear gloves because I couldn't shoot my rifle with gloves.) To protect my bottom I wore long underwear, OD pants and outside I had fatigues. Altogether I must have worn four layers of clothes."

As a result of the brutal winter of 1944-1945 in Europe, he developed frozen feet. He receives disability benefits for service-related ailments of malaria and peripheral neuropathy due to frozen feet from the service.

Students speak up

After "Keeping Memories Alive" was published, I received many requests from Lowcountry community groups, schools and professional organizations in South Carolina to give presentations. They wanted to see and hear these veterans "up close and personal." When I asked our vets if they would be willing to speak at these gatherings, there was no hesitation in their comebacks—they all responded with a resounding "Yes!"

At the Okatie Elementary School, the students loved the presentation. Lea Tierney, a 10-year-old 5th grader, said, "It's really interesting. It's something textbooks can't tell us." Many of the students said they didn't know about the hardships of World War II. "You had a lot of nerve," 11-year-old Savannah Oswald told Jean Crumlich when she spoke about life on the home front during WW II. "I just think that's pretty cool," said Savannah.

Yes, the kids were delighted with all the vets and surviving spouses that participated in this event. But all of us on the panel agreed that these kids were pretty terrific, too. We were very impressed that they were so well-mannered, polite, respectful and truly interested in our story. I later remarked that their teachers and parents were doing a good job. If these kids are the future of our country, we will be in good hands.

A parting word

Permit me to add another reason why I conducted interviews. One of the greatest privileges I've had in doing them has been meeting so many wonderful, decent men and women. Their aging bodies may be frail, their faces may be lined with wrinkles and marked with age spots, but they tell their stories with pride and humility. I humbly thank them for their interviews and their service to our country.

Arnold Rosen
Sun City—Hilton Head, South Carolina

WORLD WAR II ERA VETERANS

Fred "Andy" Anderson

Fred Anderson

Fred was born on June 12, 1925 in Fall River, Massachusetts. He graduated from Durfee High School in 1943 and went to work the next Monday at Firestone Tire and Rubber Company's huge plant in Fall River, which made barrage balloons and helmet liners for the war effort. Fred tried to enlist in May, before he graduated, but the Army rejected him because he had a heart murmur. He tried again in October 1943 and was accepted. Fred was sent to Camp Blanding, Florida, an Infantry Replacement Center. After basic, he went to Fort Meade, Maryland and then to Fort Pickett, Virginia, a staging center for troops being sent to Europe.

In his own words

We sailed from Newport News, Virginia, in a convoy of 123 ships, on March 13, 1944 and arrived in Palermo, Italy on April 4—23 days at sea. We took a train half way across Sicily and then boarded British trucks. The roads along the mountains were so rough we had to divert our route many times. We arrived at a replacement depot just south of Naples, where thousands of troops were pouring in. I was assigned as an infantryman to the 45th Infantry Division (the Thunderbirds) and Company E of the 179th Regiment. We were sent up to the front lines in Anzio to join the big push to Rome.

Q & A

AR: On patrol, what did you carry with you?

FA: I carried an M-1 rifle. I threw the bayonet away; I threw the gas mask away. I carried a real light pack. We didn't have to keep our bed rolls with us because "the kitchen" took care of those and brought them up to us at night wherever we stopped to sleep.

AR: You slept out in the open?

FA: Yes, we slept in foxholes. At Anzio they were still having air raids. The first night there we had an air raid and six people were killed. We slept in covered dugouts from then on. When we got to Rome—Rome was liberated on June 4, 1944—the Germans had just left and we rolled in without much resistance. We ended up on a hill overlooking the city. And a couple of days later, we listened to the radio to hear the news about the landing of troops on D-Day. The following week was my birthday, June 12th. I got a pass to Rome and toured the city with my buddy, visiting all the famous sights, including the Coliseum and the Vatican.

On June 18 I joined our division in Salerno for amphibious training. The entire division camped out in a huge field. We remained in Salerno until August 10. Then, on August 15 we landed in Southern France. We were constantly on patrol, mostly just walking and on rare occasions riding in trucks and on tanks in the French countryside.

On September 22 we crossed the Moselle River near Epinal, in northeast France, where we had quite a battle. In fact, there is a large cemetery in Epinal. We were in the Vosges Mountains, going up one hill and down the other—taking one town after the other.

Death up close

On October 16 I was sharing a foxhole I dug with my buddy, Robert Young. We covered it with logs and branches. One night it was late and we didn't have time to cover the hole, we just hunkered down in our sleeping bags and suddenly awoke to an artillery barrage. A tree, hit by a shell, burst and landed on my buddy. It killed him instantly. I was shoulder-to-shoulder in the foxhole with him when it struck. I reached over and tried to revive him but he wasn't moving. I was in shock. We had spent many months together. My company commander told me to stay with "the kitchen" for a few days to get away from the front lines.

AR: What do you mean, "the kitchen"?
FA: Every company has its own field kitchen, always in the rear away from combat.

In November we went through the Maginot Line (named after French Minister of Defense André Maginot, it was a line of concrete fortifications, tank obstacles, artillery casements, machine gun posts and other defenses constructed after World War I along France's borders with Germany and Italy). We got shoe pacs and were one of the few outfits that had winter parkas. It had a sheepskin liner and reversible cover. It was the coldest winter in Europe.

Author's note: Profiles of Bob Holley and Earl Rogers in this book describe the brutal winter they will never forget. American POWs, forced to evacuate their camps during the last days of WW II, were ill-prepared for the march because of inadequate clothing. Many died on the march from illness, exhaustion and frostbite.

K-rations

During that period, we slept out most of the time. It was very rare that we stayed indoors. Usually the kitchen would try to get us hot coffee and soup at night. We lived on K-rations while on patrol. A K-ration box had an inner box coated with wax. If you stood it on end, cut a hole in the bottom of the package and lit it, the wax would melt and retain the heat. Thus we could make a quick cup of coffee or heat some soup.

AR: What did K-rations consist of?
FA: We had three boxes for three meals. For breakfast we had a little tin of ham and eggs.
AR: How did you open the can?
FA: I had a tiny can opener in my back pack.
AR: What did you have for lunch and dinner?
FA: Lunch was a canned entree (processed cheese or ham), biscuits, 15 malted milk tablets or 5 caramels, sugar (granulated, cubed or compressed), salt packet, a 4-pack of cigarettes, a book of matches, chewing gum and a powdered beverage packet of lemon, orange, or grape flavor. Our supper unit consisted of canned meat, either chicken pate or pork luncheon meat, with carrot and apple or beef and pork loaf, commercial sweet chocolate bar plus a packet of toilet paper tissues, a 4-pack of cigarettes, chewing gum and a bouillon soup cube or powder packet. We carried that toilet paper up inside our helmet liner so it wouldn't get wet.

It was a rough winter but we did have some kind of breaks. Back in November we had a couple of weeks R & R in the rear, up in Epinal.

Into Germany

We had entered Germany in late November, going right through the Maginot Line. In January we entered small towns and stayed in some of the abandoned houses. We had a counter-attack and another best friend was killed. I remember we were going across a field and the snow was about two feet deep. We trudged across this field with our shoe pacs on. My buddy, who was right next to me, was shot by a German sniper. He went down and we were ordered to keep moving.

We had Christmas dinner on the line and I remember that I got about 20 packages, which I opened and shared with everybody. The Germans were on a hill near us and they were singing Christmas carols in German and we were on another hill—we could hear them. It was freezing cold. I wore long underwear top and bottom, an OD (olive drab) Army shirt, a sweater, a field jacket and a parka with a wool knit cap under my helmet liner. I didn't wear gloves because I couldn't shoot my rifle with gloves on. To protect my bottom I wore long underwear, OD pants and outside I had fatigues. Altogether I must have worn four layers of clothes. That's how I survived the winter.

**GIs, Company E, 179th Infantry, Germany, 1945;
Fred Anderson in first row, right**

We had another R & R in a little town called Dongieres, close to Epinal. The mayor thought we did so much for the town that he renamed it Learyville after our company commander, Capt. William Leary. The townspeople were so grateful to the men of Company E because of the clean-up performed by our men. This little French town was Learyville—at least as long as we were there.

In March 1945 we returned to combat with the 44th Division into Germany. On March 20 we crossed the Siegfried Line and entered Hamburg. On March 26 we crossed the Rhine at 2:30 in the morning. I was the boat commander, with a major and a lieutenant colonel aboard. We had sporadic firing but got across without any casualties. We encountered bitter fighting in Aschaffenburg. Lt. Schimpf, a wonderful squad leader in our company, was killed.

AR: Did you kill any German soldiers?

FA: Yes, seven; in different places . . . On April 12, 1945, the day
       Roosevelt died, we were in Nuremburg. It was a big city, heavily

bombed, but the Nazis fought like hell. We were fighting from street to street and house to house.

AR: How did you enter Nuremburg?

FA: We walked in. We walked most of the time. Nurnberg was leveled.

AR: Did you see any stray people walking around?

FA: A few, but the city was decimated.

AR: How did the civilians react to you? Did you have any contact with any of them?

FA: Well, the civilians were humble. They really didn't talk to us. One of my best friends was killed going into Nuremberg. We got so angry we entered one of the Nazi headquarters and tore the place up.

AR: Did you sleep in any of the houses in Nuremberg?

FA: Yes, we slept in many of the homes on our advance in Germany. I remember we approached a hospital the Germans had evacuated and found a kitchen that was loaded with food. We had a feast. In most of the houses that we stayed in (the farm houses) they had preserves, chicken, fresh eggs and ham.

AR: Were people there or did they abandon their homes?

FA: Sometimes they were there; other times we found the homes abandoned. We lived pretty well in the spring. We didn't bother eating rations any more. We threw our K-rations away. We kept only the goodies (toilet paper, cigarettes, chocolate bars). The Army was basically living off the land at that time. We took whatever we wanted.

Andy in chow line, Nuremberg, Germany, 1945

After Nuremberg we captured Munich. That was in rubble but it wasn't as much of a battle as Nuremberg. In Nuremberg it was street-to-street fighting—not so in Munich.

On May 1, 1945 we heard on the radio that Hitler was dead. The next day it snowed in Munich. I was transferred to the 9th Division to stay in Europe. The 45th Division was scheduled to come home and then go to Japan. We had 15,000 men in our division. I was transferred out because Gen. Eisenhower said that anybody who served in two theaters (of war) would not go to Japan. I had served in the Italian Theater and European Theater. The 9th Army stayed as an Army of Occupation. Actually the 45th Division got home before I did. I remained in Europe for the next five months with the 9th Division.

I had a week's leave in Switzerland and went to Berchtesgaden.

Author's note: The Berghof was Adolf Hitler's home in the Bavarian Alps near Berchtesgaden. Next to the Wolfsschanze this was the place where Hitler spent the most time during World War II. In late April 1945 the house was damaged by British aerial bombs and set on fire by retreating SS troops in early May.

In November I was assigned to the 1340th Combat Engineers and sent to Camp Baltimore in France. I went to Marseille and sailed home on the USS Monticello on December 21, 1945, enjoying Christmas dinner on board. When we were approaching New York harbor on New Year's Day we all crowded the top deck and it was great to see a giant *"**Welcome Home, Well Done**"* sign on the sloping grass perimeter of Fort Hamilton on the Belt Parkway in Brooklyn. In the harbor that morning we saw the Statue of Liberty. At the pier I walked down the gangplank; the Red Cross was there with a bottle of milk.

Discharged

I was discharged on January 7, 1946, returned home and went back to my job at Firestone. I worked for about six months, then enrolled in the University of Massachusetts under the GI Bill, majoring in forestry. I lived on the outskirts of Fort Devens; there was no housing available near UMass for all the veterans. I then transferred to Amherst and spent three years there in veterans' housing. I graduated in June 1950 with a BS degree in forestry but then couldn't get a full-time job; I picked tobacco and had odd jobs. Eventually I returned to Firestone and got my old job back.

In March 1951 I was offered a job with the Navy Hydrographic Office in Suitland, Maryland. We made hydrographic (oceanographic) charts for the Navy. I worked for the government as a civil servant. We moved from Massachusetts to the Washington, D.C. suburbs. I worked there for 25 years and then transferred to the office of the Assistant Secretary of Defense for Health Affairs. It was a tri-service group involved in the development of computer systems for hospitals. I worked there for five years and then retired, in 1981.

Moving on

At that time I separated from my first wife and moved to Hilton Head, South Carolina. I met Bess Lovelace and we married in 1981. I took a real estate course and Bess opened a cleaning business. We both got jobs as caretakers at Rose Hill Plantation in South Carolina. We lived in an apartment in the Carriage House next to the Plantation House at Rose Hill. The following spring we left Rose Hill and moved to Charleston. Bess became involved in selling her special beans at the market in Charleston. It was so successful she expanded into 17 different products, all sold at the Charleston market. We were in Charleston for about seven years. Leaving in 1994, we went to Amelia Island, Florida. We visited a friend in Hilton Head who told us about Sun City, visited it, found a home to our liking and moved in 2004.

Three close calls

I was proud of serving my country in the military. It was a tough tour of duty in Europe; I wouldn't want to go through it again. I found the relationship with my buddies in Company E enriching and positive. In fact, when my first son was born I named him after my buddy who was killed in my foxhole, Robert Young Anderson. That was my first close call.

The second was on patrol on a side of a snow-covered hill in Germany. I knelt down and fired a clip of ammo at an enemy position to see if we could induce enemy fire. We got return fire and it hit me right in the helmet. German machine guns opened up and luckily I was kneeling down. An incoming round grazed my helmet and made a dent in the front. The force knocked me down. I was dazed, with severe ringing in my ears; I thought I was hit. I took the helmet off and walked away, thankful that I was still alive.

On my last close call I was on patrol and behind a tree. I reached around to get some water from my canteen but I couldn't undo the canteen from my belt clip. Finally I pulled it around and found a large wedge of shrapnel cut through the canteen. I didn't know where or when this happened. My best guess was that a piece of shrapnel from an explosion pierced my canteen and blocked the shrapnel from my body. I'm thankful to be alive and to be able to tell my story.

Sun City

Fred enjoys his retirement with Bess in Sun City. As a result of the brutal winter of 1944-1945 in Europe, he developed frozen feet and uses a walker and a cane. He receives disability benefits for service-related malaria and peripheral neuropathy (damage to the peripheral nervous system that transmits information from the brain and spinal cord to all parts of the body) due to the frozen feet.

Andy in Sun City, 2009

Fred Anderson received the following:

* Good Conduct Medal
* Victory Medal
* European Middle Eastern Theater Campaign Ribbon with Bronze Service Arrowhead
* Bronze Star Medal

A fond reunion

In September 1997 Fred attended a very special reunion with three of his buddies of the 45th Infantry Division in Anaconda, Montana. Their story was featured in an article in the *Anaconda Leader* (on September 24). An excerpt follows:

After 52 years and three recent attempts, four men who relied on each other in life and death as young men came together to share their lives and memories with one another at Fairmont Hot Springs. Three staff sergeants of the 45th Infantry Division stationed in Europe during World War II, Fred "Andy" Anderson, Duane Simonds and Bernie Lew came together this week to visit with their company commander, Bill Leary of Anaconda to whom they lovingly refer to as "Captain."

The four had been stationed together throughout Europe in the final days of WW II landing in Sicily, Salerno, Anzio and Southern France and they were involved in the liberation of Dachau Concentration Camp near Munich, Germany. They had been part of an award winning division which received our nation's highest award for gallantry in combat, the Medal of Honor. The division had more days, 511 total, in combat than any other division and had the second highest number of casualties—27,553 of dead, wounded or missing in action.

"We bonded, and we owe our lives to each other," said Bill. "There's a camaraderie that we share that people who have not been through similar life or death situations would not understand. That is why we came back together after all this time."

Walter Bachman

Walter Bachman

Walter was born on January 31, 1920 in Brooklyn, New York. After graduating from Tilden High School in 1938, he enrolled in Brooklyn College to pursue a civil engineering degree. But after a year, he left to join the National Guard, and was sent to Fort McClellan in Anniston, Alabama.

In his own words

At Fort McClellan, a new Army base was under construction by private contractors. If you were skilled, the Army would allow you to work for the contractors. I signed on and worked during my off time to earn some extra money.

While stationed in Alabama I often corresponded with Rosemary Wilson back in Brooklyn. She wrote that she would like to come down to visit me. I really couldn't afford to pay for her trip at first, but then I won $300 in a crap game and was happy to pay for her trip. I always would say, "I won my bride in a crap game!" We were married in Anniston.

Rosemary chimes in: "Walter is Jewish and I'm Irish, so we were married in Alabama. He asked me, 'Don't you want to have a wedding by a priest?' I said, 'No, we'll do that at another ceremony so that my mother and father can attend.' It was a simple ceremony in Alabama, in May 1941.

"When Walter entered the Air Corps and began training, Robin, our first baby, was born, in 1942. Walter was at Altis Air Force Base in Oklahoma. I took our six-week-old baby to see him graduate and receive his wings. Our second baby, Bonnie, was born in 1944."

My early years

My father died when I was five years old. My mother and I moved in with my aunt and uncle, who had no children. We all lived together during my childhood years, except my uncle died shortly after we moved in; my mother had to go to work, and later, as the only male in the household, I left the National Guard to find work and help support my mother and aunt.

It was very hard to get a job at that time. I remember waiting in line at a federal shipyard in New Jersey from 4 in the morning until 6:30 a.m., when they finally opened the gate. The only thing the guard gave us was an application. No interviews; no job offers. I was furious.

Just after I got married, I convinced the interviewer at Sperry Gyroscope Corporation in Brooklyn's Bush Terminal that though I had no experience working with or assembling their products, I was a fast learner and hard worker. The company took a chance and hired me. I learned to use the micrometer and worked on the assembly line, building Norden bombsights. Later, in my B-24, we used the Norden on missions. I might even have used one I put together in Brooklyn!

My supervisor at Sperry was a highly skilled German mechanic named Jake. He was a perfectionist and a curmudgeon. Jake taught me all aspects of machinery on the assembly line. When the war broke out we had to increase production. I was called back into active duty in 1941 and reported to Camp Upton in Yaphank, Long Island.

In the Air Corps

The Army was conducting tests for bomber flight crews for the Air Corps. I passed and was sent to San Antonio, Texas, where I took another battery of tests to determine my aptitude and skill level. I was selected to become a bomber pilot and went to a variety of air bases for further training—from Texas to bases in Pine Bluff, Arkansas and Coffeyville, Kansas to Altus Army Air Field in Oklahoma, and to B-24 training in Mountain Home, Idaho, near Boise.

Walt in cockpit of trainer, 1942

Author's note: Construction of Mountain Home Army Air Field began in November 1942 and officially opened August 7, 1943. The 396th Bombardment Group (Heavy) was the first unit assigned and its planned mission was to train crews for the B-17. However, before the first B-17s arrived, plans for the field changed and the 396th was transferred to Moses Lake, Washington. Mountain Home airmen began training crews for the B-24 Liberator. The first group was the 470th Bombardment Group (Heavy), which trained at Mountain Home from May 1, 1943 until January 1944, when the unit moved to Nevada. The 490th Bombardment Group (Heavy) replaced the 470th and trained B-24 crews until it deployed to England in April 1944. The 494th Bombardment Group then replaced the 490th, once more training Liberator crews.

B-24s to the fore

I completed B-24 pilot training and went to Fairfield Air Base, Fairfield, California. It is now the home of Travis Air Force Base. I met my crew and none of them were ever in a B-24 before, except my engineer who was building B-24s at Consolidated Aircraft in Willow Run, near Detroit.

Author's note: More B-24s were built than any other American airplane. It edged out the B-17 on most performance criteria (speed, range, bomb load). Its crewmen claimed 2,600 enemy aircraft shot down. With its great range, it performed anti-sub work in the Atlantic and heavy bomber support in the Pacific.

We flew our own plane overseas from Fairfield. We landed at Hawaii, then went to the island of Kauai, which became our training quarters. We trained as a group and were officially assigned to the 494th Bomb Group, 867th Squadron.

Our crew flew 40 missions in the Asiatic-Pacific Theater. We flew 10-hour flights over the water and encountered Japanese attack planes only when we neared our targets.

Walt Bachman (front row, right) and flight crew

We used to land on the Island of Leyte in the Philippines. The air strip was a steel mat put up by the Seabees. I got hit pretty bad one day. Part of the plane's tail was gone, my number 3 engine was also gone—which is where you get your hydraulic for brakes. We had 10 in a crew—pilot, co-pilot, bombardier, navigator (all officers) plus the engineer, radio operator and the rest were gunners.

Q & A

AR: What was your altitude during your missions?

WB: Usually 10,000 feet.

AR: Did you do any strafing?

WB: Only one time when we were in an operation to take out Japanese battleships and cruisers. We swooped down and did "skip bombing." We came in and bounced the bombs on the water toward the target. We were on duty until after the atomic bomb was dropped on Hiroshima.

Back to the States

When the war ended, I received orders to return to the States. I started my journey home on October 5, 1945 aboard a troop ship. Our planes were too beat-up to fly across the ocean. We docked in San Francisco on October 28, and I returned to Rosemary in Brooklyn for a much-needed leave. I was honorably discharged on January 1, 1946 at Fort Dix, New Jersey with the rank of captain.

I was offered a position as operation officer for the Far East Air Force, with the rank of major. The position really called for a lieutenant colonel. I did not accept the offer, which was extended to four of my other flight leaders (all captains). They all declined, too. We were anxious to get home and become civilians.

When I returned home I applied for a position with the New York City Police Department as a pilot. I actually took the exam for the NYPD while working for Sperry before the war. When I inquired about a position, I learned that I had passed with flying colors and was immediately hired as an NYPD pilot. I flew a variety of aircraft including single and two-engines Grumman amphibious planes out of Floyd Bennett Field. I left the Police Department after working five years.

Q & A

AR: What was your primary job after the service? Which job did you work at longest?

WB: I worked for Harvey Radio in Manhattan as a sales manager and vice president and subsequently went into the electronic business for 20 years. I had a building on Long Island. The name of my company was Conco—Connecting Components Corporation. We sold specialized connectors for all components on an airplane.

I retired and we went to Florida in 1982 and lived there for 20 years. We have been coming to Hilton Head, South Carolina for about 37 years to visit our daughter and grandchildren. We moved to Sun City in 2005.

Final impressions of military service

I believe the military did more for me than any schooling I ever had. The service gave me a perspective on life. It was remarkable experience and I will never forget the people that I met and served with.

I remember the day we flew our 40th and last mission. In my outfit, you were required to complete 40 missions and were allowed to select your 40th. Usually, I discussed the missions beforehand with my crew, but in this particular case, I made up my mind that I was going to take the 40th no matter where it was headed because whatever got me to 39, would get me to 40, and to be blunt, I am not a big believer in fate.

The night before the CQ (charge of quarters) came in and whispered, "Captain, there is a snooper mission to the Indian Ocean." On a snooper mission, it was weather reconnaissance and observing. This was to be a weather mission to the Japanese Islands, for a forecast the Air Corps wanted. When the CQ left, the other three officers in my crew came over and asked me, "Where are we going?" I didn't tell, but they instinctively knew how I felt. Later I told them that our mission was a snooper mission to the Indian Ocean. Nobody challenged me. I believed they felt, that as our pilot, if I got them to 39 missions, they would trust me to "get them home."

We completed our mission without incident and headed home. As we approached our field, one of our gunners came up to me and asked, "Captain, on our approach, are you going to buzz the field?" (Buzzing the field is flying low over the field—a maneuver that frightens all, except the pilots, and a tradition for pilots on their last mission.)

I told him I would think about it as we neared our base. I discussed it with my co-pilot and decided to make a routine approach and landing. I was thankful that I had completed all 40 missions and brought our crew home safe. For our final mission I made a routine landing. I had nothing to prove!

Walter received the following decorations and citations:

* Distinguished Flying Cross
* Asiatic-Pacific Theatre Campaign Ribbon
* American Theatre Campaign Ribbon
* Air Medal with 7 Oak Leaf Clusters
* American Defense Service Medal
* World War II Victory Medal
* Philippine Liberation Ribbon

Walt and Rosemary in Coffeeville Air Base, Kansas, 1943

Walt and Rosemary in Florida, 1990

Walt's co-pilot, John Crawford, pays him a visit in Sun City, 2007

Elaine Barlett

Elaine Barlett

Elaine Barlett was born on December 24, 1923 in Swea City, Iowa—a small town settled by Swedes. She graduated from Swea City High School in June 1941 as valedictorian, but jobs were scarce. She worked in a "5 & Dime" store and at the switchboard of the local telephone company, where she answered with, "Number please?" and plugged the cable into the switchboard panel.

Elaine's short-term goal was to make enough money to get away from home. She also took the State Civil Service exam. She excelled in speed typing, but no typing jobs were available. She left Swea City and found a job in Forest City, Iowa, headquarters of Winnebago Industries, which manufactures motor homes. She roomed with other girls and found it was a bare existence;

they had to pool their money and sometimes didn't have enough to eat. After the Pearl Harbor attack, Elaine returned to Swea City.

In her own words

Navy posters

One of my many part-time jobs was working in the local post office. I would look at all the World War II patriotic posters and liked the Navy poster best. I thought: Here was a way to get away from home (I couldn't afford to go to college) and to be independent and yet have some control of my own life. It was a chance for me to make a decent salary and to know that I would be taken care of.

The recruiting station was in Des Moines. I went there at least twice on the train and stayed overnight to take the necessary physicals. I was sworn into the WAVES (Women Accepted for Volunteer Emergency Services) on December

24, 1943. Following orders I went by train with lots of other enlistees to Hunter College's Bronx campus in New York City. Hunter gave up several classrooms to accommodate Navy courses. I was enrolled in the Radio Operator Program and took courses in radio theory, typing and Morse code, in which I excelled. We went through several stages of physical training, too, at the Hunter gym, and lived in high-rise apartment buildings near the campus that had parquet floors. We had to steel-wool-clean the floors every week, before inspection. Years later I read that the Navy had to replace all the parquet floors because they were ruined by scrubbing with steel wool. We lived on the sixth or seventh floor and had two girls to an apartment with one bathroom, where we slept on bunk beds and had no other furniture. We marched on brick streets to and from our living quarters to school. I was part of a singing platoon that congregated in the morning and marched while singing songs.

Q & A

Arnold: How long did the Hunter College boot camp training last?

Elaine: It lasted about five months because we did not get shipped out right away. It took a long time to get our complete uniforms. Instead of issuing them at once, the Navy gave us a money allowance that was supposed to cover the basic things that we needed. We never had our uniforms all at one time. Instead, about once a week we would go to the "Ship's Store" and see what they had available.

Arnold: After boot camp, what was your rank?

Elaine: I was seaman 3rd class.

Arnold: What was your next assignment?

Elaine: The Navy asked you where you would like to go. I thought I would like to work on the East Coast, but the Navy assigned me to Radio School at the Naval Training School at Miami University in Oxford, Ohio. We had to wait for new classes to start, so I stayed at the Hunter facility and stood guard duty at the main gate, often guiding visitors throughout the building to the offices and classrooms. We even escorted visitors underneath the buildings through a labyrinth maze of huge underground tunnels in the basements and sub-basements.

At Oxford, we took Morse code, typing, radio theory and electronic wiring. My advanced typing class was a real challenge but I was able to achieve 90 words a minute with no errors. We had 30 to 35 students in a class and lived in old University of Miami barracks.

Elaine at University of Miami, Oxford, Ohio, 1944

**Graduation exercises, U.S. Naval Training School (Radio),
University of Miami of Ohio, July 1944**

Taking on Japanese Transmissions

My next assignment was at Supplementary Station School (D/F and Intercept), Bainbridge Island, Port Blakely, Washington. I traveled on the ferry across

Puget Sound to reach the base. At the main gate I requested permission to come aboard. Even though I did not board a ship, it is Navy tradition when you report to a new base to "request permission to come aboard."

On base, I noticed an array of high antennas and huge towers. I wondered what I was in for. When I made a phone call in the barracks I could hear background sounds of strange code transmissions through the phone headset. The transmissions had so much power that they resonated into the phone lines. During class we were told that we were going to learn a new code to supplement our knowledge in Morse code. We started slowly with pencil and slowly built up our speed receiving the code until we transitioned into typing the code as it came over our headsets. There were several drop-outs who couldn't keep up with the requirements and/or the stress of learning this new code.

I remained in the States as an intercept operator 3rd class. At that time, during the war, the Navy did not deploy WAVES overseas in combat zones. My primary job was copying code.

We worked in a secure building at Bainbridge Island, intercepting and copying Japanese transmissions. These messages were from shore to ship or ship to ship. The high-powered antennas allowed us to listen in to their broadcasts throughout most of the Pacific Ocean. We sent the copied messages to a decoding center. We each had our own receiver on a desk with a typewriter. You could detect a new Japanese transmission as they would transmit "V's di di di dahhh . . . .". The Japanese kept a pretty uniform schedule. They would broadcast shore to ship their orders for the day and every Japanese ship would receive their own messages. We had both Navy men and women working in the radio room. I still keep in touch with some of the WAVES I worked with.

It was an erratic schedule. We worked long hours with little sleep and drank lots of coffee to keep awake. Many of the radiomen and women dropped out because they couldn't take the pace and the pressure of constant monitoring and copying of code.

"SAVE O SAVE"

After a while, you got to know the particular idiosyncrasies of the sender and could identify him without having met him. I would copy the same sender for a long time, which had a real advantage because you just knew (especially if he had a stutter in his transmission) who he was. On my last day I was listening to a transmission and the Japanese sender broke into English (in Morse code): "SAVE O SAVE! WE ARE SINKING!" His ship was in the midst of battle and it was going down. I almost felt like I was losing a friend.

When the war ended the Navy didn't keep us for long. I was sent back to Great Lakes Naval Station in Illinois and was discharged with the rank of radioman 2nd class. I went back to Iowa and then to Michigan, to get married. I had met my husband-to-be—Peter Steffens—in the service, where we did the same work. We moved to Paw Paw, Michigan, where our son, Jeff, was born. I worked for Upjohn Company as an accountant in the Export Division. Peter was a tool and die man for Sentinel Radio and Mad Man Muntz (an electronic retail chain). We later moved to Chicago and bought a home in Glenview, Illinois. The marriage ended in 1969. During the next five years I worked and went to school at Indiana University.

I married Jack Barlett in 1974. We lived in Fort Wayne and Chicago. Jack received an assignment as a manufacturer's engineer and transferred to Spain and then to Mexico. He retired in 1997. Desirous of a warm climate, we moved to Arizona and lived there until 2003, when we moved to Sun City—Hilton Head.

Final impressions of military service

It was the best thing I could have ever done for myself. So many girls get married just to get away from home. Well, I didn't get married for quite a while. I was having a great time in the WAVES, made a lot of friends and got to travel to a lot of places. At Hunter College, we would go into the city any time we weren't on duty and go to theatres and shows and dine in our favorite restaurants. I remember at the Roosevelt Hotel, they held Sunday afternoon tea dances. It was like singing Karaoke-style. The band leader would ask anyone to get up and sing. I remember I got up and sang with the band.

A courageous cancer survivor

Following cancer surgery three years ago, Elaine has limited social activities. She keeps busy by reading and writing and is blessed with good neighbors and a close circle of friends.

Elaine at home with mom, dad and sister, 1945

Elaine at home in Sun City, 2009

George Baronowski

George Baronowski

George was born on January 2, 1921 in Brooklyn, New York and lived in the borough's Greenpoint section. He graduated from Queens Vocational High School in 1939. When World War II broke out, George, who was working for the Mobil Oil Company, wanted to join the Air Corps, but failed the test because of vision problems. Attending church one day in

Brooklyn, he met a Merchant Marine cadet who suggested he apply to the Merchant Marine Academy. George did so, was accepted and became a student cadet at Kings Point, Long Island in New York on July 15, 1942. (His older brother, Stanley, went into the U.S. Army, and younger brother, Henry, into the Marines.)

In his own words

When I entered the academy, buildings were under construction. We had a two-year cram course in 18 months that involved assignments aboard vessels at sea—the only school to do so—as well as classroom work, especially in marine engineering. During the war, we lost 142 cadets while training at sea. My job on the ship for these missions was as an engineer cadet in the engine room. I worked with an oiler, fireman and an engineer who was in charge of the watch and got signals from the bridge.

My first assigned sea duty was on October 10, 1942. I was sent by train to San Diego and boarded a brand new troop ship, the SS Mormacport, while they still were working on it. We sailed to the South Pacific, delivering U.S. Marines and war materials to Wellington and Aukland, New Zealand; Noumea and Nepoui, New Caledonia; and Bora Bora, in the Society Islands. When we dropped troops off in Auckland, I marched with them down the street. At that time all the New Zealanders were in Africa, fighting the Germans under Field Marshal Rommel.

We picked up wounded and handicapped U. S. Marines from Latouka and Suva in the Fiji Islands and transferred them back across the Pacific to the Naval Hospital in San Diego. Then we sailed for repairs and reloading to San Francisco. On April 8, 1943 I was reassigned back to the Merchant Marine Academy in Kings Point for advanced training that included propulsion systems, electrical systems, refrigeration systems and necessary shop work to successfully operate a sea-going vessel. On June 15, I received the USMMA Scholastic Attainment Award. On January 3, 1944 I received a commission as an ensign in both the U.S. Maritime Service and the U.S. Naval Reserve.

Other sea duty tours

* From February 1 to May 2, 1944, as 3rd engineer aboard the SS Uruguay. (See the subheadings below, **"Danger at sea"** and **"Meeting my brother in Liverpool,"** for highlights of this mission.)
* From June 2 to November 2, 1944, as 3rd engineer aboard the SS Mormacswan, carrying cargo between South America and the United States along the Atlantic Coast (promoted December 4 to lieutenant junior grade in the U. S. Maritime Service).
* From January 17 to March 15, 1945, as 2nd engineer aboard the SS Mormacrio, carrying war supplies to U.S. armed forces. We sailed along the coast through the Panama Canal to Portland, Oregon. Upon assignment completion in Portland, I crossed the U. S. by train to return to New York.
* From May 1 to September 4, 1945, as 2nd engineer aboard the SS Ferdinando Gorges, a lend-lease cargo ship, to be transferred in Seattle to the Soviet government.

After completing each voyage, I was required to fill out numerous reports pertaining to the mission and submit these reports to our captain. I sailed on many ships—troop ships, cargo ships and oil tankers—during the war. The most dangerous ship, of course, was an oil tanker. If you ever got hit, boom! Goodbye, you are gone!

I applied for discharge from the War Shipping Administrator and received it on May 28, 1946. Upon receiving as well my Certificate of Continuous Service in the Merchant Marine, I had officially completed my World War II active duty. I remained in the Naval Reserve until October 19, 1953, when I received my honorable discharge from the Navy.

Back to civilian life

I married Julia Dzwonczyk on January 9, 1944 at St. Stanislaus Kostka Church in Brooklyn, on graduating from the Maritime Academy because as a cadet midshipman, you could not be married while attending classes. We spent our honeymoon at Lake Placid, New York.

Julia and George, circa 1943

Wedding, January 9, 1944

When I returned from the service I had my marine engineering license and was rehired at Mobil Oil as a steam and diesel engineer. I remained with Mobil for 33 years. When they closed their plant in Brooklyn, I was the last person on the job (as an engineer); they disappointed me, because management had promised that I would remain. Instead they made me a field engineer and wanted to send me to Michigan. I really couldn't move because of family obligations. I was at a crossroads in my life, whether to remain or leave Mobil.

At home one day, my oldest daughter, Barbara (the others are Christina and Debra), was looking in the newspaper, *Newsday*, and told me, "Dad, they're looking for an engineer at the Merchant Maritime Academy!" I was a member of the Academy Alumni and knew several of the officers. I called a friend who was well-connected with the Academy. He strongly suggested that with my solid engineering background, I should apply for the job. I did so, went for an interview and was hired.

I quit Mobil on a Friday, spent two days—Saturday and Sunday—in retirement and the next day, Monday, I reported to work at the Academy as an engineer. We sold our home in Brooklyn and bought a house in Kings Point, on Long Island. After working as an engineer for six years the job became very time-consuming as I put in many hours of overtime without overtime compensation. I was hoping for a change to lessen my work load. As luck would have it, the Academy had an opening for a general foreman, to take care of the grounds with a staff of 88 men. I applied and was hired. The common grounds and landscaping had to be immaculate for the ceremonies and events at the academy.

Moving on

I finally retired from the Academy at Kings Point in 1985, and we bought a home in Florida. We had so many good friends who used to live in Brooklyn and had moved to Florida, near us in Jensen Beach, on the Atlantic coast. We had marvelous times getting together with each other and enjoyed an active social life. But over time our friends were moving or dying—six couples passed away.

Daughter Barbara was living in Sun City, South Carolina. We bought a home near her and moved to Sun City in March 2004. We liked it here but unfortunately my wife died in 1992 and I have been a widower all these years. I belong to the Veterans Association, the Widow and Widower's Club and I help with the newsletter. But now I have some "old age ailments" that slow me down. At 88 years old, I was proud to be inducted into the Sun City Veterans Association's "Over 85 Club."

Impressions—and dangers

I enjoyed my military career. It was exciting but quite dangerous. Statistics show that one out of 26 died in the Merchant Marine during World War II (largely from sub attacks). You would think that the Marine Corps had the biggest percent of casualties but they had one out of 34 to die in combat. I met so many good buddies while serving and I am thankful I survived the war.

When I graduated from the Academy, I was assigned as a 3rd engineer to a troop ship, the Uruguay, a huge, converted cruise ship. This was my first duty as an officer during the war. We picked up U.S. Army troops in Boston. As we left the harbor on the morning of February 12, 1944, our generator burned out. We had no electricity. We were towed back into the pier and unloaded all the troops. We remained in Boston for two weeks until General Electric sent technicians to install a new generator. We reloaded the ship, the troops returned and on February 28 we sailed out to rendezvous with a convoy of cruisers and destroyers bound for Europe. We had one alert where the cruisers were dropping depth charges to take out German U-boats lurking under our convoy. I was down in the engine room and could hear the sound of the depth charges exploding near us. It shook the whole ship. The dust and debris from the pipes and ducts above me was trickling down my face like a river from the vibration of the depth charges. Did we get them? Nobody knows! They didn't tell us. But the wolf packs were out there.

Author's note: The wolf packs had a devastating impact on Allied shipping. The U-boats usually hunted in what was called "wolf packs" where multiple submarines would stay close together, making it easier for them to sink a specific target. The U-boat was essentially a launch platform for its main weapon, the torpedo, though they also laid mines. By the end of the war, almost 3,000 Allied ships (175 warships; the rest were merchant ships) were sunk by U-boat torpedoes.

Meeting my brother in Liverpool

During the convoy in 1944, the Britannic, a British troop ship, was behind the Uruguay. In March we went up the Mersey River to Liverpool and docked astern the Britannic. I had off watch and was authorized free gangway (to leave or return any time). I disembarked from the Uruguay and when I passed the troop ship Britannic along the dock, I heard someone call down to me, "Hey George!" I was amazed for it was my brother Stanley, who was in the U.S. Army's 8th Armed Division. I came to the gangway of the Britannic and tried to go up to see my brother but the U.S. Army MPs stopped me. An Army major came to the end of the gangplank to see what was happening and after convincing the major and showing him my ID cards, I was permitted up to the top of the gangplank. They announced on the ship's loudspeaker for Stanley to come to there.

We finally met and hugged with all troops along the railing shouting, "What's going on?" We talked for about an hour and then they made me leave because they were about to unload the troops. I waited at the end of the gangplank and when my brother came down I marched to the train station with him but could not enter. I went to the nearest telegraph office and cabled my parents, "ARRIVED SAFELY, MET STANLEY," hoping to get word to my brother's wife, Lottie, and my Julia. I learned later that all the telegram said was, "ARRIVED SAFELY." The censors in England removed the words, "MET STANLEY," for security reasons.

George, Julia, Lottie and brother Stanley, circa 1945

My two brothers survived and returned home to raise families. Stanley also worked at the Mobil Oil company plant in Brooklyn and Henry moved to Hawthorne, California and was employed by the Department of Parks.

George in Sun City, 2009

Robert Blust

Robert Blust

Bob was born on September 5, 1924 in Council Bluffs, Iowa. His family struggled through the Depression; his father was laid off by the Union Pacific Railroad, although rehired later. Prior to the Japanese attack on Pearl Harbor in 1941, his older brother enlisted in the Army Air Corps. Then, in the spring of 1942, while still in high school, Bob received a letter from the Army inviting those over 19 years old to take a test in Omaha to become a cadet in the Army Air Corps Reserve. Bob passed the test and was sworn in on his mother's birthday—December 7.

In his own words

On February 23, 1943 I received a letter asking me to report to the Omaha Post Office to be shipped out to Jefferson Barracks and begin basic training. At Jefferson we were put in canvas tents with a small stove. We received shots that made me perspire, while being chilled in the cold February weather. Though practically every one of us got sick, we completed basic and were ready to ship out. But at the railroad station they took our temperatures; I had 102, was diagnosed with pneumonia and sent the hospital. I was there for a month before assignment at Jamestown College in North Dakota for six months.

Author's note: Jamestown College received federal funding for an Army air cadet training program during World War II. In 1939, a federal law was passed allowing the War Department to send servicemen to colleges and universities for academic and flight training. JC joined other schools across the nation participating in the Army Air Cadet Training Program—the first four months of cadet training consisted of courses of English, geography, mathematics, history, physics, medical aid and physical training.

While at the college, I went out on a double date with a GI buddy who set me up with a blind date from Jamestown, home on leave from nursing training in the military. I kept thinking of her after I was shipped out to Santa Ana, California—a processing center that conducted tests interviews, physical and mental exams to determine whether we would be pilots, bombardiers or navigators.

A medical test revealed a spot on my lungs, but an x-ray the next day cleared me. However, I missed the start of my class and had to lay around for another 30 days for the next class. I completed the course and was assigned to flight school in Ryan Field, Tucson, Arizona where I was selected to become a pilot. After primary training, I soloed on a Ryan PT-22 plane. My next station was at Minter Field, California, where I flew PT-2 single-engine planes—and ended up with an instructor who was always cursing and bad-mouthing everything I did. I asked my superior officer to assign me another instructor. He took me up for a check flight, then told me, "It's a good thing you came to me, because this instructor wrote you up and was going to kick you out of the service." He assigned me a new instructor and I graduated with flying colors.

Bob, first row, right, Ryan Field, Tucson

A busted nose

On my final advanced flight training segment I was assigned to fly the "Bamboo Bomber"—a twin-engine airplane made of metal and wood. The wood was glued onto the plane. I completed this segment successfully, graduated as a 2nd lieutenant and was assigned in 1944 to Bergstrom Field in Austin, Texas, used for pilots flying invasion gliders and the twin-engine Douglas C-47s. There were too many students, so I got held back until the next class was formed. To get flying time, pilots had to ride in gliders as co-pilots (you had to fly at least four hours to get flight pay). Once I was flying in a night formation tow when the tow line broke off. We had no landing lights, and it was pitch black outside. The pilot made a circle over a clearing and we landed in a field. The pilot had the wheel to brace himself upon impact but I had nothing to brace against. Wham! I went up against the wheel on the right side and busted my nose. At the hospital the flight surgeon was on leave and I had to lie around there for 30 days. When he returned, he told me, "I'll give you two choices: one, I break your nose and fix it and you might get kicked out of the service, or two, you go back to duty as is." I said, "I'll go back to duty!"

I went back to duty and the nose healed itself. We flew DC-3s. They were a pleasure to fly and I was getting top grades in training flights. We completed the course and then had to take additional training on C-46s. To me, flight training was fun. I really enjoyed it! Fort Wayne, Indiana was my next stop, to pick up a plane where our crew was assembled. I was the pilot and a co-pilot, mechanic and radio man rounded out my crew.

Carrying cargo and crews

The war ended in Europe but the war with Japan was still raging. I had orders to fly our brand new Curtis C-46 with my crew to India. We assembled in Miami and cargo was loaded on our plane, to be dropped off in Africa. Our flight route took us from Miami to Puerto Rico to the northern coast of South America and to the eastern coast of Brazil. On board we carried four sets of crews plus I had my own crew and a navigator. We planned to leave Brazil at night on the last leg of our trip. Our navigator had to navigate by the stars. At our briefing they projected a tail wind for our first stop, 1,389 miles away on isolated Ascension Island, of volcanic origin in the South Atlantic Ocean. But after five hours out the navigator said we had a head wind, not a tail wind. The trip took much longer than five hours.

We finally arrived in the morning. Ascension Island had a runway right on the ocean. It went uphill a third of the way and downhill a third of the way before it leveled out. We took off for the Gold Coast of Africa, 1,600 miles away, to drop off cargo. The next leg of our trip brought us to Casablanca, Morocco; Tripoli; and a layover at Cairo, where our mechanic performed some maintenance on the plane. The downtime let us do a little tour of downtown Cairo plus visit the Great Sphinx of Giza, on the west bank of the Nile River. The next day we took off and flew over Jerusalem and Dakar, the capital city of Senegal, on the Cape Verde Peninsula. We landed, disembarked—and whew! It was 120 degrees. They didn't gas us up because it was too dangerous with such heat. We took off early next morning and landed on a British air base on the western coast of India. Our next stop was Delhi, then Dinjan, in the eastern part of the country.

Flying over the hump

I was assigned to the 1st Troop Carrier Squadron of the 10th Air Force in the China-Burma-India Theater of Operation. The men of the squadron were in Burma when we arrived and they relocated to India. The squadron pilots, flying DC-3s, were all given brand new C-46s. When the Japanese cut off the Burma Road, the only way to get supplies and equipment to the Flying Tigers and to the Chinese who were struggling to survive was to fly it over the hump. The Flying Tigers was the popular name of the 1st American Volunteer Group (AVG) of the Chinese Air Force in 1941-1942. The group consisted of three fighter squadrons with about 20 aircraft each. It trained in Burma before the American entry into World War II with the mission of defending China against Japanese forces. I had 37 roundtrip missions over the hump, with a 4-man crew—myself as pilot, a co-pilot, mechanic and radioman. The only armament we had were .45 pistols. We had parachutes.

Bob peers out window of C-46 on the flight line in Dinjan, India

Loading jeep to fly over hump, to Chihkiang, China, September, 1945

Author's note: The hump was the name given by pilots who flew over the eastern end of the Himalayan Mountains from India to China to resupply Allied forces. The region is noted for high mountain ranges and huge parallel gorges and transverses the upper stretches southeast Asia's larger rivers: Mekong, Irrawaddy and Salween. "The rockpile," as the pilots called it, also had impenetrable jungles, insect-infested swamps and, worst of all, often unpredictable, vicious weather. On flight from India to China, there are three prominent ridges with deep valleys between them.

In flight over the hump, heading for Nanking China

Bob standing in "Tent City" base in China

Relocating to China

After the war with Japan ended we relocated to China. We took all our equipment—including huge transformers for electricity. We lived in "Tent City," a base where the Flying Tigers had been. We had to transport the Chinese 82nd Army from Central China to Nanking—a city that was "raped" by the Japanese.

Author's note: The Nanking Massacre, commonly known as the Rape of Nanking and known in Japan as the Nanjing Incident, refers to a six-week period following the capture of Nanking, then capital of the Republic of China, on December 9, 1937. International tribunals have found that during this period the Imperial Japanese Army committed atrocities such as rape, looting, arson and the execution of prisoners of war and civilians rising to the level of war crimes.

After the Nanking mission we shifted to Hankou, an industrial city in China to move another Chinese Army to Peking. The theory behind these moves was to keep Chang Kai-Shek's troops a step ahead of the advancing Chinese Communist Army.

Chinese 6th Army loading onto planes

These tedious transport missions dragged on for days—including flying the Chinese Army "comfort girls," dressed in Army uniforms, who were nothing more than prostitutes or professional "camp followers" for the benefit of the soldiers. Before one flight one of our captains lined up all the Chinese in the airplane and went down the aisle feeling their breasts to see if there were women on board. We would fly them anyway, to Peking and other designated cities.

Bob at right and American CO with 92nd Chinese Army

Ticket for home

Our ticket for home was 100 missions. We were running out of pilots. There was a fighter squadron in the India-Burma-China Theater of Operations where the CO (commanding officer) volunteered these guys to co-pilot for us. These guys never flew a C-46 before, had little or no experience and didn't fly with instruments. When they encountered bad weather during a mission they would usually bail out. On one mission I flew, with bad weather over our station, I circled down to land. On my right, my volunteer co-pilot was sweating like crazy. When we landed, he looked at me and said, "How the hell did you know where you were at?" I was experienced flying in bad weather and was able to visually spot land-based sites that I remembered from previous "fly-overs." After we completed our missions of transporting Chinese troops, I was sent to Shanghai and we gave the airplanes to China. I boarded a troop ship and sailed back to the States and home.

Our ship docked in Seattle and I signed up for another year. What was I going to do after the military? I was given a 15-day leave and decided to go to Minnesota to visit Lorraine Peske—the girl I had a blind date with in

North Dakota, in 1943. I proposed to her, she accepted and we were wed in St. Paul, Minnesota on February 6, 1946.

My next assignment was at Chanute Air Force Base in Champlain, Illinois, where Lorraine got a job at the base hospital. We bought a house from a military family at a very attractive price. My rank at Chanute was still 1st lieutenant (I was promoted in India). Released from active duty and placed in the Reserves, I worked part-time in a department store during Christmas and decided it was time to get a college education. I enrolled in the University of Illinois, to major in civil engineering, but the field did not appeal to me as a career. I took the test for the Post Office and got a job while flying bombers weekends at Chanute, then was called back to active duty when the Korean War broke out. Unfortunately, they put me on non-flying status and shipped me to Francis E. Warren Air Force Base in Cheyenne, Wyoming. I finally received a letter from the Air Force, offering to put me back on flying status. I was sent to Scott AFB where I took some training to get my instrument ticket updated.

On to Thule

I received a letter from Washington, D.C. that stated, "Anyone who has postal experience will be transferred to Thule Air Force Base in Greenland." Thule is the U.S. Air Force's northernmost base, above the Arctic Circle and 947 miles south of the North Pole on the northwest side of the island of Greenland. The orders stated that your wife couldn't go with you—and no "ifs ands or buts." They were building a SAC (Strategic Air Command) base at the time. Thule's main mission was to function as an operations base for SAC strategic bombers, supporting SAC B-36s, B-47s and KC-97s. In 1957, SAC activated the 4083rd Strategic Wing at Thule, consisting of B-36 bombers. I ran the Post Office, which handled civilian, Army, Air Force and Navy mail. We distributed the mail as soon as possible; it represented "the highlight of the day" in this desolate environment. We got all kinds of packages—big boxes of liquor were received, mostly to American civilian sub-contract workers on base. These guys made big money and didn't pay taxes up there. They used to say there were a lot of women up there, all behind the trees. But the funny thing was there are no trees in Greenland. We slept in very well-insulated barracks that were raised from the ground.

It was truly a unique experience being up there in the Arctic. The Eskimos would visit us at our barracks. There were occasions when Eskimo women would even sleep overnight in the barracks. These unauthorized visits were quickly stopped by order of our commanding officer. Family values were bizarre for Eskimo families. Bearing children was considered the prime function of Eskimo women. However, there was a notion that living in the cold Arctic the women had a hard time getting pregnant. In fact, if Americans visited an Eskimo family, the Eskimo husband would want you to sleep with his wife because the men had trouble getting the wife pregnant. When the ruling Danish government found out about this, they told the Eskimos they could no longer go over to the American base nor could they invite Americans to visit them.

My tour was supposed to be for six months but the Air Force later decided to keep the men at Thule for a year. Twenty-four hour days in summer and 24-hour nights in winter made for erratic sleeping. I worked myself until I just "gave out." My tour of duty at Thule was for a year but I did manage to get a 15-day leave to go home.

With very few women stationed at Thule, there was a beautiful blonde attached to the U.S. Weather Station. She came into the Post Office one day and the clerk at the window was bowled over and speechless when he saw her. He came out of the cage and said to the other clerk, "Go out and take over my station, I can't talk to her. It will be all gibberish!"

There were only two weapons—pistols—on that whole base. One was in the communications center and I had the other. The U.S.S.R. could have landed a plane with 20 or 30 troops and taken over the entire base. We had no security. It was weird! In early spring the military allowed us to order any equipment we needed. Supplies (fuel, vehicles and heavy equipment) were sent by ship. Food was flown in on a regular basis on large cargo planes. They sent jeeps and weapon carriers with no cabin enclosures. How did they expect us to drive these wide-open vehicles in the Arctic? They were more suited for desert use. Gen. Curtis Lemay was furious. He flew to our base and found out they didn't send any tugs that are used to pull the planes around the air strip.

Spraying skeeters

My tour ended and I was sent to Langley Field in Virginia attached to a Spray Squadron. We had three DC-3s that were retrofitted with a fuel tank in the cabin piped up to the wings to disburse spray against mosquitoes. Our mission was to spray all the military bases up and down the East Coast every week, including Cape Canaveral and the missile site. My wife moved in with me near Langley, where I was finally promoted to captain.

Once, when we had a severe infestation of mosquitoes at Cape Canaveral, our unit dispatched three planes that sprayed the entire area. I returned after a week and was told by the operations officer that I had shut down a missile launch because of our spraying. I said, "You talk to the veterinarian, he said the base was fine!" We also sprayed over the U.S. Military Academy at West Point, New York and the Charleston Navy Base.

I retired from the service in 1968 with 23 years of credit and the rank of lieutenant colonel. Prior to my retirement from the service I was able to work for Ozark Airlines as a captain thus overlapping two jobs until I retired when I reached 60 (as stipulated by Federal law). Unfortunately, my wife Lorraine was diagnosed with intestinal cancer and passed away on February 6, 1983—exactly 37 years from the day we were married.

Captain Bob Blust, Ozark Airlines pilot, 1962

Bob and Lorraine, 1983

Final thoughts

I was honored to serve my country in the military and extremely grateful to have had the opportunity for the education and training to pursue a career that I truly loved. It was a great experience. I had fun. When I retired from the airlines it was a time to get out because it wasn't fun anymore. The airline industry was chaotic. As pilots, we were burdened with a myriad of rules, regulations and restrictions.

I met Elsa Gustavson, my present wife, when I was living in Maine. Elsa and I now enjoy retirement in Sun City, South Carolina. We moved into our beautiful home in 1997.

Bob at home in Sun City, 2009

Charles Burton

Charles at Mare Island

Charles was born on August 31, 1922 in Louisville, Kentucky. After graduating from high school in 1940, he went to work making plumbing fixtures for American Standard, which operated 24 hours a day, seven days a week. He was working the late shift the Sunday night that the news came over the radio: Pearl Harbor had been bombed. A worker near Charles was running a big cutter when he heard the news—then held up his hand and said, "Look, I cut the thumb out of my glove!" Blood started squirting but because he was so distracted he didn't feel it at first. Charles explained: "If you took your eyes off them wheels the blades would cut your hand." It was a sad night; not much work was done after that news.

In his own words

I enlisted in the Navy in October 1942 at a recruiting station in Louisville and took boot camp in Great Lakes, Illinois. My rank at graduation was seaman 2nd class, and I received orders to go to Mare Island, California, assigned to the underwater demolition team. I then had orders to report to the USS Dixie somewhere in the South Pacific.

Painting of USS Dixie in Charles' den

Q & A

Arnold: What kind of ship was the Dixie?
Charles: It was a destroyer tender AD-14—one of the largest tenders in the fleet. We could pick up a standard destroyer and set it up on our deck—that's how big it was!
Arnold: How many men were on the ship?
Charles: I would estimate close to a thousand.
Arnold: What was your rank?
Charles: I was a yeoman 1st class.
Arnold: What were your duties?

Charles: I was in personnel administration. I transcribed shorthand and typed, worked for Admiral Halsey as his private secretary aboard the USS Dixie. It was the flag ship for the 3rd, 5th and 7th fleets. All the big admirals planned the South Pacific battles aboard the Dixie. I had top secret clearance and sat in on most of the meetings and briefings.

Arnold: How were you transported from Mare Island to the USS Dixie?

Charles: I sailed on several ships across the South Pacific looking for the Dixie. It took three or four months to find it. Every time I went someplace I learned that the Dixie had just departed.

Arnold: When did you finally get on board?

Charles: In early 1944 at New Hebrides Island.

In his own words

We were in 17 major battles and sailed as part of an armada of battleships, cruisers, destroyers and carriers. We were in charge of all the repairs and keeping the other ships well-stocked. We had the big guns. We were the first American ship to go into the Philippine Islands—17 days of battle going into invasion of Leyte Bay. The Dixie took a hit by a Japanese suicide attack bomber and sustained a six foot hole in our hull down below the water line. We had to send for the largest dry dock in the world to raise us out of the water. The huge floating crane finally got to us just in time. Our ship was about to capsize because it was listing at a 45 degree angle—a little bit more and we would have surely capsized. During the battle I got hit in the head with shrapnel but managed to remain on board as it healed. The Battle for Leyte Gulf was the largest naval battle of World War II and, by some criteria, the largest naval battle in history. Our ship was huge! It was 17 stories high, 535 feet long and 70 feet wide.

As we steamed into the many islands in the South Pacific, we could only get 14 miles out because the Dixie was 30 feet under water and we couldn't anchor in shallow water. Our long-range cannons would wreck havoc on the enemy on shore. We never went on shore but stayed aboard ship. Life on board was hectic; food was good although most of it was dehydrated. But they had ways of fixing it up.

Author's note: The Dixie alternated between Noumea and Espiritu Santo in support of operations in the Solomons from November 1942 to March 1944, and then went to the Solomons, where she was based at Hathorn Sound. Among other battles the Dixie was at the Gilbert Islands, New Georgia Islands, Yap Island, Iwo Jima, Wake Island, Pilou Islands and the Philippines. In September 1944 she arrived at the huge fleet base at Ulithi, serving there until February 1945. Her essential services were next given at San Pedro Bay, Leyte, where she remained until the end of the war. She provided service to ships on occupation duty at Okinawa and Shanghai.

Headed home

Charles sailed home on a cargo ship and docked at Seattle in December 1945, then took a cross-country train to Philadelphia where he was discharged as a yeoman 1st class and signed up for the Naval Reserve. He was awarded the following medals:

*   Commendation Ribbon from President Roosevelt for service above and beyond the call of duty
*   American Area Campaign Medal
*   Asiatic-Pacific Medal with 6 stars (each star represents a battle)
*   Philippine Liberation Medal
*   Good Conduct Medal
*   China Service Medal
*   Occupation Medal 1 star

As a reservist Charles was called back into active duty in 1950 and served on the USS Oriskany, a carrier with squadrons of fighter planes; he was assigned to Composite Squadron 33. The ship sailed to Korea and provided air support during the war.

Charles returned to Louisville and went back to work at American Standard as a machinist apprentice, then left and went into the insurance business for the next 27 years. He retired at 59. Charles married Jean Burnett on December 18, 2001; his first wife died in 1996. Jean and Charles moved to Sun City in 2007.

He never regretted his military service. "If I hadn't been married," he said, "I would have stayed in. I'm just thankful to be here. I served my country, survived the war and am happy to be in Sun City."

In 2008 Charles was diagnosed with congenital heart disease. The doctors gave him four months to live. His heart was beating at 20 percent of its normal capacity, so slow that there wasn't enough pressure for blood to circulate to his lower extremities. If he walked out the door of his house onto the street and back he experienced shortness of breath. There was no feeling in his lower legs. He was grateful to the love and support of his daughter and son-in-law, who lived nearby. Charles also was thankful to the local Hospice and the visiting nurses that provide additional care and support toward the end.

Charles in Sun City

Author's note: Charles Burton died on January 28, 2009 at his home in Sun City, one month after I interviewed him.

S. James Capossela

James Capossela

Jim was born on November 22, 1925 in New Rochelle, New York. He graduated from high school in 1942, worked at several part-time jobs and then enrolled at Ohio State University. After completing the first quarter he received a draft notice for induction into the Navy and reported to Whitehall Street in New York, in March 1944. The government was drafting men into the Marines, Army and Navy; at Whitehall, when Jim arrived, they had four lines—Marine, Navy, Army and Coast Guard. They placed him in the Marine Corps line. Jim asked the guy alongside, "Do you want to go into the Marines?" "Yeah!" he said. They switched places and that is how Jim entered the Navy.

In his own words

After my induction I reported to Sampson, New York, near Geneva in the Finger Lakes area, for a five-week stint of boot camp. After boot camp I went to radio school at Bedford Springs, Pennsylvania from April until graduating in November. Then the Navy sent me down to Camp Bradford in Virginia—an amphibious training base. I was later transferred to Fort Pierce, Florida, another amphibious base. I worked with the underwater demolition team. On July 1945 I was shipped out to San Diego, California on a troop train. The war in Europe was over, but the war continued in the Pacific. We shipped out aboard the USS Ostara (AKA-33), an amphibious cargo assault ship. We sailed to Hawaii and then onto Eniwetok and onto the Pacific Theater and Asia. When we left Hawaii we were carrying over $2 million in payroll for all the military in the Pacific Theater.

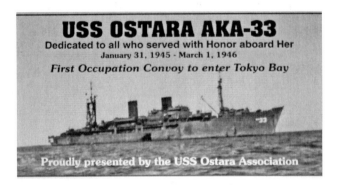

USS Ostara poster

Q & A

Arnold: Where did you sleep on board?

Jim: On board I went down to our assigned compartments where the racks (beds) were stacked two and three high. I found an open rack on top, right under a ceiling fan and grabbed it. It probably was the worst thing I could have done because that rack was always dirty because everybody and his cousin slept on it. The one advantage was sleeping near the fan because it kept me cool.

Arnold: How was the food?

Jim: Excellent.

Arnold: Were you ever seasick?

Jim: Only once. When I left San Diego the ground swells were turbulent and the water was extremely choppy.

Arnold: How many were aboard the ship?

Jim: About 400.

Jim on board the Ostara

Transporting human cargo

We went to Haipong, in French Indo-China—now Vietnam. We picked up 1,000 Chinese soldiers to sail to Chingwangtao (Manchuria) in November 1946. They wore pith helmets and short pants, and were very poorly equipped. We had to clean out the ballasts to make room for the Chinese soldiers. They slept in the holds of the ship below the lower part of the interior. One of them was climbing up the Jacob's ladder and cut his foot; two days later he died from lockjaw. We had to throw the body overboard. Two others died from dysentery; living down in the hold of a ship was cramped and at times stifling hot. Their bodies were thrown overboard, too. As a radio operator, I copied an incoming message from headquarters that said, "When they (the Chinese soldiers) die, place them in a sack and weigh them down and throw them over." This was probably the result of a directive from the Chinese military authorizing our crew to take this action for health reasons.

When we left Northern China in November, it was freezing. These poor guys come up out of the holds of our ship wearing short pants, sandals and tee-shirts. They marched these guys off our ship and loaded them onto little coal cars and drove them off into the hills. They eventually joined Chiang Kai-shek's Nationalist Army. (Chiang served as generalissimo [chairman of the National Military Council] of the Republic of China from 1928 to 1948.)

Mistaken call sign

The war in the Pacific had ended back in August while we were up in northern China near Manchuria in Chingwangtao. Our convoy of ships was receiving messages relating to the end of the war in the Pacific and orders to depart for home. I was frantically copying the messages and listening intently to hear our call sign NTOI, among the messages that would order us home. I copied NTOE instead of NTOI in one of the messages and disregarded it because it was not our call sign. For two days ships were going home and we were floating around until the "Old Man" (commanding officer) got furious. "Open up the key and get a CONFIRMATION on that message," he said as he burst into the radio room. I listened to the transmission again and lo and behold it was NTOI (our call letters)—and the message was that our ship was ordered to return to the States. My error in not recognizing our call sign caused a two-day delay in returning home. The men on board were furious. They wouldn't let me in the chow line and they put salt in my rack—playful indignation of my error (but never malicious). We sailed to San Diego and arrived on December 17, 1945.

I was discharged in Lido Beach, Long Island on June 5, 1946. I was held back because I put in for a disability—for which I was awarded $11.87. My final rank was radioman 3rd class.

Back home

Jim returned home to New Rochelle, New York and went to Ohio State University, where he graduated with a degree in marketing and business administration and met Joanne Shuster. She was a registered nurse from a small town in Ohio, Wapakoneto. They were married in Columbus on June 19, 1948. Joanne had graduated and worked as a nurse while Jim was still in school. They rented an apartment in Columbus; Jim, receiving money from the GI Bill, also had a part-time job at an old slaughter house across the Olentangy River while attending school, one of many part-time jobs. After he received his degree they moved to Pelham, New York and lived with Jim's parents. His first job was with the Neptune Auction Room, as a bookkeeper making $49 a week. They moved to Dayton, Ohio, where Jim found a sales job with Sears Roebuck.

In his own words

I always loved to travel. Many times I would just "pick up and leave." Whenever I moved to a new place, I never had a job waiting for me. Perhaps it was my adventurous spirit. We stayed in Dayton with our two sons for a few years but I always liked Florida, where I was stationed in Ft. Pierce and enjoyed the surroundings. We packed up and left, where my father had a house and we lived with him for a while. Eventually we bought a house in Hialeah. By then we had four sons. I worked for Richards's Department Store in Miami for about eight months and then worked as a sales rep for Viceroy Cigarettes, which were made by the Brown & Williamson Company. I never smoked. As a matter of fact I was the only guy on my ship who never smoked.

Joanne never really liked Florida. My parents said to me, "Why don't you come home? There's a house for sale in Pelham." So in 1957 we moved back to my familiar territory.

The job I held the longest, for 28 years, was with the Rawlings Sporting Goods Company. Before that I was working for Tech Tape; they wanted me to move to California. My wife said "No!" so I quit. On a trip to New York City, I went into the Spalding offices—and who should be there but a guy I went to high school with. He said to me, "Jim, they're not hiring here but Rawlings is hiring. Go down and see them." It helped me land a job there that I was an Ohio State graduate, because OSU was a huge account at Rawlings. I was interviewed that Friday and they told me to report for work next Tuesday as sales rep. When I started I had 13 accounts in the NYC territory.

Opening day panic

The morning of April 17, 1964 I was in the Rawlings warehouse in Englewood, New Jersey. George Zuckerman, who bought equipment for the

New York Mets baseball team, called in a fit of panic. "Jim," he yelled, "you've got to help me! I forgot to order the bases, home plate and the pitching rubber, do you have them?" I checked the inventory—they were there in stock. We threw them in my station wagon and I took off speeding to Shea Stadium in Flushing Meadows, New York. When I got there the police were waiting for me. They opened the barriers in the parking lot so that I could pass through and drive directly on to the field. Construction workers were painting outfield signs and fresh sod was being laid in the outfield as the teams took batting practice. And there on the field were Lindsey Nelson and Bob Murphy (Mets announcers) talking to the crowd. The field crew was anxiously waiting to install these critical pieces of equipment. They raced over to my station wagon and removed the items. The field crew manager said to me, "Jim, thank you very much—now get off the field!" I drove off the field and headed home, turning on my radio as I headed along Grand Central Parkway. Breathing a sigh of relief, I listened as the first pitch was thrown to officially open Shea Stadium. It dawned on me that I was a small part of baseball history, because without those pieces of equipment, the game would have never started. I will never forget that day. By the way, the Mets lost to Pittsburgh, 4 to 3.

More moves

Our family remained in Westchester County and our four children attended Pelham High School. After many years living in Pelham I decided to leave because of a misunderstanding related to new personnel and new management policies. It was time to move again. Again, I didn't have a job and by this time my wife said to me, "If we're going to move, you're going to pack everything—I'm sick and tired of moving!" We moved, and bought a house in Richardson, Texas, outside of Dallas. We were there a few years when Rawlings called me and sent Joe Lombardi (brother of famous football coach Vince Lombardi). He urged me to return to work. They offered me the most undesirable territory—the New York City area. Nobody could hack it. All the sales reps quit when they were assigned there. It didn't bother me, because I enjoyed meeting new people and new challenges. We moved to Oradell, New Jersey until I retired from Rawlings, and Joanne and I pondered on a place to retire.

My wife confessed to me that she always wanted to live in North Carolina. We moved to Charlotte in 1989, but Joanne developed cancer in 1990 and wanted to return home. We moved to Cincinnati, where we remained until she passed away from ovarian cancer in 2000. I remained in Ohio for a year and decided to go back to Florida to the Villages, a premier active adult retirement community in central Florida. I enjoyed living there and stayed put for five years. My traveling and adventurous instincts "kicked in" and that's when I decided to move, in 2006, to another active community facility: Sun City—Hilton Head. I enjoy the amenities and a new circle of friends in this wonderful place.

Final impressions of military service

No regrets whatsoever! I loved military service. I met a lot of wonderful people. And the Navy gave me an opportunity to travel to places like Hawaii and the islands of the South Pacific—Eniwetok, Guam, Saipan, the Philippines, Okinawa as well as Chingwangtao, China and French Indo-China—places I would never dream of going to if I lived in a different time. I will always have these memories—some bad but mostly good!

Jim at home in Sun City

Allen Haskell Casey

Haskell, wife and daughter, 1944

Author's note: World War II Navy veteran Allen Haskell Casey moved from Sun City, South Carolina to the nearby Victory House Veterans nursing facility in Walterboro in 2008. At 99, he is the oldest member of the Sun City Veterans Association. His wife, Dorothy, and daughter, Doris, kindly helped with this profile.

Allen Haskell Casey was born on March 21, 1910 in Hill City, Texas. He dropped the first name and likes to be referred to as Haskell. His mother liked the name because she was fond of Gov. Charles Haskell of Oklahoma.

Haskell went to Tarleton College in Stephenville, Texas and then to Missouri as assistant manager of a Woolworth store.

In Dorothy Sorensen's own words

I was working at an F. W. Woolworth store in Maplewood, Missouri when Haskell was transferred there. I was a counter girl on the sales floor but was transferred to the office because I was proficient in office skills; earlier, I graduated from high school and learned bookkeeping and other office skills in a business school. The entire work force was girls, and all of us took notice when this nice-looking young man came into our store. Fortunately he was attracted to me. And it will be 72 years in June (2009) that we are together. We had our first date in August 1936, I received my engagement ring in December and we wed on June 19, 1937.

We lived in an apartment near the store. When he was transferred to St. Louis, I got a job as a bookkeeper in a towel and linen supply company. Woolworth transferred Haskell frequently to supervise and manage during the company's expansion in the St. Louis area. In 1943 we were blessed with the birth of our daughter, Doris.

My brother, Tom Sorensen, a Marine pilot, sent me a note: "Dot, I'm going to give baby Doris her first airplane ride." Two weeks after that, he was killed in a plane crash.

Q & A

Arnold: Where did your brother die?
Dorothy: He was killed right off the coast of Georgia at the Pensacola (Florida) Naval Training Base. He was in flight doing target practice. His buddy, flying alongside him, watched as his plane went into a spin and later said, "I knew he was doing everything in his power to pull out of it." Tom crashed in the ocean and they never found him, despite an extensive search. My mother and dad took it awfully hard and I did too because when he was born, I was five years old and almost dying from vaccinations. I developed an infection that almost entered my heart and the doctor told me (I was screaming bloody murder) he was going to

bring me a baby brother for Christmas. Tom was born the week before Christmas.

Haskell was just as upset about Tom being killed as I was. He said, "I think I'm going to enlist to serve my country." He didn't have to go into the military, at 33 years old.

"Bring the baby"

Arnold: When did your dad enlist?
Doris: My dad entered the service on March 6, 1944, in St. Louis.
Arnold: Where did he take boot camp?
Doris: San Diego and from there he was sent to Bremerton, Washington.
Dorothy: When the Navy shipped Haskell to Bremerton Naval Base, he called me and said, "Bring the baby and come out." I asked him, "But what if you ship out before I get there?"
Doris: In 1944 mom got in the car from St. Louis, Missouri and drove west.
Dorothy: And I'd never driven over a mountain range before, much less with Doris in the back seat. I went to the pediatrician and asked him, "Is it safe to take the baby?" Haskell was anxious to see Doris.
Arnold: How did you manage? They didn't have car seats for babies at that time.
Doris: That's right! I was in a cardboard box in the back seat of the car for the entire trip.
Dorothy: I took another girl with me who had a baby even younger than Doris. She also wanted to see her husband, who was stationed with Haskell; so here we were two women wandering from St. Louis to Bremerton, Washington in 1944. We rented a little place not far from the base and were able to spend some time together from May to August. Haskell was then shipped to Mobile, Alabama and processed to board the USS Basilan (AG-68), an electrical supply ship. It sailed around the Pacific and provided installation and repair of pipes for fresh water on board ship. Dad was a metalsmith; he cut pipes.
Doris: It's a shame we couldn't have done this interview two years ago because my dad was very alert. He just turned 99 on March 21 (2009).
Arnold: Do you visit him often at the Victory House in Walterboro?
Doris: Yes, we go at least once a week.

On board the Basilan

The Basilan departed for the Pacific on December 8, 1944 and after stops at Guantanamo Bay, Cuba, and in the Canal Zone, arrived at San Francisco on February 10, 1945. During April and May she served at Ulithi, Caroline Islands, as a supply and repair ship. On May 20, she departed for Leyte, where she continued her supply and repair duties until September, when she proceeded to Shanghai, China, via Okinawa and Korea. Haskell and his crew sailed home on December 9.

Q & A

Arnold: The war ended in the Pacific in August 1945. Did Haskell remain in the Navy?

Doris: No, he was discharged at Lambert Field in St. Louis.

Arnold: What did Haskell do after he was discharged?

Doris: They put me in the back of the car and took off for a grand tour of the West.

Dorothy: We fell in love with that area of the country around Bremerton, Washington. We thought we would go back there and start our life together. He applied for a job but nobody was hiring anybody. Haskell said, "We got to go back east. It's futile here." We returned to St. Louis and rented a house.

Doris: My dad started selling Guardian Service cookware. He eventually worked for Cook's Paint.

Dorothy: They transferred us from St. Louis to Oklahoma City and then to Kansas City and back to St. Louis. Haskell worked for another company, as a salesman for United Steel & Wire Company (a complete line of shopping carts and wire merchandising displays). I remember as a child when we moved to Kansas City, he managed the elite, flagship Cook's Paint store in the brand new Plaza Mall in Kansas City.

Arnold: What company did he stay with for the longest period of time?

Doris: He worked as a painter for the Missouri National Guard in St. Louis and that became his longest job. He was kind of a jack-of-all-trades. My dad built the house that we lived in. He was very handy. He could build or repair almost anything. He was handy with other things besides painting but he enjoyed painting and was good at it.

Dorothy: He also rebuilt car engines.

Doris: He was a civilian contractor for the Missouri National Guard for 14 years and at the age of 65 he retired.

Snow birds

Arnold: Did you stay in St. Louis after retirement?

Doris: At that time mom and dad became snow birds.

Dorothy: I retired because I had a business working out of my home, renting films to churches and organizations (in the days before videos and DVDs). When I reached 62 in 1977 we took off in our trailer and headed for Florida. We were thinking about "wintering in Florida." We arrived in Florida and found that it was the "love bug" season. If you were outside you could be covered from head to foot. I said to Haskell, "Let's get out of here quick. I don't ever want to see these bugs again!" We headed along the coast going west. Haskell had an aunt in Wichita Falls, Texas and we stopped off to see her. We ended up "wintering in Texas" on the Mexican border and buying a place in Mission, Texas. We lived there for 25 years—six months down and six months back in St. Louis.

Arnold: When did you all decide to come to Sun City?

Doris: That wasn't their decision. That was mine. When I retired I said "I'm moving south!" My parents probably would have preferred if I had picked a place in Texas. We stopped in the Sun City in Texas and although we liked the houses, the people just weren't as warm or friendly as I would have liked them to be. My husband, Dan Natale, and I came down here to Sun City—Hilton Head for a vacation. I had never been east. We found this area to our liking. I noticed how green everything was. It was beautiful! And I talked Dan into buying a place after our third visit. We bought in 2001.

Mom and dad had moved in with us in St. Louis in 1994; dad was 84 at the time. When we moved full time in May 2002, we had a little car caravan from St. Louis. I was in one car, Dan in another, my dad and mom were in another and my aunt and uncle was in yet another car. At that time dad was 90 years old and he drove all the way down here.

Arnold: When did Haskell develop his ailments?
Doris: Two years ago. He was doing fairly well for his age but was having a little stability problem. I had gotten him a walker but he was very proud and didn't like assistance with aids or help from anyone. He didn't use it a lot but was unstable and that's why we decided that he move in with us. Two years ago he had a major stroke and since that time has had recurring strokes. He was on the front porch when he had a major stroke. It didn't really affect his speech and he kept saying, "I think I had a stroke!"

When we took him to the neurologist the doctor confirmed that he had a stroke. That was the beginning of a deterioration of his health. He was in the hospital at Coastal Carolina for a month and then he was admitted to a private nursing home for a month. When we brought him home mother and I took care of him. Eventually he was having too many falling episodes. It was reaching a point where the three of us had difficulty lifting him up from the floor. In September 2008 he had a scary episode. While sitting at the table he passed out. We called 911 and they took him to Coastal Carolina Hospital. When we took him back home he continued to deteriorate until we reached a point where it was growing exceedingly difficult to take care of him. We had been on the waiting list for the Victory House Veterans Nursing Home in Walterboro. A spot opened up and we were able to admit dad into this brand new facility.

Author's note: Victory House is a 220-bed, state-of-the-art nursing care facility operated by Advantage Veterans Services of Walterboro for the South Carolina Department of Mental Health. It has 126,000 square feet on a 20-acre site. With a staff of 250, the facility is one of the most modern of its kind in the United States. It has three nursing units with 56 beds each, as well as a 52-bed secured dementia unit.

Arnold: What is the present diagnosis of Haskell?

Doris: He is in a wheelchair. He can't walk because there is no link from his brain to his feet. When we visit him we find he is somewhat disoriented. He still knows who we are but he talks irrationally. His hearing deteriorated and I think that's a big part of dad's problem because when he can't hear and/or understand, he can't respond.

Arnold: What about eating?

Doris: He is not able to feed himself anymore, but his spirit remains positive. He was never really a negative person. I don't think you can reach the age of 99 without a positive outlook on life.

Final impressions

Doris: I asked him, "Dad, why did you join the Navy?" He said, "I always liked the Navy!"

Dorothy: I wondered about that, too, because he had friends in different branches of the service but for some reason was always very partial to the Navy. Since he had his choice—he wasn't drafted—he chose the Navy.

Daughter Dorothy Natale

Haskell Casey in Fisher House, 2009
Allen Haskell Casey died on August 16, 2009.

Joe Catanese

Joe Catanese

Joe Catanese was born on December 21, 1924 in New Brunswick, New Jersey. He enlisted in the Navy after graduating from high school in June 1943. Joe completed boot camp in Newport, Rhode Island with the rank of seaman apprentice; was assigned to Electrician's Mate school in Newport; and reported for duty on board the USS Ranger, a CV-4 aircraft carrier. Ranger, begun in 1922, was the first American carrier designed as such; previous carriers were converted from other ship types. Joe would spend three years at sea on board the Ranger.

In his own words

We shipped out of Boston. As an electrician's mate my job was primarily to repair and maintain refrigerators and small motors aboard ship. I slept in the lower deck in a 3-tier bunk bed.

The Ranger transported troops to Casablanca. On one Atlantic crossing the weather was rough and the ocean was extremely choppy. We had over 2,000 soldiers on board. It took 11 days to cross the Atlantic. We never went straight, the ship changed course frequently. Most of the troops on board never left the "john" or their rack for days—they were incapacitated with severe seasickness.

USS Ranger, 1990 U.S. Navy photo

The USS Ranger launched aircraft on submarine patrols. We sailed in a convoy that included the Tuscaloosa and the Augusta cruisers plus five destroyer escorts. We were on submarine patrol in the Atlantic for quite a while. I was promoted to seaman 3rd class.

Our aircraft consisted of Grumman TBFs, Wildcats and Marine Corsairs. The Ranger was one of the first ships that brought jets aboard, mainly for practice landing. Twenty-six jets aboard and they carried 26 off. Their landing gear was not strong enough on impact when it "hit the deck." When the hook grabbed the jet, the force went on the front wheels and the front wheels would just collapse. The practice landing of these experimental jets were a total failure—all crash-landed!

P-40s on deck, U.S. Navy photo

Wildcat landing on Ranger, U.S. Navy photo

We made many Atlantic Ocean crossings carrying troops and aircraft to Casablanca. On one of these trips we carried a load of B-36s Convair Peacemakers—disassembled and crated in boxes. By the spring of 1945 the German Navy was in disarray and our submarine patrols were infrequent.

We still sailed with a convoy of destroyers and two cruisers—they were part of our team because a carrier never traveled alone. I had three years of sea duty aboard the Ranger, until 1946. We had storms in the North Atlantic where we had to strap ourselves into our bunks to avoid falling out.

When the war in Europe ended we sailed to the South Pacific, stopping off in San Diego and Hawaii. While the Ranger was the first carrier built as such, the Saratoga and the Lexington were being built as cruisers but because of the treaty establishing the League of Nations, the U.S. was limited as to war ships and they couldn't be built as cruisers. At that time the members of the League didn't think aircraft carriers were going to amount to anything. American aircraft carriers had a wooden flight deck; the English had steel.

"All Hands to General Quarters!"

When the call to General Quarters (GQ) is made, the crew prepares the ship to join battle. Off-duty or sleeping crewmembers report to their stations and prepare for action. Watertight doors between bulkheads are shut and security is increased around sensitive areas such as the bridge and engineering rooms.

There were many lulls in our sea duty. The captain decided to initiate a physical training day aboard ship. I remember the first day he ordered all off-duty seamen to report to the flight deck to engage in calisthenics. There were 1,800 seamen on the flight deck. When they started the jumping jack drill, can you imagine the thunderous noise it made from 1,800 seamen hitting the wooden flight deck at the same time? The men below the flight deck were so frightened that an "All hands to General Quarters!" was sounded. They thought it was a torpedo attack. Needless to say that ended all further exercise days.

We were in San Diego when the Japanese surrendered and the war ended. The celebrations were wild. I was the last one off the ship. On VJ day, the Ranger had amassed a total of 77,906 landings, second only to the number amassed by the Saratoga, seven years her senior.

Departing San Diego on September 30, 1945, Ranger embarked civilian and military passengers at Balboa in the Canal Zone and then steamed for New Orleans, arriving on October 18. We were there along with the battleship Mississippi. Following Navy Day celebrations, she sailed October 30 for brief operations at Pensacola. After arriving at Norfolk, the Ranger entered the Philadelphia Naval Shipyard November 18 for overhaul. She remained on the eastern seaboard until decommissioned at the Norfolk Naval Shipyard on October 18, 1946.

Discharge—and Sun City

I was officially discharged in May 1946 with the rank of 2nd class electrician's mate. I returned to New Brunswick and worked for New Jersey Bell for 37 years. I have been married for 59 years. I met Julia Zwolinski—my bride-to-be—on a blind date. I was 24 and we wed in 1949. We are blessed with four children and four grandchildren

I had a very positive feeling about my service in the Navy. I was proud to serve my country.

I retired from the phone company in 1983. We used to visit Hilton Head, spending many enjoyable winters there. We saw Sun City being built, and on return to New Jersey on one of our usual trips, came home to two major snow storms in one week. We said to each other, "What are we doing here?" And the only place we thought about was Sun City. We came down here in 2005 and bought our wonderful retirement home.

Joe in Sun City, 2008

Walter Choplick

Walter Choplick

Walter was born on June 5, 1927 in Shenandoah, Pennsylvania and graduated from West Mahanoy Township High School in 1945. He enlisted in the Navy in his senior year, took boot camp in Bainbridge, Maryland and was at Camp Perry, Virginia when armistice was declared in Europe on May 10, 1945. He was ordered to report to the Naval Construction Battalion Center (CBC) in Port Hueneme, California, West Coast homeport of the Navy's mobile construction force.

In his own words

At Hueneme, we boarded a troop ship, were issued helmets, boots, green fatigues, carbines and backpacks and set sail for Japan. En route we stopped at island chains in the Pacific to drop off mail. We reached our final destination at Tokyo Bay a week after the armistice was signed, ending the war in the Pacific. In Tokyo we saw the remnants of a city bombed out as a result of our air raids. The Japanese were walking around with surgical masks for protection against airborne pollutants. I was sent to Yokosuka Naval Base with 10 of my buddies, where we slept on cots in tents. In Yokosuka there was a submarine base where the Japanese had built caves on the side of a mountain to store bombs, ammunition and a variety of weapons.

A military gamble

That August, upon the return of the surrender delegation to Japan, complex demobilization machinery went into high gear: the rapid, orderly repatriation and disarmament of the Japanese armed forces. In the overall picture, enormous military risks were involved in landing initially with "token" United States forces. (Our unit landed a week after the surrender.) The Japanese mainland was still potentially a colossal armed camp, and there was an obvious military gamble in landing with only limited American troops.

But the Japanese had not waited for the Allied forces to appear before they started to disband their Army and Navy. By September-October 88 percent of the Army was demobilized. The occupation troops soon found the bulk of their activities directed towards supervising disposition of war material. The demobilization program functioned smoothly and efficiently on its own momentum and reports to American military headquarters were monotonously uniform: "No disorders; no opposition; cooperation continues."

(Author's note: The occupation of Japan by the Allied Powers but mainly carried out by the United States, started in August 1945 with Gen. MacArthur as supreme commander and ended in April 1952.)

I was assigned to the Bomb and Ammunition Disposal Unit. My job was to arrange for Japanese workers to take the ammunition and armaments out of those stored caves in Yokosuka and load it on trucks to be driven out to the bay, then loaded onto barges and dumped into the ocean. Some of the workers were injured while unloading the weapons and cordite. (During the war the Japanese fired their big guns with black powder and cordite, a family of smokeless propellants used in firearms and artillery.) Cordite burns like gasoline. On one occasion I saw a barge blow up in the ocean. One of the workers lit a cigarette on board to cause the explosion. All on board were killed.

Cordite loaded on barge

Munitions cave in Yokosuka, Japan

Q & A

Arnold: You didn't handle the cordite, did you?

Walter: No, the Japanese were doing it but we were there alongside them.

Arnold: You weren't assigned sea duty on a specific ship?

Walter: No, I was stationed at Yokosuka Naval Base. My rank was seaman 1st class.

Arnold: How long was your tour in Japan?

Walter: We arrived in September 1945 and completed our job in April 1946. The Navy was discharging you on the basis of points accumulated. They told me I couldn't return home until I went to rest camp (R& R). I was sent to a resort town, Shiga Heights. We went skiing and I broke a leg trying to avoid hitting a tree while going down the slopes.

They took me to a Japanese hospital but were unable to X-ray my leg because their machines could not display the ligament images. I was sent to another hospital where they stabilized my leg in preparation to returning home. I reported to a naval officer for processing. He asked me, "Why don't you stay in the Navy?" I said, "I'm lame and lazy and want to go home. Why should I stay in? The war is over and I want to go home." He asked, "What outfit are you in?" "Bomb and Ammunition Disposal Unit," I said. "Oh," he said. "You get out of here while you are still ahead!" When I returned to the States I was admitted to a military hospital and made a full recovery. I was discharged in July 1946.

Back home

Walter passed the test to enroll in Penn State University under the GI Bill but was not admitted because that fall the class was full. He had to wait for the 1947-48 class, attended for a year, then left: "I wanted to get out before they threw me out!" Walter went into business for himself, and on October 8, 1950 married Gloria Balkiewicz—she was from his hometown, Shenandoah.

In his own words

I started my own company, Choplick Concrete Burial Vault Company, in 1948 from scratch and drew customers from Shenandoah and surrounding areas. I had to purchase all the materials—a cement mixer, planks, cemetery equipment and molds for the vaults. At the end of 1948 I started making the vaults and stored them in the empty yard next to my house. I made the vaults in a small two-car garage. I took the completed vaults out of the garage and stored them in our empty lot. We did business with the local undertakers who, in turn, sold them to the families of the deceased. I sold about 30 or 40 a year. When the business started to grow, I dug out a foundation on my empty lot and erected a building. When I received orders from the undertaker, I placed the vault on the truck and drove it to the cemetery and to the grave site with tents and lowering devices, which was included in the sale of the vaults. I was in the business for 56 years and retired in 2004.

On to Sun City

We originally went to Florida and looked at the homes but didn't like what we saw. We looked at Sun City and bought a beautiful, spacious home. Gloria said, "Walter wants to go back to Pennsylvania every year. He was born in that house so it's sentimental."

Looking back on my military service, I found it to be an enlightening and adventurous part of my life. I was glad to be of service to my country. I was 17 years old and wanted to be in the Navy. I never fired a shot! But when we took those bombs out everything else seemed easy. I felt I made a worthy contribution toward the orderly repatriation, demobilization and disarmament of the Japanese armed forces.

Walter and Gloria at home in Sun City

Sylvester and Jean Crumlich:
the Home Front

Sylvester Crumlich

I can sympathize with the young families of today who are separated because of war. In 1943, Sylvester H. Crumlich, my 28-year-old husband, was inducted into the Seabees, leaving me at home with my baby, Arla. This is my story of "life on the home front" during World War II, with a bow to Pat.

—Jean May Crumlich

Sylvester "Pat" Cromlich was born on April 7, 1915 in Cumberland County, Pennsylvania. He graduated from Mechanicsburg High School in 1934 and earned a full athletic and scholastic scholarship to Albright College in Reading, Pennsylvania but had to assume management of the family farm when his father died. He also worked at a builder's hardware store and eventually took a job as a dispatcher with Sinclair Pipeline.

In Jean's own words

Pat and I were high school sweethearts. He was a football player and I was a cheerleader. We were married July 1, 1939. He was 24 and I was 20. Our honeymoon was delayed until Labor Day. We went to Atlantic City. The dark clouds of war were building in Europe and while in Atlantic City we heard the news that the Nazis invaded Poland. All signs were imminent that World War II was on the horizon.

Pat said. "If I'm drafted, I'll go! I won't take a deferment, I'm an able-bodied man."

He left on our fourth wedding anniversary when he got his notice to serve. I was six months pregnant and they gave him a deferment until the baby was born. We had our first and only child, Arla, in March 1943. He could have gotten a deferment because of his job but he didn't and his boss said, "Well, Pat, why don't you go down and take the physical and see if you can get in the Seabees?" He was accepted, took basic training at Camp Perry in Williamsburg, Virginia and won an advanced rating of petty officer 2nd class.

Hardships

What was ahead of me? I was frightened. After our daughter was born I had to get on my feet. I remember crying all day trying to figure out a budget of $78 a month. Where would I live and how would I care for the baby? Allotment checks were the same every month, although there was one stretch where I didn't get a cent from August to February. I thought we were going to starve! When I finally got the back money, it was like hitting the lottery.

Jean at home, 1944

I promptly put the money in the bank, like Scrooge! I made all of Arla's clothes and all of mine. Each month when the check arrived, I budgeted for airmail stamps, money for the paper boy, the milkman and groceries. I took Arla to Western Auto for toys, games or puzzles. She had a dollar to spend. One year we didn't get Christmas gifts from Pat. He couldn't wrap them himself because of censorship. The Navy had men assigned to package gifts and only then could they be mailed. I remember the postmaster at Mechanicsburg called me once and offered me a job. I would be the first woman to work in the Post Office. He said, "Jean, the men said they could work with you better than anyone, and the pay is $45 per week." It almost killed me to turn him down, but there was no one to care for the baby. My mother couldn't help because of her health. I was very disappointed.

A risky car trip

Pat finished his boot camp training in the middle of August and was going on his first liberty. I decided I was going to take Arla and spend a night with him. Pat said not to come but we went anyway. My friend, Mary Doyle, whose husband worked at Sinclair, said we'd go together; she took her four-year-old.

Everything was rationed—tires, gas, and food. Money was also rationed with me! We bought a used 1941 Studebaker and ordered new tires. Before the order was completed the government "froze" tire sales. My generous friend Mary took tires off her car and put them in the trunk. She took her gas ration book if we needed it. About ten miles from Camp Perry, we had a blowout going up a steep hill. I got a jack out and blocked the wheels. A car roared down the hill with two young men as passengers. They did a U-turn and came back to us. When they saw the children, their faces fell but they put Mary's tire on my car and got us going.

We arrived in Williamsburg hot and tired. There was no air conditioning and we all needed showers. Mary took Arla and bathed her in the sink in a public restroom. She used Fels Naptha, strong laundry soap, as soap was rationed during the war. I sat on the curb wondering what to do. I kept asking people for room information. Finally someone gave me an address and directions to a house on the outskirts of town.

We drove out and found an elderly couple in a small house. They were gentle people. The man had only one arm. They looked us over and we were a sight! Finally they said, "You can stay if the baby doesn't cry." I said, "She's a good baby, but I can't promise you she won't cry." The man agreed and we had a pleasant stay at their home.

Pat's liberty started after a dress parade at Camp Perry, where he led his platoon through drills and formation. I was really proud of him. In six weeks those men learned a lot and we all grew up in a hurry. That trip was worth more than I could ever say.

Shipping out

He shipped out from San Francisco in 1943 and sailed to Hawaii and then on to the South Pacific. In the long war years we exchanged letters—our only source of communications. His were always censored. Sometimes I wouldn't get mail for weeks and I was depressed. I used to make four or five trips to the mailbox looking and hoping.

Pat was a shipfitter in the Seabees. That was a Navy enlisted rate requiring a range of skills involving the uses of metal, including plumbing. The "plumbers," as they were called, often went in ahead of the actual construction of buildings. They put in the roads and runways for the airports. Pat island-hopped around the South Pacific to wherever he was needed.

There'll be bluebirds over,
the white cliffs of Dover,
tomorrow, just you wait and see.
There'll be love and laughter
and peace ever after,
tomorrow, when the world is free.

Everyone in America waited for the words of this song (most popularly sung by Kate Smith) to become a reality. Finally, on May 7, 1945 V-E Day (Victory in Europe) arrived, the day of Germany's surrender, officially ending the European phase of World War II. V-J Day (Victory over Japan) was to follow on August 15, with Emperor Hirohito formally signing Japan's surrender on September 2. Peace at last!

Typhoon at Okinawa

At that time his port of embarkation was Okinawa. There was a typhoon brewing, heading for Okinawa. The Navy ordered all ships that were moored to sail out to sea. Pat's ship sailed just before the typhoon hit. It was the biggest typhoon to hit the island. On October 9, when the storm passed over the island, winds of 80 knots (92 miles per hour) and 30-35 foot waves battered the ships and craft in the bay and tore into the Quonset huts and buildings ashore. A total of 12 ships and craft were sunk, 22 grounded and 32 severely damaged.

Pat arrived in San Francisco and processed out in Baltimore as petty officer 1st class. I had put all the money I could into a savings account. This really surprised him because I had enough to make a small down payment on a house before he came home.

Just before he came home, however, I told Pat Arla didn't like beards. Pat stopped in the YMCA in Harrisburg to shave before taking the bus to Mechanicsburg. The baby had been talking to a clean-shaven picture of her dad for months. When he first saw her she said, "You want to see the duck?" We were having duck for dinner.

Back to work

When he returned he had his "lame duck" patch signifying his discharge. His job was waiting for him and he went right to work. His main career was with Sinclair—it became Colonial Pipeline when he retired, in 1980, and we moved a lot. We lived in Ohio, New Jersey and Myrtle Beach, South Carolina. We stayed there 17 years, and then came down here to Sun City. We liked Myrtle Beach, but as Pat's health began to fail—our daughter had bought a house in Sea Pines and since she was our only child—we decided to come down here. We moved to Sun City in April 1998. But he never joined the Vets group here because he was walking with a cane and had difficulty with his equilibrium.

He died December 9, 2000. I am here 10 years. I pray for families separated by the present wars. I know it is not easy to wait on the "home front" at any time. I've been there. May God bless the military and their families!

Jean at home in Sun City, 2009

Jim Donnelly

Jim Donnelly, with wife, Barbara, and son

Author's note: Janet Donnelly, daughter of Jim Donnelly, was kind enough to help me with this profile. When I visited Jim at the Fraser Health Center, an assisted-living facility at Seabrook, Hilton Head, South Carolina, in April 2009, he was unable to conduct an interview. His son, Dennis, was with him at the time. Jim suffers from memory loss as a result of Alzheimer's disease. Daughter Janet was able to provide me with documents, photos and some memories of Jim's military service.

Jim was born on January 10, 1921 in Bay Ridge, Brooklyn, New York. He attended New Utrecht High School and left school to work as a carpenter and welder at Weld Master Company in Brooklyn. Jim enlisted in the Army Air Corps July 15, 1942.

After basic training he was assigned to Radio Operator School at Truax Field in Madison, Wisconsin for 14 weeks and became qualified to fly as first radio operator on NAFW C-47 and C-53 aircraft. Jim served as aerial radio operator in Africa and Italy attached to the 1329th Army Air Force and the 1252 AAF Base Unit. On one of his flights from Casablanca to Tripoli on August 5, 1944 Pilot 1st Lt. Hessen—filed the following report:

Delay at beginning of trip at Casablanca due to maintenance. Finally changed airplanes. Time in Algiers was cut down somewhat. Tripoli operations very slow and caused delay before leaving station. Sick passengers taken care of in Algiers. Enlisted men's quarters in Tripoli very poor and Officers sleeping quarters should be fumigated

Flying over the hump

In May 1944 Jim was sent to central Burma and assigned to the 1306th AAF, India Wing, India China Division, where he flew missions over "the hump"—the name given by Allied pilots to the eastern end of the Himalayan Mountains over which they flew from India to China to resupply the Flying Tigers and the Chinese government of Chiang Kai-shek.

Jim in Burma (on right), awaiting a flight over the hump

Jim in Burma, waiting for USO show

These missions involved flying as a crew member on C-54 transport planes carrying troops and supplies. Jim was a radio operator and part of a four-man crew (pilot, co-pilot, mechanic and radio operator). In September 1946, Jim took part in probably the greatest skyways troop movement in history, as the Army Air Force began flying the first of 80,000 Chinese soldiers and their equipment to reoccupied areas of eastern China. The missions included transporting two Chinese armies to Shanghai in the largest and most complex operation ever undertaken by the U.S. Air Force in the Far East. Jim's unit, the Air Transport Command, had to divert a substantial number of C-54s from the hump route to accommodate the flights within China. Jim's planes were based in eastern Bengal. He was awarded the Distinguished Flying Cross, American Service Medal, the Asiatic-Pacific Service Medal and the World War II Victory Medal. Jim didn't talk much to his children about his military experiences. Daughter

Janet does remember that on one of her dad's missions the plane made a crash landing. Jim was wounded and hospitalized as a result.

In her own words

My dad was discharged from Fort Dix, New Jersey on November 26, 1945. He went into carpentry for the Woodworking Trade Company. He never graduated from high school nor did he enroll in school after serving in the military. While dad was at Radio Operator School in Madison, Wisconsin my mom, Barbara Dorothy Hagerty, visited him there. They were married on October 13, 1942 in Madison. My mom was from Brooklyn, too; they lived next door to each other and met before the service.

I was born in Brooklyn on December 21, 1947. I went to St. Martin Catholic School. We moved to Long Island when they were building the Levittown homes. Dad bought a small Cape Cod home on 3691 Martin Street.

Author's note: Brothers Bill and Alfred Levitt built relatively inexpensive mass housing for veterans returning from World War II by applying mass-production techniques in a village in central Long Island, New York.

Since dad was a skilled carpenter, he erected extensions on the home and did extensive remodeling of our modest home of two bedrooms downstairs, a small kitchen and a small living room. We were eight children—four boys and four girls—and we had four bedrooms. We quickly became the biggest house on the block. I hear some of my friends describe their traditional Thanksgiving or Christmas dinners and they say, "I'm having ten people over for Thanksgiving dinner!" I would be amused and think to myself that we had this every day, for every meal. I went to Catholic school but everyone else went to public school.

Q & A

Arnold: Did your dad work as a freelance carpenter or did he work for a company?

Janet: He worked as a union carpenter; he worked freelance and had several jobs.

Arnold: He reported to the union and they would assign him jobs?

Janet: Yes. And a lot of times he worked on his own.

Arnold: Did your mom work?

Janet: No, not until we were all grown. She took a job in the church. She prepared food for the priests, then would come home and prepare food for us.

Arnold: So his primary job was carpentry?

Janet: Yes. He retired and moved from Levittown to Florida. They moved down to Florida in 1977 into a mobile home community.

Arnold: Did he continue to do carpentry work in Florida?

Janet: He was on his own. When my mom died in 2000 he remained in Florida for a couple of years and then dementia (Alzheimer's) was starting to set in. When Hurricane Wilma devastated Florida in October 2005 my brother's mobile home was destroyed so he moved to Sarasota and took my dad with him. I eventually brought him with me to South Carolina and moved him into the Riverside at Belfair, an independent assisted living facility. I had VA assistance, limited health insurance and social security that helped pay for his living expenses.

Always a patriot

My dad flew the American flag his whole life. When he moved to Palm Beach Gardens, Florida in June 1979 he lived in a little mobile home area called Garden Walk. It was his goal to encourage all his neighbors to honor America by flying the flag. To recognize residents that displayed their flag he would present them with a "certificate of appreciation" that he and my mom created. My mom died in 2000.

When Jim moved to South Carolina he resided in an assisted living facility in Hilton Head. Janet says, "Medicare paid for it but we were losing all of his savings." Her objective was to try to get her dad into the Veterans Victory House at Walterboro, South Carolina, a special veteran's nursing home. She said to me, "I don't want to but I have to. Well, he can't be on his own; you saw him."

Jim at Fraser Health Center, Hilton Head, April 22, 2009

Janet's dream came true when Jim was admitted to Victory House in May 2009. The Veterans' Victory House: Home of the Greatest Generations is a 220-bed state-of-the-art nursing care facility operated by Advantage Veterans Services of Walterboro for the South Carolina Department of Mental Health. The nursing home is 126,000 square feet on a 20-acre site with a staff of 250 and a 52-bed secured dementia unit.

Jim Emswiler

Jim Emswiler

Jim was born on August 16, 1920 in Elkhart, Indiana. His parents moved to Columbus, Ohio when Jim was a year old. After graduating from high school in 1938, Jim went to Los Angeles and was working for Lockheed Aircraft Corporation when Pearl Harbor was attacked in 1941. He returned to Columbus, enlisted in the U.S. Army Air Corps in January 1942 and was sent to Patterson Field and then to flight training schools. After stops at Thunderbird Field in Phoenix and Minter Field in Bakersfield, California, Jim received his wings and commission at Luke Field in October 1942.

His next assignment was at a yet-unnamed, large dry lake bed in California—now called Edwards Air Force Base—where he trained on a

Lockheed Lightning P-38 aircraft. The P-38 introduced a second engine to American fighters. A tricycle landing gear and twin-boom configuration were other major innovations.

In his own words

I was sent overseas to North Africa and assigned to the 12th Air Force. We flew P-38s. I loved the P-38. I was the only one on board—a single seater. I was a reconnaissance pilot but I trained as a fighter pilot. No guns, just cameras. We originally landed at Oran, on the Mediterranean coast in northwestern Algeria. At my next base, in Algiers, the base commanding officer was Elliot Roosevelt, son of the president. I flew out of Constantine.

(Author's note: The reconnaissance plane that had the earliest and greatest influence for the Americans in WWII was the F-4, a factory modification of the P-38E, which replaced the four guns and cannon with four high-quality K-17 cameras. The Lightning in its reconnaissance role was so well-liked by military strategists that hundreds of gun-equipped P-38s were field-modified into camera-toting F-5 variants.)

P-38 reconnaissance plane over Maison Blanche Airport—photo taken by Jim Emsler flying alongside

As a reconnaissance pilot, I took photos of airfields and railroad yards in North Africa. We had a camera mounted at the head of the pilot's cabin.

There were three different cameras, a 6-inch and two 40-inch cameras. After landing, the film was processed by specialists so that bombing sites could be analyzed. My stay in North Africa was brief. I flew only 10 missions and then was bitten by a mosquito and came down with malaria. The Air Corps sent me to a hospital in Algeria. My weight was down to 108 pounds and I was shipped back home. I recovered shortly and married my high school girl friend, Violet Eddy, from Columbus, in 1943.

I was then sent to Will Rogers Field in Oklahoma City, where I remained for nine months. I wanted to go back overseas, and received orders to ship out to Italy. I was sent to Bari on the east coast of Italy and flew 46 more missions as a reconnaissance pilot in a P-38. One day I decided to take my P-38 and fly over Berlin, while the war was still going on.

Q&A

Arnold: What made you do this?

Jim: Just an impulse! It turned out to be an historic flight, the first from Italy over Berlin, and I did it on my own initiative.

Arnold: You didn't have orders?

Jim: No.

Arnold: Did you file a flight plan?

Jim: No. I just decided I wanted to go. I flew over Berlin at about 25,000 feet and a couple of days after that, the 15th Air Force, which was based in Italy, bombed Berlin because of the flight I made.

Arnold: After you returned from the flight, did you get bawled out?

Jim: Oh, no. They were quite thrilled with it. I made a second flight over Berlin after the 15th Air Force bombed the city. I led a flight of four P-38s, each escorted by two P-51s (Mustangs). When over Berlin, one of my P-51s got out of formation and flew right in front of me. I thought, this is a hell of a way to die. Fortunately, I took evasive action and avoided a mid-air collision. On another occasion I had made several passes over Budapest. When I looked behind me I saw hundreds of flak bursts. I immediately took evasive action, but the flak followed me until I got out of range. It was scary.

Photos from on high

In addition to the usual photos of airfields, railroad yards and other enemy facilities in Europe and Africa, Jim took such images as:

— the bombed-out city of Munich
— Dachau concentration camp
— the canals of Venice
— Pisa and its leaning tower
— The Alps around Salzburg
— Hitler's hideaway, "The Eagle's Nest," in Berchtesgaden

Bombed-out city of Munich

Luftwaffe airfield, Munich

Hitler's hideaway, "The Eagle's Nest," in Berchtesgaden

In his own words

I had to make a single-engine landing once. When I first was in training at Edwards the commanding officer had the radio equipment removed to make room so another pilot could squeeze in with me on a training flight. We took off and the other pilot asked me, "Would you like to try a single-engine landing?" I said, "Well, sure," thinking he had done this before. But he said he hadn't, and he had to go around making a proper approach—quite a dangerous thing to do in a P-38. The first time I flew a P-38 solo I was instructed to buzz the field. Just as I approached, one of my engines cut out. I just circled around and landed on the lake bed.

Incidentally, there were four of us in the room when I graduated flight school at Luke Field. All three of my roommates died within three months after we graduated together. Two of them were in training. When they took off on a practice flight their engine cut out and they couldn't control the plane. It flipped over and they were killed in the crash. My other roommate was killed in combat over Sardinia.

When the war ended in Europe, I was sent home. I expected to be shipped to the Pacific, but Japan surrendered after the atomic bombs were dropped on Hiroshima and Nagasaki. I was finally discharged in Indianapolis with the rank of major.

Recognition

Jim received the following medals for his military service:

* Silver Star
* Distinguished Flying Cross
* Presidential Citation
* Air Medal and six oak leaf clusters

Back to civilian life

Jim was 25 years old when he was discharged. He returned to Columbus, reunited with his wife and was happy to work in his father's electrical appliance business. His love of flying prompted him to serve in the Air National Guard, where he was able to fly P-51s.

When Jim was 40 years old he returned to college and earned bachelor's and master's degrees in history at Ohio State University. He taught school for about six years in junior and senior high school in a small town east of Columbus.

Jim had been a stamp collector all his life and sold stamps for about 10 years. He lives in Island West (a golf community in Bluffton, South Carolina) with his daughter, son-in-law and granddaughter.

Asked about his thoughts of military service, Jim replied, "It was positive. I enjoyed it. It was really the highlight of my life."

Jim at home, 2009

John Guarneri

John Guarneri and bride Lillian, on their wedding day

Author's note: I never met John Guarneri. His daughter, Nina Lafamina, was kind enough to show me his papers and photos from World War II, including love letters that John wrote to Lillian Billella. They struck a chord with me and are at the end of his profile. For soldiers, letters home can be as much about personal therapy as communication—a way to process the loneliness of separation, exorcise demons on paper and remember love and family in the midst of combat or monotony.

John Guarneri was born on June 29, 1920 in Palermo, Italy. His family immigrated to the United States on October 19, 1921 and settled in Brooklyn, New York. After graduating from Brooklyn High School of Automotive Trades in June 1938, he worked for National Rebuilt Motors in Brooklyn until he was drafted into the Army, along with his two brothers (Carlo and Salvatore), on July 21, 1942. John completed basic training at Camp Upton, New York. He worked as a postal clerk at several Army bases and then transferred to his principle MOS as an automotive mechanic.

His unit was deployed to the South Pacific on April 23, 1943 and sailed to New Caledonia, arriving on May 13. During World War II, the French South Pacific colonies of New Caledonia, French Polynesia and the New Hebrides joined the Free French Forces. Assisted by Australia, the South Pacific colonies became vital Allied bases in the Pacific Ocean.

John's overseas tour ended on March 28, 1945. He returned to the States on April 17 and was discharged on October 3 at Pine Camp (later Camp Drum), New York.

**John and Lillian celebrating discharge from Army
in Coney Island with Army buddy**

John met Lillian Billella at a neighborhood dance. Her father was very strict, but a romance grew, an engagement followed and the couple was wed on

May 6, 1945 at St. Joseph, Patron of the Universal Church. They went to Niagara Falls for their honeymoon and returned to their home in Brooklyn, moving to Smithtown, Long Island in 1964. They had two children, Jack and Nina.

He worked for the New York Sanitation Department for a few years, then became a transit patrolman for 26 years. He retired in 1977, then worked part-time for Geico Insurance to 1988, taking photos of cars. John died on February 26, 1988 and Lillian died on September 24, 2005. Nina lives in Hauppauge, Long Island.

Transit Patrolman John Guarneri

Love letters from the front

Daughter Nina saved a box of documents and letters from her father to his intended. He wrote to her almost daily. The letters are in their original hand-written envelopes with postage stamps that range from three to eight cents. The two below serve as good examples of John's unwavering adoration and love of Lillian. Punctuation and spelling appear as they do in the original letters.

New Caledonia
March 8, 1945

"Suddenly my heart sings"

My dearest beloved,

Whakaho, yip-yips—you finally done did it. I guess you know what I am driving at. Yep, you are right beloved. It's about the picture you took with the . . . and they were . . . no, OK, I better stop. I have gone far enough. I love you beautiful. I love you above all. Doris Day just finished singing, "Suddenly my heart sings." It's a beautiful song, darling; just like you my love.

I am feeling fine, darling and I hope to hear the same from you all at home. I received a letter from your friend, Jeannie today, and darling, she is always telling me of how much you always talk about me, and how much you miss me. Oh darling, how much I love you. You don't know how much you mean to me. You are everything I live for. I love you darling, more than life.

Honey when I start reading in your letter that you took a picture with the skirt on, my heart skipped a beat. But OK, I have to wait at least a month before it gets here. Say, honey, how about an enlargement of it. Boy, I'm going nuts, darling. But darling, you realize why. It's because I love you so much and you mean the world to me. Tonight I saw the movie, "Meet Me in St. Louis." It was OK, but nothing what they built it up to be.

So I see that Chubby's brother broke some girl's heart that works with you. A lot of guys that are stationed here have been getting those letters. Some were almost married and their girls tell them that they are going with someone else. What beats it all—a fellow down here has been away from his wife two years, and she told him she gave birth to another child. Boy, what this war isn't bringing out in some people! All I have to say, honey, that when love is true and deep like ours, it will never die. I love you darling. You are the love of my life. Darling, you're driving me nuts trying to figure out what you are sending me for Easter. But I have it darling. It gives me something to look forward to. But couldn't you have told me dear? I hope you had a swell time on your last outing your club had. Where did you go? Hope you all took pictures.

Darling, in your last letter you mentioned that you wanted to buy a suit, but you didn't get it because it cost about $50 or $60. Darling, I mean this! The next time you tell me something like that, I am really going to be angry with you. Darling, how many times do I have to tell you, that whenever you want, something and you are short of money that you should go get it out of our account. What do you think we have it for? Honey, for Easter I want you to go and draw out about $100 and buy yourself a real good outfit, complete. Please darling`, and then take a lot of pictures. I am going to see if you are going to do me that pleasure. I love you darling. I love you more than anything in this world.

Sweetheart, I guess I'll leave you with a special kiss and say good night my beloved wife. I love you.

My love and kisses to mom, pop and Sally. A million special love kisses to you, my beloved wife. I love you.

Regards to all,

Always and affectionately,
All my life,
Your beloved husband,
I love you truly,
Johnny

New Caledonia
March 19, 1945

My dearest beloved sweetheart,

Hello darling: I love you. Writing you a few words dear, letting you know that I am well, and feeling in the best of health. I'm hoping to hear the same from you. Darling, I better hurry up and get home, for you may not want me anymore. Boy, I am slowly getting old. Today I am twenty four years old.

Honey, if this damn war wasn't going on, we would be, by this time, the parents of at least three beautiful children. There is nothing slow about me, is there darling?

Oh well honey, some day them good old days will come for you and me. You know, dear, I was supposed to have bought a couple of cases of beer so we would have had a little party tonight. But the boys were one step ahead of me, and they bought it. It sure made me feel good in how they thought of me.

Incidentally dear, as I am writing, I feel as if I am sitting on air—ahem, I wonder why? I have had the blues all day long today, dear. Because I know that you must have been thinking of the times we were together. But honey, this war can't last forever, and some day we will be together again, just as we belong. I love you darling. I love you above all.

Well beloved, I am enclosing a fifteen dollar money order in this letter. Boy, our bank account is steadily growing. Darling, what do you think we are going to do with it when I get home? No, don't say it's going towards our home, because it's not. I have about $2,400 home myself. Darling, we have everything ready; all we need now is to hear that solemn word of "Peace." I love you darling. I love you. I know what we are going to do with that money dear. Someday I will take you to New York to the best fur coat store in the city and buy you the best in the house. We will sure look good going on our honeymoon.

Today our company gave us fellows a formula to fill out pertaining to what our American Army experiences were and are. They are going to have published in our hometown paper. I gave the name of the following papers—Brooklyn Eagle, Daily News, Daily Mirror. So honey, be on the lookout—you may come across it in the paper.

I still haven't received the package your mom sent me, but I hear that some boats came in so I hope they were on one of them. My darling, its one o'clock now, and the boys are still in bed. So I guess I will close now and put the light out.

My love and kisses to mom, pop and Salvatore and a million love kisses to you my beloved wife. I love you above all. Regards to all our mutual friends,

Affectionately as ever,
Your beloved,
I love you darling
Always and forever yours
Love,
Johnny

John Hango

John Hango

John was born on August 9, 1924 in Woodbridge, New Jersey and drafted into the U.S. Army (as a junior in Woodbridge High School) on March 23, 1943. After completing basic training in Fort Dix, New Jersey, he took further training in Alabama's Fort McClelland and Camp Rucker. In November John stood ready to board a troop ship in Newport News, Virginia bound for North Africa.

In his own words

As we were lined up waiting to board the ship, a riot started—a bunch of Southerners against Northerners. I assume one or more of the GIs began making disparaging remarks and that must have ignited this full-blown riot. The rest of us couldn't believe what we saw. The MPs broke it up, arrested the participants and locked them up on the ship. They were court-martialed when we landed in Tunisia. I have no idea what eventually happened to them.

It took us 30 days to sail from Virginia to Tunisia. We slept and ate topside for the entire journey. Below deck they had racks for us to sleep on but it was hot and humid down there so we preferred being topside. Thirty days at sea! One night we felt the ship do a 180-degree turnabout so that another ship in our convoy could take our place. About three hours later that ship blew up. A torpedo got it. All you could see was fragments flying out of the water. It was an ammunition ship that blew up. We arrived in Tunisia without any more incidents.

I was in a replacement unit. In Africa I was assigned to Company I, 157th Infantry, 45th Division (Thunderbirds). After two months we went to Anzio, Italy as replacements. At Anzio we stayed in the mountains until May 1944, when we were ordered to the front lines to face combat.

On patrol

On patrol we had several encounters with German troops but I managed to survive. As we walked on patrol we passed mine fields and shells were falling around us. I remember seeing dead GIs on the side of the road with bullet holes in their bellies and blood seeping out of their stomachs. I couldn't stop because I would have been a sitting duck. Some were still alive but we were ordered not to stop to help them but to keep moving. It was a terrible experience. I continued to participate in patrols until I got wounded. Anzio was invaded before our unit got there.

Author's note: The following excerpt is from The Fighting Forty-Fifth, *compiled and edited under supervision of the Historical Board of the 45th Infantry Division.*

The silence of the mist-shrouded morning was misleading. It gave no warning of the hell that was to be Anzio The lonely stretch of Italian coast looked gaunt and uninviting to the first Thunderbirdmen who hit the beach on the heels of the 3rd—the Marine Division.

The 179th Infantry landed in the Anzio-Nettuno harbor on January 22, 1944, within 24 hours after the assault troops hit the beach. The initial landing was extremely successful, and the beachhead forces pushed their lines as far out as their small number would permit. The enemy had prepared few defenses in this sector—they had not progressed beyond hasty field fortifications, trenches, some barbed-wire road blocks and a few mine fields.

By the last day of the month, the entire 45th Division had completed debarkation on this little point of sand some 30 miles from Rome. Infantry troops took up defensive positions at once, for it was established by air reconnaissance that the Germans were rapidly bringing in reserves to oppose any advance in the direction of Rome.

After the invasion, about a month or two later, the Army began sending in troops to replace the paratroopers that were wounded. My rank at that time was private 1st class. We left on May 29. When the attack began, we encountered fierce firepower. As the shelling grew intense, I laid down along the railroad tracks for protection. A mortar shell exploded near me and I got sprayed with shrapnel. I was gravely wounded in my right shoulder, buttocks and ankle. I laid there for two hours trying to get up but just couldn't! I had no strength. It started getting dark and I must have passed out.

Author's note: John's attack was described in The Fighting Forty-Fifth, *pages 74-75:*

Tired from their night march and the constant stop and go that mark a frontline relief, the men settled into their shallow slit-trenches and relaxed as best they could. Dawn was approaching. There was silence for awhile and then suddenly from far away came the sound of approaching shells, then the screams, rumble and crash as the projectiles hit. The men huddled in their holes and waited tensely as the shelling increased. Over the noise of the explosions came the distant sound of enemy guns. Shells blew men out of shallow trenches. The cry of the wounded—"Medics, medics"—pierced the air. To the cramped, nervous men crouching to the ground, the barrage seemed endless, but suddenly the shelling ceased. Across the rocky flat from Aprilla rolled German light tanks and behind them charging infantrymen.

The full brunt of the enemy assault struck the Division. Riflemen and machine gunners cut down the German infantry, but three German tanks completely overran the left platoon of the Company.

Q & A

AR: What happened when you were wounded?

JH: When it got dark, I started crawling back to where I thought I came from. I was crawling on an open field. I must have passed out because I heard someone say, "Here's another one!"

AR: What did you have with you—a backpack and a rifle?

JH: Not much of a backpack.

AR: What kind of weapon did you have?

JH: It was an M1903-bolt action rifle. I was a sniper.

AR: What else did you carry?

JH: A canteen and extra ammo. After I heard someone say, "Here's another one," I must have passed out—that was the last thing I remembered. The next thing I knew I was on an airplane. I was going back to Naples. When I got back to a military hospital I slept for three days. They couldn't get me up. They kept slapping my face but I couldn't stay awake. I finally woke up and they started treating my wounds and I underwent surgery. I was reclassified as a non-combatant because I had no strength in my right arm. I was moved to the 235th Field Hospital in Naples and later transferred to France. I was assigned as a postal clerk and then to the officer's mess unit—all non-combat assignments. The Army did not want me to go back into combat.

AR: So basically once you got hit, the war was over for you?

JH: Yes, as far as combat was concerned. The *Woodridge Star Ledger* in New Jersey had an article in the paper about my encounter:

> *Purple Heart, PFC John Hango: Wounded in Italy on May 29, 1944, PFC John Hango has been awarded the Purple Heart Medal. Nineteen years old, PFC Hango was inducted on March 27, 1943 and trained at Fort McClelland and Camp Rucker, Alabama. He was assigned to overseas duty in September, 1943. Two*

other brothers are also out of the country. They are: Corporal Stephen in England and Private George in Newfoundland.

I got orders to sail home from Le Havre, France on November 17, 1945 and arrived in the States on November 30. The ship was one of those converted cruise liners—the George Washington.

Discharge—and awards

John was discharged at Fort Monmouth, New Jersey on November 30, 1945. He was awarded the following decorations and citations:

* European-African-Middle Eastern Ribbon
* Good Conduct Medal
* Purple Heart Medal
* Distinguished Unit Badge

Liberation of Dachau

Although John did not participate, his unit (the 157th Infantry, with the 191st Tank Battalion in support) along with British Army units was part of the liberation of the Dachau Concentration Camp shortly after noon April 29, 1945.

Author's note: Dachau, 1933-1945, will stand for all time as one of history's most gruesome symbols of inhumanity. There our troops found sights, sounds and stenches beyond belief, cruelties so enormous as to be incomprehensible to the normal mind. Dachau and death were synonymous.—William W. Quinn, 7th U.S. Army.

At 10:30 a.m. I Company of the 157th Infantry and elements of M Company (3rd Battalion) are dispatched in the direction of the concentration camp. Forward elements of I Company enters the concentration camp after finding and inspecting a trainload of dead prisoners. Pfc. John Degro of Burton, Ohio is believed to be the first American liberator to enter the concentration camp and come within view of the inmates.

Company I soldiers reach the inner compound where inmates are imprisoned. The crematorium and gas chamber are soon discovered. Pandemonium reigns and dead bodies are everywhere.

The American GIs in a frenzy of horror and anger gun down some 122 captured German soldiers—most of them Waffen SS. Dozens of inmates break out of the prison enclosure and kill approximately 40 guards, some with their bare hands. Private John Lee of I Company later told newspapers that he was personally involved in at least 60 of the killings.

In total, over 200,000 prisoners from more than 30 countries were housed in Dachau of whom two-thirds were political prisoners and nearly one-third was Jews. About 25,000 prisoners are believed to have died in the camp and almost another 10,000 in its sub-camps, primarily from disease, malnutrition and suicide. In early 1945, there was a typhus epidemic in the camp followed by an evacuation, in which large numbers of the weaker prisoners died.

For further information on Dachau see:

scrapbookpages.com/Dachau Scrapbook/ . . . /SoldiersKilled.html

www.humanitas-international.org/archive/dachau-liberation

www.**45thinfantrydivision.com**/index14.htm

Q & A

AR: What did you do when you were discharged?

JH: I returned home to Woodridge, New Jersey. I was 22 years old and had a hard time finding a job. The military had a "52/20 Club." This provision enabled all former servicemen to receive $20 once a week for 52 weeks a year while they were looking for work. Less than 20 percent of the money set aside for the 52-20 Club was distributed. Rather, most returning servicemen quickly found jobs or pursued higher education. I did eventually get a job with Copperworks, a copper mill in Perth Amboy, New Jersey.

Mildred Pickers

In 1947 I suffered an appendicitis attack and was told by my doctor to go to Perth Amboy hospital early next morning. Mildred Pickers was a nurse at the hospital. When I arrived on the floor, she asked me what I was doing there. I said I was scheduled for surgery to remove my appendix. She was a little perturbed because at that time of the morning the nurses were just changing shifts and were busy doing paperwork from the last shift. She told me to go in a special room, and get undressed. Nurse Mildred returned and began to shave the area where the surgery was to be performed. At that time the hospital was being renovated. While she was shaving me, all of a sudden the razor slips out of her hand and falls down a hole to the floor below. She had to go downstairs and retrieve the razor and come back up. My room had an opening in the floor where pipes were coming up from the floor below.

The surgery was successful. While I was recovering I was attended by several other nurses. One morning I had the following exchange with another nurse:

"You know Miss Pickers? I want to take her out for a date!!"
"No, I don't think so!"

"Will you ask her?"

"No, not me!"

"You ask her!"

"No!"

I finally told her (halfheartedly in jest), "You ask her today. If you don't, I'm going to grab hold of you!"

Mildred walked into the room and said to me, "I hear you want a date with me?" I said, "Yeah; what's wrong with that?" She says, "Nothing; but I'm too old for you; I'm older than you are!" "So what; I don't care. I still want to go out with you."

I was in the hospital for about a week. A day before I was to be discharged, I asked her, "Do we have a date?" She says, "Oh, all right!" We did have our date. A romance, courtship and wedding followed and we were married for 59 years. Mildred died in March 2008. She was from Salem, New Jersey and received her Certificate of Nursing from Perth Amboy General Hospital as an RN. She was a nurse at the hospital for four years and as a lieutenant in the WAVES during World War II served in the Philadelphia Naval Hospital.

Just before I met Mildred I went to work for Johnson & Johnson Surgical Division in Brunswick, New Jersey. I started out as a slitter helper (we cut tape in various dimensions). After six months I was transferred into shipping, then to production control as an expeditor and I became a production control scheduler. My final 17 years I was a production supervisor. I worked for J & J for 36 years and retired in 1984.

Mildred and I went to the Poconos and stayed there for 10 years. Then we moved to North Carolina where my daughter, Carol Aita, and her husband had a business. I have one son, John Jr. We lived there for 10 years and then moved to Sun City, Hilton Head—South Carolina in 2003.

Thoughts of military service

I think all kids around 18 or 19 should be in military service—to give them a sense of responsibility. Not because we want them to go to war, but I don't feel the kids of today are getting the education in schools that they need to function in a complex world. I am not blaming the teachers. I blame the parents because they are not instilling a proper foundation for their children. If you don't have a proper foundation you will lack the necessary attributes to succeed in life. If you are in the service you are told what to do and you either do it or suffer the consequences. If a kid is home and the parents ask them to do something, and the kid refuses, often times there is no consequence; the parents might just let it go. In the service you do it, or else! It's a matter of discipline. The service gives you a sense of maturity, responsibility and respect for authority.

Why tell your story?

I wanted to tell this story for my grandchildren. I have three grandchildren and two great-grandchildren. They don't know about wars. There are going to be wars—whether we like it or not. I don't know and I hope not.

I'm humble about the small part I played in World War II and I'm proud that I had an opportunity to serve my country in a noble cause. For my children and grandchildren this may be a-once-in-a-lifetime trip. When I and my fellow vets are gone, our stories will remain in this book giving our children and grandchildren a chance to know us better.

John at home in Sun City, 2009

Viorica and George Hawley

Viorica Hawley

Author's note: This profile differs from the typical military veteran profile published here and in my first book, "Keeping Memories Alive." It is the story of two brave, caring and compassionate people, Viorica Bretoi and George Hawley, and their efforts to help some of the eight million displaced victims of World War II in Europe. Viorica served as a member of UNRRA (United Nations Relief and Rehabilitation Administration) and George served in the U.S. Army.

Viorica was born on September 18, 1916 in St. Paul, Minnesota. At age 15, she graduated as valedictorian of South St. Paul High School, enrolled in Lancaster Business College of St. Paul and then won a scholarship to study at Macalester College (in St. Paul). She went on to the University of Minnesota, graduating with a BS degree in social work in 1937.

Q & A

Arnold: What did you do after college?

Vi: I was enrolled in a graduate program (in social work, at Minnesota) and got a job at an Armour Company meat-packing plant.

Arnold: What did you do at Armour?

Vi: I worked for four men in the kosher meat department, for the Jewish market. I was their Girl Friday. I did the secretarial work and calculations to determine cost.

Arnold: Where did you work after Armour?

Vi: In 1938 I was hired at the International Institute of the YWCA in St. Paul as activities director. I remained there until I went to California in 1942. During the war, the government started the USO (United Service Organization), which had branches in all the major cities. I was a USO volunteer.

In her own words

The International Institute had branches in the YWCA and later became an independent agency. I was at the Y in St. Paul one day and a recruiter happened to be there for the USO. I took the interview, completed the application and was hired. I was sent to Vallejo, California at Mare Island Navy Yard. My job title was associate director. I was sent to New York for additional training and had a stint at a USO Club in Indiana before returning to Vallejo.

In 1944 I was offered a job in Oakland as personnel counselor for the Aviation Annex of the Navy Supply Depot, a position established to help civilian defense workers employed in the main supply base for Naval Aviation in the Pacific Theater of Operations. I dealt with employee grievances and job and housing problems that affected morale and work output.

I also enrolled in two evening classes at the University of California at Oakland. One was International Organization, the other was Spanish. In my International Organization class the professor told me a recruiter was expected to visit from UNRRA (United Nations Relief and Rehabilitation Agency) and he thought I would be a natural for the job.

I took the interview and soon after received a telephone call at the Navy Yard. I thought it was someone giving me a line when he asked me if I could report to Washington, D.C. in a week. I answered, "Are you kidding me?" I finally realized that he was a bona fide executive from UNRRA and they really intended to hire me to join an orientation course in Washington the following week. I took a physical exam at the Navy Hospital in Oakland. In those days it was very difficult to book a cross-country flight, so I went by train. The train was packed with GIs; they were sitting, and standing, in the aisles. I arrived in Washington, enrolled in an orientation course that lasted several weeks and then received my overseas shots and uniforms.

Saving the children

I was appointed a child welfare specialist for UNRRA in Austria. In July—it was 1945—I was sent to England on the Santa Rosa, a hospital ship used by the military. The war was still going on in the South Pacific and we sailed across the Atlantic in a blackout. Victory in Europe (V-E Day) had been May 8, 1945, when the World War II allies formally accepted the unconditional surrender of the armed forces of Nazi Germany and the end of Adolf Hitler's Third Reich.

Upon arriving in England I was sent to Jouleville, France (Eisenhower's headquarters), which was an UNRRA team staging area. I was assigned to a team of five, with an American director, a French assistant, a Dutch nurse, a Canadian supply officer and Australian and American drivers. We drove in two British Army trucks. I sat in the back with my meager possessions—a duffle bag and a small backpack. I remained in post-war Europe for two years, mainly in Austria.

As a United Nations agency, UNRRA was charged with relief and rehabilitation work for all Allied civilian populations displaced or left homeless by World War II. In 1947 the name was changed to the International Relief Organization. UNRRA teams were deployed to the most heavily damaged areas to try to save starving children and their elders. The most pressing task was locating and caring for children who were lost or homeless, and whose parents were dead or missing.

A heart-rending task

Temporary shelters were located; medical aid, food and clothing were provided; and attempts made to identify and locate relatives of these youngsters. After identity was established and physical and mental rehabilitation was sufficient to withstand the trip, railroad convoys were set up and staffed by UNRRA to return the children to their native soil.

Children being transported from Austria to Poland, from Viorica Hawley's collection

In August 1945 our team of five was assigned to take over a DP (displaced persons) camp the British Army had set up for us in the mountain town of Admont, Austria. This had been a Nazi mountain cavalry post. We had a large number of Polish, Ukrainian and Yugoslav DPs. In early 1946 I was moved to Ebensee, Austria with a Canadian director, Rudi Bialuski, to set up a temporary children's home in Rindbach, near Ebensee, that was formerly owned by the family of the famous music composer Felix Mendelssohn.

Before winter set in a permanent home for displaced children was established in Bad Schallerbach. This site was formerly a Cur Heim (German for rest home) that had been used by employees from Vienna who took advantage of the mineral springs nearby to help their arthritis and other ailments. Classrooms and barracks to house the children and staff were constructed. The children and staff were from all parts of Europe but German was spoken throughout. A Polish adult was assigned as a teacher and a 19-year-old Polish boy, Richard Borowski, was assigned to supervise and counsel the boys.

Author's note: Viorica had a language course in German in college and was able to speak it well. She accompanied the children on many train rides across Europe. The Polish Red Cross played an important role in identifying and locating homes for the children and worked very closely with the UNRRA teams. Viorica received special letters of recognition by the Polish Red Cross and UNRRA. Thousands of children were involved, and their situations were often heart-rending. Admont and Bad Schallerbach, home for so many displaced children, were near the Ebensee and Stein Kogel concentration camps, which were converted by the U.S. Army and UNRRA into staging areas for secretly repatriating members of the Jewish faith from Eastern Europe to Palestine.

Children in classroom in Admont, Austria, 1946, from Viorica Hawley's collection.

Ebensee Concentration Camp

Following is copyright American-Israeli Cooperative Enterprise, reprinted with permission.

Ebensee Concentration Camp, together with the Mauthausen subcamp of Gusen, is considered to be one of the most diabolical concentration camps ever built. Its main purpose was to provide slave labor for building enormous underground tunnels in which armament works were to be housed.

Rising at 4:30 a.m., the prisoners dug away at the tunnels until 6 p.m. Work soon was done in shifts 24 hours a day. There was nearly no accommodation to protect the first batch of prisoners from the cold Austrian winter. Bodies were piled in heaps; every three or four days they were taken to the Mauthausen crematorium to be burned. The dead were also piled inside the few huts that existed.

The prisoners wore wooden clogs. When they fell apart the prisoners had to go barefoot. Lice infested the camp. In the morning food rations consisted of half a liter of ersatz coffee; at noon, three-quarters of a liter of hot water containing potato peelings; in the evening, 150 grams of bread. Due to this ill treatment, the death toll continued to rise. The camp was surrounded by a barbed wire fence, small towers with machine guns and shacks for the SS.

Two tanks from a squadron of the U.S. Third Army liberated Ebensee on May 5, 1945. By that time, there were around 18,500 prisoners in the camp. Jews made up approximately one-third of the inmates. Other groups of prisoners included prisoners of war, political prisoners, criminals, Russians, Poles, Czechoslovaks and Gypsies. There were inmates of 20 different nationalities in Ebensee, but the Jews were treated more harshly than other prisoners. Toward the end of the year, their number in Ebensee increased to 40 percent.

George Hawley

In the words of Wayne Hawley

My mom spent two years after the war in Admont and Bad Schallerbach, Austria. During that same period, my dad, George Hawley, was stationed in the Army in Ebensee. He entered the Army as a private and landed in Europe on D+ 13—thirteen days after D-Day. Dad went through all the enlisted ranks except two and then he got a battlefield commission as a 2nd lieutenant during the Battle of the Bulge. After the war, Dad was an artillery officer in the 8th Armored Division. The Army assigned him to an engineering district while they were staging for the invasion of Japan. His unit was slated for the first day's invasion of the island of Honshu. The Army brass knew they were going to sustain a large number of casualties in a ground invasion of Japan. This invasion never occurred as the Japanese surrendered after the atom bomb was dropped at Hiroshima and Nagasaki.

My dad's job at Ebensee was to turn the concentration camp into a displaced person's camp. Many of the surviving prisoners were still at the camp. A lot of the Holocaust survivors at Ebensee had nowhere to go. What our government was secretly doing was taking a lot of these Jewish men and women, who had no place to go, and ferrying them by train to the coast of France and shipping them to Palestine. The British didn't know we were doing this. Palestine was still under British rule. The survivors were sick, anemic and in various stages of shock. Dad told me he was outraged and disgusted to see the horrific conditions of these inmates. I asked him once, "What was your worst encounter during the entire Second World War?" He said, "Wayne, my worst day was when we liberated the concentration camp at Bergen-Belsen. That was the most horrible thing I ever saw in my life." At Bergen-Belsen he said the people were so emaciated it was pitiful to see. The GIs who liberated these camps were also overwhelmed with sorrow and immediately began feeding the prisoners—not knowing that gorging of food would result in severe gastro trauma and death.

Author's note: Bergen-Belsen was a concentration camp near Hanover in northwest Germany. As the first major camp to be liberated by the allies, it received a lot of press coverage and the world saw the horrors of the Holocaust. Some 60,000 prisoners were present at the time of liberation. Afterward, about 500 people died daily of starvation and typhus, for a total of nearly 14,000. Mass graves were made to hold the thousands of corpses of those who perished.

German female guards loading dead prisoners onto truck after the camp was liberated by the British on April 15, 1945—Photo courtesy of the Holocaust Research Project

In 1946, Belsen served as the largest DP camp for more than 11,000 Jews and the lone Jewish-only camp in the British zone of Germany. Within three days the refugees formed a camp committee that organized political, cultural and religious activities, such as searching for relatives and spiritual rehabilitation. More than 20 marriages were performed daily during the first few months; more than 2,000 children were born to survivors. An elementary school was founded in July 1945, attended in 1948 by 340 students. A high school started In December 1945 was partly staffed by the Jewish brigade. A kindergarten, orphanage, yeshiva and religious school were also formed. The DPs also wrote the main Jewish newspaper, Unzer Shtimme (Our Voice), in the British zone.

Many of the DPs wanted to immigrate to Palestine, but they faced strict British immigration policies. Clandestine military training sessions held by the Haganah were performed at the camp in December 1947 to prepare DPs for immigration to Palestine. Free departure from the camp was prohibited until 1949. By mid-1950 most of the DPs had left and by 1951 the camp was empty. Most of Bergen-Belsen's DPs immigrated to Israel, the United States and Canada.

My father saw some pretty rough stuff during the war. During the Battle of the Bulge, he nearly got killed. As a forward observer riding in a tank he and his crew suddenly sustained a tremendous explosion. The tank crew didn't know what hit them. It was an 88 round that pierced the front armor plate. Everyone else in his tank got killed, but luckily Dad, in the turret, got blown clear. He received a battlefield commission for gallantry in combat. During the attack he was wounded in his leg by a bullet. The doctor told him to put in for a Purple Heart award but he denied the incident—he never admitted he got shot, nor did he ever tell me he got shot until about 2000. "Yeah," he said, "I got shot. (But) I never really told anybody." He pointed to his leg and showed me his scar. He turned down a Purple Heart because, he said, the wound wasn't bad enough.

Working together

While Dad's mission was to reconstruct the former concentration camp at Ebensee into a displaced persons camp for the adults, my mom was busy helping the displaced children. In the occupied countries Hitler had taken, blond-haired, blue-eyed children—the *wunderkind*, for his so-called super race—away from their families and brought them to Germany and Austria. Mom cared for, sheltered and fed some of these blond-haired kids and other children that were displaced from their parents. There was a large group of children from Poland who were shipped out to Austria during the Nazi invasion for safety reasons. Nuns also kept a large group of these children.

Fate and circumstances brought Viorica Bretoi and George Hawley together. Mom's group cared for the children and Dad provided shelter and food for the displaced adults and Allied prisoners of war. He took prisoners of war from the Russian, Polish and Czech and any Allied armies and placed them on trains bound for their pre-war homes. My mom had basically the same job—she located the children's parents or surviving relatives in the occupied country. Because the Germans were such good record-keepers, Mom's team and the Red Cross could locate most of their homes. Meanwhile, Mom and Dad met because they worked together.

Courtship and marriage

She tells of his proposal: "We were dating in Austria, and I told him that I was planning to join the International Relief Organization when I return to the States." He said, 'Are you or are you not going to marry me?' That was his proposal to me! I'll never forget it! We got married in Bad Schallerbach and the burgermeister of the town performed the ceremony."

George Hawley was born on December 23, 1920 in New London, Connecticut and joined the Army in 1943. He made a career of the Army and retired after 33 years with the rank of colonel. A veteran of World War II, Korea and Vietnam, he was awarded the Legion of Merit. (He was a forward observer for four months during the Battle of the Bulge in World War II, and someone in the Army figured out that the life span of forward observers—whose main job was to spot, before a mission, where enemy artillery and positions were—was measured in minutes.)

Viorica and George lived in military housing for most of George's career. Their first stateside base after the war was at Fort Knox, Kentucky, where he was assigned to the Universal Military Training unit that was being planned. Viorica and George had three children—Brian, Karen, and Wayne.

Journey to Sun City

George's superior officer at Ft. McPherson in Atlanta, Georgia, Maj. Gen. Samuel L. Reid, was a native of Charleston. In 1973 he invited George and Viorica to visit him at his Royal Pines Country Club for the weekend. This led to buying a home nearby, on Lady's Island in Beaufort. They enjoyed their spacious home for many retirement years. When George became ill and the home was too big to care for, they visited Sun City in Bluffton, South Carolina, found a home to their liking, with a separate apartment for son Wayne, and moved in 2001. In April 2002 George died. At present Viorica lives in the home with Wayne.

Col. George Hawley

Willard Gray Herring

Gray Herring

Gray was born on August 25, 1922 in Clinton, North Carolina. He left high school in spring 1941 to work on the family farm. The next spring Gray received a draft notice. Because he didn't want to walk (in the Army), he joined the Navy. After boot camp at Great Lakes, Illinois, he was sent to Fargo Barracks in Boston and requested submarine duty. Instead he was assigned to the newly-commissioned battleship Massachusetts, where he spent the rest of World War II, in the Atlantic and the Pacific.

Mileposts at sea

Author's note: The following describes outstanding missions and mileposts recalled by Gray Herring, and drawn from the book, "A Pictorial History of the U.S.S. Massachusetts."

We went for a few shakedown cruises right out of Boston in the Atlantic, and then headed for Africa. I was a 5-inch gun loader . . . .

Early on November 8, 1942, a large task force of American warships and transports, with the Massachusetts as flagship, moved in toward Casablanca in French Morocco. It signaled that the United States was now ready to throw its might across the seas. French fleet units, including the huge new battleship, Jean Bart, were at anchor in the harbor. The American force approached slowly, under orders not to fire unless resistance developed. Suddenly star shells lit up the sky. Rear Adm. F. C. Griffen, in command of the American force, gave the agreed signal for action—"Play ball!"—and they were in one hot engagement . . . .

When general quarters sounded, I was in an enclosed gun mount and began to load shells and powder . . .

In this battle the Massachusetts was credited with sinking three enemy ships and silencing shore batteries. She returned to the States and her battle-tested crew was granted leaves and liberties. On February 6, 1943, the battleship left Portland, Maine and after passing through the Panama Canal proceeded to Noumea, New Caledonia. In April the Massachusetts pushed into the Coral Sea as a member of a task force group supporting operations against Russell Island. The following month she was back in the Coral Sea again, this time covering operations against Munda, New Georgia, in the Solomon Islands. Her final operations in this area took place in late August and early September when she supported action against Vella Lavella. There followed a lull during which the ship was based first at Effate in the New Hebrides and later in the Fiji Islands.

For the next 11 months the Massachusetts was in battles in the Gilbert Islands, the island of Nauru, Taroa, and Maleolap atoll.

On February 1, 1944, the Massachusetts helped cover landing operations on Kwajalein, the world's largest atoll. The landing went "according to the book" and within a few days the fleet anchored at Majuro—the first pre-war Japanese territory to be occupied by American forces.

In mid-February the Massachusetts took part in a surprise attack against the Japanese stronghold on Truk. Some 209 Japanese planes were destroyed and various types of ships were sunk or damaged. Navy pilots flying Kingfishers (a two-seat amphibious aircraft) launched air strikes in the Marianas. During the rest of February and March the Massachusetts bombed and strafed Saipan, Tinian, Ota and Guam.

After 15 months of Pacific duty, the Massachusetts headed back for the States. She landed in Puget Sound and by next morning the first leave parties went over the side. Within less than two months the Massachusetts headed out again.

More action

Strikes were made against Leyte, Cebu, Negros and Panay Islands. In the invasion of Leyte, the force made new air strikes against the Philippines. During the period October 22 to October 27, the Massachusetts took part in the Battle for Leyte Gulf. . . .

Author's note: The Battle of Leyte Gulf, also called the "Battles for Leyte Gulf", and formerly known as the "Second Battle of the Philippine Sea," is generally considered to be the largest naval battle of World War II and also one of the largest naval battles in history. It was fought in waters near the Philippine islands of Leyte, Samar, and Luzon, October 23-26, 1944, between naval and naval-air forces of the Allies and those of the Empire of Japan. On October 20, U. S. troops invaded the island of Leyte as part of a strategy aimed at isolating Japan from the countries it had occupied in South East Asia, and in particular depriving its forces and industry of vital oil supplies. The close of the battle found all three Japanese forces taking part in the encounter fleeing in defeat, the great majority of their ships having been either sunk or seriously damaged.

Tokyo bombed

In mid-February the Massachusetts took part in the operation that had been the goal of naval planning and strategy for many months—the first raids by carrier planes on Tokyo. As American planes bombed the homeland of Japan, the Massachusetts was a principal supporting force, lying less than 70 miles from the coast of the main Japanese island of Honshu and 117 miles from Tokyo . . . .

Just did his job

There were many days at sea without seeing any signs of the enemy. This did not mean, however, that we were relaxed. Then, even more than when in battle, it meant that all personnel had to be alert, ready for any emergency such as going to General Quarters at all hours of the day and night. Watches and routine functions competed for the 24 hours a day, and the ship, a home for 2,500 men, had to be kept in good repair—every gun and piece of equipment had to work. As for me, whatever my feelings were didn't count; I just did my job.

> *General Quarters or Battle Stations is an announcement made aboard a naval warship to signal the crew to prepare for battle. When the call to General Quarters (GQ) is made, the crew prepares the ship to join battle. Off-duty or sleeping crewmembers report to their stations and prepare for action. Watertight doors between bulkheads are shut and security is increased around sensitive areas such as the bridge and engineering rooms.*

The Massachusetts had been in port for a total of 70 days since starting out on the first Philippine operation, August 20, 1944. Most of these days were spent in Ulithi atoll, which is typical of the Pacific bases—plenty of water surrounded by sandy, palm-topped islands. One of these dunes was designated as a recreation center where thousands upon thousands of liberty-famished officers and men were landed. Baseball diamonds, horseshoe pits, basketball courts and swimming areas were provided for their amusement. One correspondent termed Ulithi "Heaven without women." Yet those days in port were soon to be prized.

Q & A

AR: What was your rank?
GH: I was a seaman.
AR: What was your sleeping quarters like?
GH: We slept in bunks. It was three or four high.

AR: How was the food?
GH: The food was good.
AR: Did you ever get seasick?
GH: Only in typhoons.

Stormy weather

The Japanese were not the only opponent in the Pacific. The weather frequently proved to be a difficult adversary. The first typhoon came in Ulithi on October 3, 1944. The entire task force group hurriedly got underway and by the time she started through the channel, visibility had dropped to zero.

The next typhoon, one of the worst in Naval history, struck while the Task Force was refueling off Luzon. Heavy seas and winds forced discontinuance of fueling operations. On December 18, 1944, the storm struck with all its fury with screaming winds and mountainous seas. Many ships sustained damage. Luckily, the Massachusetts suffered only minor damage. The third typhoon struck in June on June 5, 1945. Estimated winds were better than 100 knots. The ship passed through the "eye" but again came through with only minor damage.

Statistics to be proud of

We had so many battles and bombarding that it is difficult for me to remember them all. In addition to the torpedoes and bombings, I remember the Japanese kamikaze suicide attacks diving at us—30 or 40 Japanese planes coming in all at once.

AR: What about any injuries to crew?
GH: We had one guy—I don't know how he passed away on our ship.
           He was buried at sea. I don't know whether he was in an accident
           or died as a result of wounds.
AR: How long was your tour on the Massachusetts?
GH: Three and a half years.
AR: Did you travel mostly in convoys?
GH: Yes, we wouldn't move without four destroyers alongside of us.
           Whenever we were in battle they were still there. If the enemy
           fired a torpedo at us, instead of us "taking it," they would take
           the hit. They protected us.

AR: Near the end of the war what happened when Japan surrendered?

GH: We had a complement of 100 to 200 of Marines on our ship at all times. The Marines were ordered to disembark at the end of the war when Japan surrendered. We were given the choice to volunteer to be sent to Japan to secure the mainland. I told them, "Not me! I had enough!" The Navy did get quite a few sailors to volunteer, though. They sent them over on a platform vessel from the battleship to a transport ship. We sailed home and docked at Bremerton, Washington. I left the ship, traveled to Nashville, Tennessee where I was discharged on December 20, 1945. I traveled to Florida where my mother lived.

Jenny Lou Jones, 1946

Jenny Jones was living in Jacksonville, working for a Packard dealership. My sister, Mary (she lived there with her husband, an elementary school principal), brought me to the dealership and introduced me to Jenny on Oct 20, 1945. Our courtship lasted two years and we were married on September 11, 1947.

Wedding day, September 11, 1947

After the wedding we lived with my mother in Jacksonville. I went to work for Railway Express. I rode the train and handled freight. When Railway Express went out of business, I took a job for the Jacksonville Coach Company as a bus driver for five years. My longest job was with the Army Corps of Engineers as a civil service employee, where I worked in the printing department. We did all the printing and specifications for Cape Canaveral. I received a Special Achievement Award as part of a team that printed 43 million units of offset material during 1975. This was the largest number of units printed during any fiscal year in the printing plant's existence.

Jenny and I lived in Cocoa, Florida. I worked for the Corps of Engineers for 17½ years, which gave me a total of 20 years, including military service time. I retired on June 16, 1980. We moved up to Waynesville in the mountains in North Carolina and I kept busy with some carpentry and farm work. We eventually returned to Florida and built a house where we lived from 1994 to 2000. Our son bought a home in Hilton Head Island. When we visited him we visited Sun City and moved in April 2000. We have four children, seven grandchildren and two great grandchildren.

Proud to serve

I enjoyed my service in the Navy. I had the opportunity to work with a dedicated and committed group of sailors and officers on board the USS Massachusetts. It wasn't always easy going but it was an important part of my life and I am proud to have my story in this book.

Gray and Jenny at home in Sun City, 2009

Jim Hoel

Jim Hoel

Author's note: This profile, which differs from the format of others in this book, was written largely with the help of Rick Hoel, Jim's son, for which I am deeply grateful. Jim served his country with honor, distinction and some riveting experiences.

Jim was born in Canby, Minnesota on September 2, 1921 and moved with his parents, Omer and Olive Hoel, in 1935 to Evanston, Illinois. In February

1942, Jim left the Harris Bank of Chicago and enlisted as a cadet in the Army Air Corps. He was trained to be a bombardier and navigator.

On May 17, 1943 Jim and his crew took off at Bury Saint Edmonds base in England with 10 other B-26 bombers. One of the 11 turned back before crossing the coast and made it safely home on one engine. The other 10 planes were shot down, and 40 of the 60 airmen in those 10 planes lost their lives that day.

My father was 22 years old. His life changed forever that day. He describes it in his own words.

Hit by flak

Our B-26 Marauder was flying less than 50 feet above the North Sea to avoid German radar. At this altitude things happened fast at over 200 miles an hour. As our plane passed over the Dutch coast, what looked like a massive 4th of July fireworks show of small arms fire loomed before us. Ahead to the left, our lead plane was hit and in an instant was gone, snap-rolling and crashing upside down into a sand dune. The shock of my friends' certain deaths swept over me but a burst of tracers brought me back to our own problems.

Our radio operator was shouting and our pilot frantically yelled for me, the plane's bombardier-navigator, to find out what was happening in the rear of the plane. I crawled back from the nose and an enormous blast stunned me as flak ripped into the side of the plane.

The pilot shouted for us to get ready for a crash landing. I quickly strapped our radio operator into his seat, opened the ceiling escape hatch and fell to the floor bracing my back against the pilot's bulkhead. My future looked bleak. I didn't know of a single survivor from any past B-26 crash. Yet I felt strangely peaceful. My only regret was for my parents, as I pictured them receiving the inevitable "missing in action" and, later, "killed in action" notices.

The plane smashed into the Maas River at 250 miles an hour and split in half on impact. The front section sank like a submarine in a few seconds. I was underwater but able to stand on the plane's floor and push our radio operator out of the hatch ahead of me. We struggled to the surface for air. In a moment, our pilot and co-pilot burst to the surface and the four of us swam towards shore. Our turret and tail gunners never made it out of the Marauder.

When we reached the river's bank, a young German officer was waiting. He pointed his rifle at us and in perfect English stated: "For you I think the war is over." On a bank behind us 20 more German soldiers pointed their weapons at us. We had no idea what would happen next. I glanced at my wrist to check the time but my watch was gone.

Stalag Luft III

Stalag Luft III was originally a POW camp for British RAF officers. Due to the overflow of captured Allied forces, the Germans started putting American officers (my dad arrived with the rank of 2nd lieutenant) in the camp, one of several in the area. The Luftwaffe was in charge. Stalag Luft III was the site where prisoners dug escape tunnels they named Harry, David and Charley, which led to the movie, "The Great Escape."

Author's note: On the night of March 24-25, 1944, 76 Allied prisoners of Stalag Luft III, 100 miles southeast of Berlin, escaped through a tunnel named "Harry." Within days most were recaptured. An outraged Hitler had 50 of them shot, an appalling abrogation of the Geneva Convention, to which Germany was a signatory. Twenty-three were reincarcerated. Three made it to freedom—a Dutchman and two Norwegians, all flyers with the British Royal Air Force.

In any war, you get a combination of people from all over the world with expertise ranging from engineering, digging, structural design, architecture and mechanics to bracing the tunnels. With all this talent, one could build a whole camp. In the Stalags, the Luftwaffe, when they did follow the Geneva Convention, allowed British and American officers to oversee the men within their barracks under their own military hierarchy. The Luftwaffe fed and guarded the prisoners but did not really manage their military duties. In many POW German camps for non-officers, prisoners endured slave labor, working in armament and war material factories.

My father had a brief opportunity to escape while being transported the same day he was shot down. Put in a room and left alone, he had a chance to jump out of a second-story window, but hesitated for fear he would break a leg.

In the camp it was the duty of an American soldier to try to escape. The prisoners had assigned roles. They took elaborate steps to hide the tunnels they were digging under stoves and sinks but were caught several times. Periodically the SS—which didn't trust the Luftwaffe—would enter the camp and conduct a sweeping search to look for anything suspicious, turning the place upside-down for anything related to digging an escape tunnel.

Playing a penguin

My dad was what they called "a penguin," because he would fill pouches attached to a string around his shoulders with dug-up sand and dirt, then outside pull the string to let the pouches slowly empty onto the ground as he shuffled around, his feet patting down the earth. Over time he and fellow "penguins" dispersed all that sand and dirt so slowly that the Germans never caught on. My dad has told me so many stories about life in the camp—and not all sad. There was a lot of camaraderie and humor. For the most part, however, it was a difficult existence. Some time before they finally made the great escape, the American officers were transferred into another Stalag Luft. The actual "great escape" was only with British prisoners, although American prisoners helped dig the tunnels.

The Germans recaptured most of the prisoners who escaped that one time, lining up 50 and shooting them in the back of the head—pretty clear that it was an execution. But when the RAF commander asked how many of the escapees were wounded, the Germans replied, "None, they were all trying to escape." So much for the Geneva Convention!

Toward the end of the war, the barracks my father was in—originally designed for six to a room—had 12 to14 per room. Things were getting bad; the POWs were being fed less and less. Germany was losing the war. Hitler had this plan to march all the American soldiers to locations where he might be able to use them as hostages for negotiating demands.

The Death March

The Russians were advancing from the east across Europe. Hitler ordered a mass evacuation of POW camps. My dad was involved in "The Death March," which sent 10,000 men for up to 70 miles during one of the coldest winters in European history. It was brutal. The prisoners were told to get their clothes and meager belongings together and assemble outside. Their clothes were totally inadequate for winter weather. Their coats, if they had any, were tattered and torn. One guy had cut himself when he had to relieve himself and tried to cut a patch out of the side of his pants to clean himself. It was horrendous. Along the way, time and again men could just not go any further. The fatigue, bitter cold and lack of food were too much to bear. The Germans would walk them for an hour in the bitter cold—and while they were walking they were sweating. When they stopped for a break to rest the sweat just froze to their bodies. Some couldn't continue; they just lay down and died.

A random act of kindness

One day during The Death March my dad noticed a farm house way off in the distance. He saw someone coming from the farm house toward the ragged line of 10,000 marchers stretching across 20 miles. As the person walked closer my dad saw that it was an old woman, in that freezing weather, with a pot of tea in one hand and a cup and saucer in the other. She walked up to one of the GIs and said to him, "Would you like a cup of tea?" And she gave it to the GI. One normally would think, how does that help—helping just one man? But it was a gesture, a symbol that my dad remembers that inspired the men who saw this gesture as a single act of kindness.

They reached Moosburg, which was a prison camp just northeast of Munich. Conditions there were horrible. The camp was built for 15,000 POWs but already housed over 100,000. Allied prisoners were packed 12 to a cabin. On the day the war ended, the German guards just left the prison camp. My father at that time weighed about 110 pounds.

After being freed, my father traveled to Dachau and saw what was going on at the recently liberated concentration camp there. He was one of the first observers into the camp to view the horror, and still doesn't talk much about that event.

His parents never knew when he was coming home (he did get a leave en route in Paris). After he returned to the States, the Chicago-bound train he was on made a short stop close to his parents' house. He left the train, walked home and knocked on the door. "Hello!" he said when his folks opened the door. Among a hundred other stories of the war, here is one that stands out.

A German neighbor

While he was being interrogated, a German officer came in and got permission to have a word with Lt. Hoel. The interrogator stepped out of the room and left the two men alone. The German officer, who seemed about my father's age, looked at him and said, "You know, I was born in Evanston!" The German talked on in perfect English; my dad figured this was a trick. So he started to talk about the neighborhood, and asked where the German had lived. Near the corner of Main and Hinman, he replied.

My dad thought, "The Germans really do their homework." The two talked back and forth, reminiscing about names and places in Evanston; finally my dad decided he would trick the German officer.

Dad: One of my favorite places was the local ice cream parlor, and you might also remember the place on Main Street.
German: Oh yes, I remember it well.
Dad: Do you remember when you walked in and you turned to the left, to the soda fountain counter?
German: No, no, you walk in and you turn to the right to the soda fountain counter.

That response confirmed to my dad that this German officer was for real. "How did you get here?" my dad asked.

Some time before the war, Hitler invited dual citizens—Germans who lived in America—back to Germany as visitors. Then Hitler kept them in Germany as conscripts to serve in the German Army. If circumstances were different, these two guys might have played on the same high school football team instead of facing each other across a table in a Nazi POW camp.

Evanston, Illinois—August 27, 2003

The ringing woke me at 6:30 a.m. At 82 years old, I wasn't usually up at this hour. I reached for the telephone and fumbled with the receiver. "Hello?" I said. "Is this Jim Hoel?" the distinctly British voice asked expectantly. "Yes," I said, confused. "Did you fly in a Marauder airplane in the war?" I again said yes though I hadn't thought about the Marauder for some time. "We've got your watch," the caller said excitedly. I was ready to hang up and go back to sleep

*but asked, "Just what watch are you talking about?" My watch was sitting on
my bed stand. "The one you lost when your airplane crashed in 1943." I was
stunned. All of a sudden, 1943 seemed like yesterday.*

Until he received the phone call, my father had not thought about his watch
since the day his Marauder went down 60 years earlier in the Maas River.
After spending two years as a prisoner of war in Stalag Luft III and helping
to dig the tunnels made famous in "The Great Escape" movie, my father
returned from the war only to get on with his life. The phone call on August
27, 2003 brought him a flood of memories.

How his watch ended up in England remains a mystery to this day. The
watch had special significance. It had been given to him by his employer,
The Harris Bank of Chicago, in February 1942, as a departing gift after
my father had enlisted as a cadet in the Army Air Corps. The watch was a
beautiful Swiss Gallet Chronograph, which my father had used to navigate
his Marauder. His name and address were engraved on the back.

Jim's watch recovered

Peter & Tiny

The watch was discovered when Peter Cooper, a 56-year-old truck driver in Kirton, England, was visiting his neighbor, 89-year-old "Tiny" Baxter. Tiny showed Peter a watch he had kept for years in a drawer with other collectibles. He had been an engineer for the British forces during World War II and after the war his mother gave him the watch when he returned home. Unfortunately, how the watch traveled from the bottom of the Maas River in Holland to Tiny's mother in England is anyone's guess. Tiny simply never thought to ask her.

When Peter noted the inscription on the back of the watch, he asked Tiny's permission to have a friend search the Internet for the owner. The search found my father listed on several sites identifying survivors of World War II plane crashes. With the help of several contacts in the Chicago area, Peter located my father and placed the call. After the call, Peter sent him the watch, which then was repaired. It still works just fine.

Writing my father's story, I find myself taking my own journeys back in time, and musing about my own life and experiences with my father and my entire family. It's been humbling. After all, if any number of things had happened just a bit differently on May 17, 1943, I wouldn't be here. My father is regularly feeding us with memories of events that at the time may not have seemed significant, but today carry poignant meaning—little things that bring back a flood of emotions and hold incredible lessons about human suffering and the importance of one person's efforts on behalf of another.

The final story

A few years ago Jim visited England and the scene of his plane crash in Holland with his son Gil, and met Peter Cooper, who had returned his watch. In Holland they were greeted by the entire town as heroes. But for Rick's father, many of the memories that the watch reawakened don't fit simply into a "good news" story. While in Holland, he visited the graves of many of the men who were lost that day. It is important to him that people understand the whole story, which is more about the men he served with who didn't return—the real heroes in Jim Hoel's eyes.

Jim returns to Holland, photo near the Maas River

How very lucky I am that my father is alive and well today at 87—he still lives in Evanston. I've gotten to know my father so much better by visualizing his life at 22 years old.

I also better appreciate a simple fact—the struggles I have today, with economic conditions mostly, are far less difficult and much easier to bear when I think of the much greater challenges that prior generations—my father's in particular—have had to face.

Rick Hoel practiced international law in Chicago and Hong Kong before moving to the Lowcountry. Now a broker with Realty Management Advisors in Bluffton and a freelance writer, Rick is a member of The Island Writer's Network.

Rick Hoel

Bob Holly

Bob Holly

Bob was born on June 17, 1924 in Erie, Pennsylvania. After graduating from Strong Vincent High School, Bob worked for Burke Electric Company for a short while before enlisting in the Army in April 1942. He was ordered to board a troop train for North Carolina. At the end of his journey, he stepped off the train and was greeted by a sergeant who said, "Welcome to Airborne!" His buddies asked, "What's Airborne?" The Army, they figured, volunteered for them. Bob was sent to Camp Mackall, North Carolina where he trained in glider flying. He found the gliders to be very fragile aircraft; the Army gave him a chance to join the paratroops. He volunteered and was sent to Camp Forest, Tennessee. The Army brought all the instructors to Jump School from Fort Benning, Georgia.

Q & A

Arnold: Where did you go after Jump School?

Bob: After going on maneuvers in Tennessee, we were shipped out of Boston on a troop ship and landed in Swindon, England in December 1944. It only took us seven days to cross the Atlantic.

Arnold: What did you do in England?

Bob: We were issued passes to go to London on the weekend. I met a girl there, like we all did. She invited me for Christmas Eve dinner. That morning they blew the whistle to fall out in formation. We were told, "Proceed to the supply room and draw out two bandoliers of ammunition and six hand grenades; you're going over. The Germans broke through the lines. We're going into battle!"

They flew us over the English Channel in a C-47 and we landed in France. On Christmas Eve, instead of eating a nice dinner in England, we were digging foxholes. We stayed in the area until February 26, 1945. We didn't wash or shave for two months and froze all the time. We were in combat in the Battle of the Bulge and I got wounded in March 1945—hit by a shell fragment in the eye.

The Battle of the Bulge

The Ardennes Offensive (16 December 1944-25 January 1945) was a major German thrust launched towards the end of World War II through the forested Ardennes Mountains region of Belgium. It was officially named the Battle of the Ardennes or the Ardennes-Alsace campaign by the U.S. Army, but it is known to the general public simply as the Battle of the Bulge, a description promoted by Winston Churchill to deliberately belittle in the public's mind at the time the serious nature of the struggle. The "bulge" was the initial incursion the Germans put into the Allies' line of advance, as seen in maps presented in contemporary newspapers. With over 800,000 men committed and over 19,000 killed, the Battle of the Bulge became the single biggest and bloodiest battle in U.S. history. The winter of 1944-45 was a historic time in Europe. For 40 days the fighting raged through some of the coldest, snowiest weather remembered in the Ardennes, indeed the coldest in 100 years.

In his own words

My worst memories of combat were trying to survive from the cold. I was cold, cold, cold! We couldn't carry much equipment in our backpack for warmth. I didn't have a heavy coat, just a field jacket and I was freezing. The Army tried to ship us overcoats but they never arrived. We just had to huddle together to keep warm. I remember taking off my paratroop boots one night. My buddy told me, "Don't do that, Bob, you'll freeze!" But my feet were so cold I took my boots off anyway to rub my feet. The next morning the boots were frozen solid and it took a long time to soften them up to get them back on. I'm still cold, after all these years! It's up here (Bob points to his head with his finger). Some guys were desperate. They were saying, "Sometimes I wish I would shoot off a finger"—as they pointed a finger in the air—"so they could take me back to the States and get me out of here."

We took a lot of prisoners. The Germans were giving up in droves. One day four of us were coming out of the woods and saw some Germans and shouted to them, "Put your hands up and lay your guns down!" Before you know it we must have had 80 German soldiers surrender to four of us. The Germans looked exhausted and they just had enough. They were freezing too! They turned in their guns. We marched them back to our camp where the MPs took them off our hands.

Q & A

Arnold: What weapon did you carry?
Bob: I had an M-1.
Arnold: What was in your backpack?
Bob: A change of underwear, a mess kit. We wore a brown OD wool cap under our helmet. During the Battle of the Bulge we were assembled into the 17th Airborne Division and were finally relieved by Gen. Patton. The Army took us out of the line and started sending some troops of the 101st Airborne home, but our unit—the 17th—went into Berlin. When a shell fragment

hit me in the eye, I was blinded for three weeks. They took me in back of the lines to the hospital where the doctor treated me. After they removed the bandages, they asked me if I wanted to transfer to another outfit. I told them that I would prefer to rejoin my old outfit—the 82nd Airborne Division. We were the first troops into Berlin. Berlin was divided into four sectors—the French, the English, the Russians and the United States. We arrived ahead of the Russians but had to wait for them to come in on the other side.

Arnold: What did Germany look like when you marched into Berlin?

Bob: It was bombed out as far as the eye could see. We met the Russians but we had the biggest sector allocated to the U.S.

Arnold: Where did you sleep?

Bob: We slept in abandoned apartment buildings that were salvageable. Some of us were in a building where you could sleep in a room with half the wall gone.

Arnold: What about meals? Did you have C-rations or hot food?

Bob: They had hot food for us.

Arnold: What did you do while you were there?

Bob: I had a lot of guard duty, guarding the German POWs. We were ordered to dress in class A uniforms—white boot laces, white scarves and white gun belts for parades for Marshall Zhukov and Gen. Eisenhower at Tempelhof Airport. That is where the freedom flights landed at the beginning of the Marshall Plan, to start bringing in food and supplies to aid Germany and begin the rebuilding effort.

Surrender

On May 7, 1945, German military leaders surrendered unconditionally to a representative of Gen. Eisenhower at Supreme Headquarters, Allied Expeditionary Force (SHAEF) at Reims in northeastern France. A document of surrender was signed. A day later, at 0001 on May 9, German officials in Berlin signed a similar document, explicitly surrendering to Soviet forces in the presence of Marshall Zhukov. May 8, 1945 became V-E Day (Victory in Europe), a day of celebration for the victorious Allies in the U.S. and Europe. SHAEF had concluded its mission and was officially inactivated on July 14, 1945.

**Soviet soldiers placing their flag on top of Reichstag,
photo in the public domain**

Berlin had been suffering food shortages for many months, caused by Allied strategic bombing and exacerbated by the final military assault on the city. Despite Soviet efforts to supply food and rebuild the city, starvation remained a problem. Almost all the transport in and out of the city had been rendered inoperative, and bombed-out sewers had contaminated the city's water supplies. In June 1945, one month after the surrender, when the Americans arrived in their sector of Berlin they found that Berliners were getting only 64 percent of a 1,240-calorie daily ration. And, Bob saw, Berlin was really leveled as a result of the Allied bombings. Occupation duties ended in June. In September, the 17th Airborne Division returned home and was disbanded.

Going home

I had enough points to go home. We boarded a liberty ship in Southampton, England and crossed the Atlantic in 17 days. It took us seven days to come to Europe and 17 days to sail back. I was sick every day. Most of our guys were seasick as well. We approached New York Harbor and it was a wonderful sight to see the Statue of Liberty. They asked me if I'd like to march down Fifth Avenue in New York City or be let out three weeks earlier. I didn't care about marching, I just wanted to go home. Most of us did. But a lot of the 82nd Airborne guys did march in a ticker tape parade down Fifth Avenue.

I was discharged January 3, 1946. We got paid $50 extra for airborne duty. In the gliders we were only getting $48 a month and you could push your finger through the side of the fuselage. And I remember riding in the gliders and many scary, bumpy landings. After discharge I returned to Erie, Pennsylvania and started work for the *Erie Dispatch* newspaper as a district manager. I lived in Erie with my mom and sister. I married my first wife in 1948 (it ended in divorce) and two years later got a job as a liquor representative for Seagram's. I started in sales and wound up 32 years later as assistant vice president. I married my second wife, Gloria Sartini, in 1982. Gloria has two children from an earlier marriage and I have 10.

Law enforcement

When I worked for Seagram's, my insurance agent told me that he had a volunteer police department in his town, Florham Park, New Jersey. "Would you like to join?" he asked. I didn't think I had the time but he assured me that I would be taught procedures, and I became a volunteer police officer working Friday and Saturday nights for four years. In 1976 Seagram's transferred me to Philadelphia and we lived near Valley Forge Park. I always had a love of horses and began to ride horses there. It was also the year of the bicentennial celebration in Philadelphia and the Wagon Train came in from across the country to participate in the celebration and parade. I met the chief one day and he offered me a part-time paid position as a police officer. I was a part of the mounted patrol unit. I eventually retired from Seagram's in 1982. I was fortunate to be placed on full-time duty with the police and remained on the force for 12 years. Then Gloria and I moved to Palm Gardens, Florida.

I still had a desire to continue to work in law enforcement and joined the Palm Beach Sheriff's Department. I went through training at the police academy and became certified for the state of Florida. I worked for the Palm Beach sheriff's department for 14 years. After being wiped out by two hurricanes during our 14 years in Palm Beach Gardens, Gloria and I decided we needed a change. Since we moved to Sun City, South Carolina I work for the Bluffton Police Department one day a week, where I do fingerprinting, answering the phone and help with walk-in inquiries.

Impressions of military service

I had a positive experience, when I look back at my military years. I served my country and was glad to be able to serve and survive the hardships of war. Today, I think every young person should have the opportunity to serve in the military at least a year. I believe they would derive a great benefit to themselves and their country.

I am a member of the 82nd Airborne Division and keep in touch with my buddies by way of emails. Gloria and I enjoy our retirement living in our home in Sun City and enjoy beautiful surroundings in the heart of South Carolina's treasured coast.

Bob was awarded the following medals for his military service:

* Good Conduct
* American Campaign
* European African Middle Eastern Service
* World War II Victory
* Purple Heart

Gloria and Bob relax in Sun City home, 2009

Ernest Karlson

Ernie Karlson

Ernie was born on July 16, 1926 in Chicago, Illinois. He attended McGregor High but graduated from Denfeld High School in Duluth in 1944 and enlisted in the Navy. After boot camp Ernie was sent to Norman, Oklahoma for advanced aviation ordinance training, then to Miami, Florida, where he trained on the PB4Y4 (a 4-engine, land-based bomber—the Navy's version of the Liberator).

Terrified—in his own words

On our first training flight on the PBY, I was assigned to the tail turret. From there I could see nothing of the rest of the plane except the extreme back edge of the rudder, and then only if I looked straight up. We had an instructor pilot to show our pilot the plane's characteristics. We did violent climbs, dives, turns and stalls which shook the plane, all magnified in the tail turret. I had to hang on for dear life and didn't know from one moment to the next whether my turret was still with the plane or not.

I was terrified! Upon landing I went to the pilot, saluted and said, "Sir, court-martial me if you will, but I will not get in that turret again." A wise man he was as he negotiated with one of the other gunners to take the tail turret and give me the after-upper deck turret, from which I could see the whole plane. Thereafter, even in practicing extreme evasive maneuvers, I could see the wings, which bent like a bird's, but I knew I was still in the plane.

As a result of the change I was content and enjoyed flying. It wasn't until my Army service, 1952-1970, including 18 months in Korea, that I learned that a coward dies a thousand deaths—a brave man dies but once. How true!

In addition to my flight training I was reassigned to San Diego to a replacement pool where we were awaiting orders to go to Southeast Asia. I was injured while on liberty and they left without me. I remained in San Francisco Treasure Island and became a shore patrolman for about six months.

I was discharged from the Navy at Alameda, California in 1946 and decided I would like to try college. My dad, a poorly-educated immigrant, had told me, "Learn to live by your head instead of your back." In chess I had learned to keep my options open, so my two years at Duluth Junior College in 1946-48 involved both pre-law and pre-business; but it became painfully apparent that I was not suited to the case method of study. So I transferred to the School of Business Administration and took Labor Relations because it had the fewest required courses.

In the Army

That left me free to take the ROTC program which, because I had two years of service, allowed me to go directly into the advanced course. I graduated from the University of Minnesota with a BBA degree and entered the U.S. Army as a 2ⁿᵈ lieutenant.

I completed the Engineer Company Officer course and was reassigned to Ft. Leonard Wood, Missouri. I received orders to ship out to Korea in 1953. While briefly in Japan, I helped process personnel records for troops coming and going. In Korea, I was assigned to an engineer battalion, north of the 38th parallel. My tour in Korea was 18 months. I arrived there 10 days before the armistice was declared. Two years in the Navy plus 18 in the Army add up to my 20-year military career.

I had three years as an assistant professor of military science at Bucknell University in Pennsylvania. I was assigned to a freshman class to teach a course in American Military History—of which I knew nothing. I spent a great deal of time preparing every lesson. Yet in every class that I taught, there was a student that knew more about the topic at hand than I did. I learned humility really quickly. When somebody would ask a question, I knew that I could recognize the correct answer easier than I could recall one. So I would turn the question back to the class. As a result there was always someone who would be happy to provide the information. I would recognize the correct answer when I heard it and gave the student credit for it.

I retired from the Army when I was the transportation officer at the Defense Depot at Mechanicsburg, Pennsylvania with the rank of lieutenant colonel.

Lt. Col. Ernie Karlson retires from the Army

Life after military service

I started sending out resumes, but all the trucking and transportation companies told me I was overqualified for any position they had. My wife, Ramona said, "Why don't you apply for a state job?" I said, "The state doesn't pay anything." She said there were many people working for the state getting along just fine. I applied at the Pennsylvania State Central Personnel Office and indicated that I was interested in working for the Department of Transportation. During the interview I noted that I was in the Transportation Corps in the Army for 16 years; I was hired on the basis of my military experience, my education background and a solid interview. It turned out that it was one of the best things that ever happened to me because when I retired, the state covered my Medicare supplement, including prescription drugs, and that has been a godsend.

A proud father

His first child, Mark, is a freelance appliance repairman. Ernie's youngest child, Eric, lives on Marco Island, Florida and works for a company that builds and maintains docks.

His daughter, Katherine Ozimek, lives in Silverdale, Washington. Her husband, retired Capt. Peter Ozimek, was a submariner in the Navy. Kathy herself retired from the Navy after serving 20 years with the rank of commander. Her specialty was aviation. Her first assignments were navigating C-130s down to the Antarctic in support of the National Science Foundation.

**Ernie's daughter, Cmdr. Kathy Ozimek,
retires from the Navy**

Ernie's first wife, Ramona, died of breast cancer in 1994 while living in Mechanicsburg, Pennsylvania. Mary Jane also lost her spouse. Ernie and Mary Jane were both married to their former spouses for 43 years. Ernie said he was very fortunate to have met Mary Jane: "I chased her for 11 years before she caught me." Mary and Ernie were married in 2005.

Sun City

In 1997 Mary Jane and Ernie went to Florida to see Ernie's son, Eric, and then took a cruise ship out of Tampa to Guatemala. When they returned they drove home to Pennsylvania. They decided to stop off at Sun City, South Carolina to visit friends but they were out of town. Ernie was ready to turn around and go home but Mary wanted to look around. They were very impressed with the visual beauty of Sun City, found a house to their liking and moved in 1998.

Impressions of military service

One evening at dinner about 1975 daughter Kathy asked her dad what he thought of the military. "Well," he said, "it has been very good to me." Ramona explained later that Kathy was thinking of applying to the Naval Academy. Ernie was dumbfounded. The next thing he heard was that their congressional representative had convened a board at the Navy Defense Depot in Mechanicsburg to interview applicants for the Naval Academy, and that the girl who did very well there was Kathy—who, like her father, loved sailing and did it competitively. When board members asked her about this, Kathy had so much to say on the subject and expressed herself so well that her interview and record were well received. Accepted into the Academy, she had a distinguished career as a Naval officer and after 20 years retired with the rank of commander.

Ernie says, "We developed a saying, Kathy and I: No matter what, enjoy it whether we like it or not!"

Bob Klatt

Bob Klatt

Bob was born on February 6, 1923 in Milwaukee, Wisconsin. After graduating from high school in June 1941, he worked at Cherry-Burrell, makers of stainless steel dairy equipment, until getting a draft notice. Bob enlisted in the Navy in January 1943 and was sent to Great Lakes, Illinois for boot camp. On May 1 he went to Armed Guard School in Little Creek, Virginia; at month's end it was on to the Brooklyn Navy Yard.

Author's note: The U.S. Navy Armed Guard Service from World War I and II is very much an unsung military service branch that provided gun crews for service aboard U.S. merchant ships. Starting in late 1941 with 1,375 ships, the service grew by the end of World War II to 145,000 personnel who manned the guns in 6,236 U.S. and Allied merchant ships. Some 2,085 died, and another 1,127 were wounded from enemy action.

Time line of missions

June 3, 1943: Detached duty as armed guard on board US Armed Merchant Vessel USS K. I. Luckenbach.

November 18, 1943: Detached duty as armed guard on board US Armed Merchant Vessel USS Charles Scribner.

September 7, 1944: Detached duty as armed guard on board US Armed Merchant Vessel USS Benito Juarez.

November 1, 1945: Assigned sea duty aboard the USS Aristaeus.

December 1, 1946: Transferred to intake station, San Francisco.

**Armed guard aboard the USS Charles Scribner,
Bob at top**

Q & A

AR: What was your job on board?

BK: My job on the ship was part of the gun crews. These were merchant ships with Navy personnel manning the guns.

AR: How many guys in your Navy crew?

BK: About 24.

AR: And your job was to man the guns? Did you ever fire the gun?

BK: No.

AR: What happened when you arrived at your destination? Did you handle the cargo?

BK: No, we had nothing to do with that at all, and nothing to do with the merchant seamen on board, either. They steered and ran ship. Our 24 Navy personnel performed guard duty for security and protection in case of an attack.

AR: How were the accommodations aboard?

BK: We slept below the first deck. The food was excellent.

AR: When the war was coming to an end, what was your rank?

BK: Gunner's mate 3rd class.

Bound for Archangel

I remember a trip I took to Archangel, Russia, bound for the Arctic Circle. (Chief seaport of medieval Russia, Archangel spreads for over 25 miles on both banks of the Northern Dvina River near its exit into the White Sea.) To get there, we sailed out of Edinburgh, Scotland in a convoy. One night two merchant ships in our convoy were hit by torpedoes—one next to us and the other, behind us. It was pitch black, but the explosions lit up the sky. We arrived in Archangel in a ferocious storm. I couldn't believe the swells that enveloped our ship. It was scary. The convoy was broken up but our cargo was secure. We had four locomotives on board. I spent my 21st birthday on the Arctic Circle. We stayed out there—stuck in the ice—for a month. We had to wait for an ice breaker to come and get us out. It was fortunate that we had food on board and plenty of heat.

Author's note: According to the War Shipping Administration, the U.S. Merchant Marine suffered the highest rate of casualties of any service in World War II. Officially, a total of 1,554 ships were sunk due to war conditions, including 733 ships of over 1,000 gross tons. Hundreds of other ships were damaged by torpedoes, shelling, bombs, kamikazes, mines etc. Foreign flag ships, especially those with Naval Armed Guard on board as well as ships belonging to U.S. territories such as the Philippines, are included in this list.

AR: Where did you arrive on your last trip home?

BK: We docked in New York. When we landed, the Navy didn't know what to do with us. I didn't have enough points to get discharged. They shipped me across the country and across the Pacific to Okinawa. I left in early September 1945. Toward the end of December I was assigned to a Navy ship to return to the States. I landed in San Francisco, was shipped to Great Lakes, Illinois and then discharged January 26, 1946.

Back to civilian life

I returned to Milwaukee and went back to work at Cherry-Burrell. My cousin made a New Year's party in December 1946 where I met Ellie Thiel. A romance ensued and we tied the knot in August 1947, and moved into her family's apartment. Before getting married I had been sworn into the Milwaukee Fire Department. It was to be my primary job for 31 years. I retired as a lieutenant in 1978. Our main fire station was in downtown Milwaukee. After I left the Fire Department we moved to Hartford, Wisconsin and bought a skeleton cottage I restored into a year-round home. I sold this home and moved to Sun City—Hilton Head, South Carolina in 2000.

Impressions of military service

I found military service very rewarding and was so thankful that I was able to serve my country, and survive. I matured as an individual, valued the experiences and enjoyed seeing other parts of the world. I remember fondly our first trip to Wales and two trips to London.

Another trip that stands out in my mind was when we sailed along the East Coast. We took off from Galveston, Texas, then went on to Iran through the Straits of Gibraltar and stopped at Marseilles before going into the Suez Canal and the Persian Gulf. These were golden opportunities that I will always cherish.

Bob at home in Sun City, 2009

Bud A. Ledbetter

Bud and Helen Ledbetter

Bud was born on February 9, 1916 in Minot, North Dakota. His mother, Frances Falness Ledbetter, was a hard-working single parent raising four children from the time Bud was four years old on an income of $22 a week from work as a tailor. Ice skating and outside play was Bud's only recreation; TV and other diversions had not yet been invented and though he never owned a bike or roller skates, his childhood was a happy one. With Bud's part-time jobs paying 35 cents an hour, he decided to join the Navy and enlisted in Minneapolis on August 9, 1935.

Q & A

AR: Where did you take boot camp?

BL: San Diego, in Company 35/21.

AR: Where did you go after boot camp?

BL: The first place was on the old, World War I USS Broome
         (DD-210), a 4-stack destroyer. I put in four years on this vessel,
         at first standing bridge watches and doing deck work and then I
         was a gun pointer on number 1 gun. I became friendly with the
         radio gang; I always was interested in electricity. I had use of the
         radio room and the typewriter and learned to type and became
         familiar with radio procedure. Within six months I became a
         radioman and spent the last two years on board the Broome as a
         radio operator. On September 1, 1939 I happened to be on watch
         and received the first message of World War II: "Germany has
         invaded Poland. England is now at war with Germany."

In his own words

On November 7, 1939 my four-year enlistment was up. I left the Navy and
returned to North Dakota and worked with my mother for a while. Then
I returned to Minneapolis to re-enlist (January 19, 1940) and was sent to a
destroyer base in San Diego. When the United States gave 50 destroyers to
England to help fight the German submarines, I worked for three months
installing new electronic equipment on some of those ships.

Then I received orders to report to the USS WASP (CV7), a new aircraft
carrier which was to be placed in service in April. My assignment, with four
other radiomen, was to install and repair all radio and sonar equipment.
This included radar and aircraft homing beacons, which were installed in
early 1940. The next year was spent training to make ready for the war we
were sure would come.

My ship was engaged in what was called "Neutrality Patrol" in the Atlantic
from ports which included Norfolk, Virginia and Portland, Maine plus others
in Newfoundland, Iceland and Bermuda. Our duties included protection
of large Lend Lease convoys from submarine and surface attacks. In spite of
all the protection the U.S. Navy and the Royal Navy could offer, hundreds
of merchant ships were sunk by German wolf packs.

Author's note: According to George Baronowski, whose profile is in this book, statistics show that one out of 26 Merchant Marine personnel died during World War II.

We were also tracking German fleet units, promptly reporting same for Royal Navy awareness. I remember one three-week sweep of the Atlantic to the Azores when we headed back to Bermuda for a much-deserved rest.

I became a warrant officer in December 1940 and transferred to the USS Princeton. The Navy sent me to a radar refresher course for a month, and I spent a year at the Naval Research Lab in Washington, D.C. That's where I met my wife-to-be, Helen Kolasar. We got married on July 25, 1943. After 65 years together, she passed away May 2, 2008 at the Naval Hospital in San Diego.

At the Naval Research Lab I graduated number 11 out of 44 in that class and was transferred to Charleston Navy Yard where I was ship superintendent for radio and sound. We commissioned about a half dozen destroyers, LSMs and even one PT boat. I was there for over a year.

I was transferred to the South Pacific with orders to install radar on one of the islands. While in the New Hebrides, I received orders to fly back to Pearl Harbor. I returned on a Martin PBM-5 (Patrol Bomber Mariner). I was in the communication pool at Pearl Harbor. I ran into a commander who I worked with at the Charleston Navy Yard. He said, "I'm looking for someone like you," and transferred me from the communications pool into Service Force at a ships repair unit in Pearl Harbor. I supervised about 24 technicians together with Seabees.

Pearl Harbor—and onward

On December 7, 1941 the Wasp had just returned from patrol and was anchored in Bermuda. I got a call that Sunday afternoon—I just had lunch—and was told that the Exec Officer wanted to see me immediately. He said, "I want a radio put in this room as quickly as possible. Pearl Harbor has been attacked!" The radio was installed and from then on we did a lot of patrolling.

When the Battle of Midway occurred, in July 1942, we were in England, operating with the British fleet. We had two cruisers—the Quincy and the

San Juan—and eight destroyers. I was a radioman 2nd class at the time. We sailed up to Scapa Flow in Northern Scotland and flew all our torpedo planes and bombers off the carrier deck. All we kept on board was two fighter squadrons. We got underway and went to Greenwich, Scotland, up the Clyde Canal into Glasgow. Our ship tied up at the King George V dock. We stayed there a few days and lo and behold down the dock were 50 Spitfire aircraft. We loaded them aboard our carrier and stowed them down below. We got underway with a couple of English battleships that joined our task force and sailed through the Straits of Gibraltar. At that time Malta was the most bombed spot in the world, with the Germans on one side and the Italians on the other—bombing the island because the British flew from there. We flew the Spitfires off to Malta and returned to Glasgow where we picked up another load of 50 Spitfires, got underway and went with the same task force. I remembered seeing a large Sutherland bomber flying up to the north—they were flying "wing" for us looking for German ships. We flew the last of the Spitfires to Malta. The RAF pilots engaged the enemy and were credited with shooting down 450 German and Italian aircraft and Malta was never bombed again.

Churchill sent us a message that said, "Who says a Wasp can't sting twice?" Many people in Malta gave us credit for saving their country.

Author's note: While the Wasp was conducting those important missions to Malta, a train of events far westward brought the carrier to the Pacific. Early in May, almost simultaneously with Wasp's second Malta run, Operation Bowery, the Battle of the Coral Sea, had been fought. That action turned back the Japanese thrust at Port Moresby. One month later, from June 4 to June 6, an American carrier force smashed its Japanese counterpart in the Battle of Midway.

During that time, the Battle of Midway was going on and the English were giving us "three cheers" because our fleet in Midway had sunk some four Japanese aircraft carriers. I think we had only one aircraft carrier in the Pacific—the Enterprise. We sailed back to Norfolk changing our squadrons and sailed to Scapa Flow to pick up our aircraft and take them back to the States. We docked at Portsmouth, then went through the Panama Canal to San Diego and picked up the rest of our aircraft squadron. A contingent from the 2nd Marine Regiment was loaded onto various transports; we had about 10 transports alongside us. We were going to make the landing at Guadalcanal. On July 1, 1942 we sailed for the Tonga Islands en route to

Tongatabu. While we were there, I remember, the Marines did a rehearsal landing for Guadalcanal. We got underway and then the Marines did go ashore at Guadalcanal.

On the morning of August 1 the first planes from Wasp's air group barreled down the deck, 16 Grumman F4F Wildcats followed by Douglas SBD-3 Dauntless dive bombers and Grumman TBF Avengers. In the first Solomon Islands battle we lost the Quincy, the Vincennes, the Astoria and the Australian cruiser, Canberra.

The Wasp is hit!

Early morning September 15 we were called to General Quarters and shot down a 4-engine Japanese bomber that apparently was scouting us. Each aircraft carrier always had four fighter aircraft airborne. We called it CAP (combat air patrol). We had most of our aircraft in the air except for one squadron. At noon, we had lunch, secured from General Quarters, and that's when we received three torpedoes on the starboard side, forward of the island structure. That caused a lot of damage, starting fires all over and igniting a 500-pound bomb magazine that blew up.

Our three hits were the result of seven torpedoes from a Japanese submarine. One of the seven torpedoes sank a destroyer. I think it was the USS Blue. Another torpedo went into the next task force and hit the battleship USS North Carolina. I got to my battle station in time to hear the word passed from the North Carolina calling the task force commander saying, "We have just been torpedoed! We are increasing speed to 30 knots." Fire broke out and everything was blowing up all over the ship. Finally I could not communicate at my battle station anymore. I was tuned to Radio 3 to keep on the air. I was on the 01 level—one level above the hangar deck. The flight deck was 02 level. I went up to the flight deck and that's when I saw some disabled planes.

The Wasp was built so that it would flood horizontally rather than lengthwise, to prevent list. The sides of our ship blew out for about a hundred feet and you could see sailors swimming on the other side through the ship. All of our water mains, which went through the keel, were ruptured so we had no water to fight fires. Our crew did the best we could for about an hour. The aircraft on the hangar deck were blown up, killing people, and shrapnel was flying everywhere. Finally I got up on the flight deck and there was another explosion. The Wasp had a wooden flight deck made of teak. I looked up forward where the elevator was and saw the flight deck was raised and warped.

A YE homing beacon was used by pilots to find their way back to the carrier when they were on their bombing attacks. When they returned there was no YE. We had all our planes in the air but they couldn't land on the Wasp. They were fortunate to land on the Enterprise. Its admiral refueled all his aircraft and sent them to Guadalcanal to land on Henderson Field. He sent out some scout planes to track our aircraft. All of the airborne planes landed on the Enterprise. They took all the small stores and the clothing they could find on the ship, piled them in the airplanes for those guys, gave them what they could and had them take off to Guadalcanal. Our airplanes refueled and also flew off to Guadalcanal, to fight the Japanese.

On Guadalcanal we had volunteer coast watchers from Australia. They were dropped by parachute on hilltops in the Solomon Islands to observe Japanese aircraft take off and land from Ribald, New Britain, home of a large Japanese air base. From their vantage points the coast watchers would say, for example, "Forty twin engine bombers taking off from Ribald, New Britain and heading to Guadalcanal." It was a big help for U.S. forces.

Abandon ship

Captain Sherman ordered "abandon ship" at 1520. All badly injured men were lowered into rafts or rubber boats. Many men had to abandon from aft because the forward fires were burning with such intensity. The captain still had control of the engine so—in the midst of terrible fire everywhere—he backed the ship where the wind was on the starboard quarter and the smoke was going over the port bow to keep the smoke away from the crew. We all abandoned ship. There were 2,000 of us in the water. About 300 were killed immediately. We didn't have life boats, we had rafts. I was in the water for about 3½ hours. We had life jackets—a kapok life jacket.

I remember a little bitter humor in the midst of disaster. Our executive officer was a regulation guy, a stickler for proper uniform attire. White socks were a "no-no" for him. Everyone had to wear black socks. There was a fireman in the water with us, an Olympic swimmer. The firemen and the engineers were the last ones to get off the ship. The Olympic swimmer swam near the raft where the executive officer was. Our stickler exec was on the life raft with 20 other guys who were all standing up. The raft was under water. They yelled to the swimmer, "Come on aboard!" The fireman yelled back, "I can't! I got white socks on!" And away he went.

I was in the water and found a sailor who was vomiting. He was really ill; his head was bobbing in the water. I grabbed hold of his life jacket and turned him on his back and pulled him along with me for the next hour and a half.

At a reunion in Boston in 1990, John Mann—the sailor who Bud saved from drowning—was re-introduced to Bud Ledbetter. He said, "Bud, I've waited all these many years to thank you for saving my life in the water after the Wasp sinking."

Q & A

AR: Were you cold?

BL: No, it was in the South Pacific and the water was not cold. But our ships launched depth charges in the water where we were. Our task force had a lot of destroyers that received submarine contacts. The destroyers continued to chase subs and launch depth charges. They probably had about 30 or 40 depth charges in the water from our ships trying to destroy Japanese subs. I don't know if anyone got hurt. But apparently the underwater explosions drove the sharks away because I never saw any sharks.

At sunset I said to myself, "It's time for me to get rescued, because if that sun goes down, the show's over!" Finally I spotted a motor whale boat that came alongside and picked the two of us up (me and the sailor I was holding). We were the last to be picked up because I got behind the rest of the group towing my guy. They transferred us onto a destroyer—the USS Laffey. When we got on board the crew of the destroyer was ordered to give us any extra shoes or clothing. When I came on board all the shoes were gone. The deck was hot so I wrapped my feet in rags for the next couple of days.

AR: How many guys were in the water?

BL: At least 2,000. All were picked up. There were lots of destroyers. I can't remember the amount of boats. The Laffey was one and the Lansdowne (DD-46) was another. Although the submarine hazard caused the accompanying destroyers to lie well clear or to shift position, the "tin cans" (destroyers) carried out the rescue efforts with persistence and determination until Laffey, Lansdowne, Helena and Salt Lake City had 1,946 men embarked.

AR: And you got picked up by the Laffey?

BL: I was on the Laffey for a couple of days and I never went below deck. I went up on the 01 level, just above the main deck, and sat outside the radio room on a battery locker. I sat there for a day and a half. The radioman would come out and bring me a cup of coffee. We sailed in to the New Hebrides.

The USS Laffey served during World War II and the Cold War. It is now moored at Patriots Point Naval and Maritime Museum in Mount Pleasant, South Carolina. It will be getting more than $9 million in repairs to keep it afloat. Jim White, a Sun City—Hilton Head resident who served as a machinery repairman on the Laffey from August 1953 to November 1956, said he couldn't be more proud that the ship will stay afloat.

Bob Wampler, also of Sun City, plans to travel among the ship's former sailors in escort. Wampler, 65, worked as a radio supervisor in the ship's main communications compartment from June 1962 to July 1965 and now serves on the Laffey Association's board of directors.

—*The Island Packet, July 2, 2009*

**Survivors of the USS Wasp on board the USS Laffey,
October 16, 1943; U.S. Navy photo**

AR: What was your condition when they rescued you? Were you ill
        or injured?

BL: My hands were bleeding and I had a scar on my head where I
        banged it against the bulkhead when the torpedoes hit. I was
        treated for my burns on the Laffey and on the Salt Lake City,
        which I later transferred to. I was on the Salt Lake City when she
        sailed for Noumea, New Caledonia. At Noumea they transferred
        me to an Army transport. I stayed on board until we finally set
        sail to San Diego. While we were on that ship I was given my
        examination for chief radioman—which I passed. We arrived
        in San Diego, and I was given 30 days leave to see my mother
        in Vallejo, California. My next set of orders assigned me to the
        USS Princeton (CG-69) in Philadelphia. That was when I was

transferred to the Naval Resource Lab for a radar refresher course. I was transferred again for one year to Radio Material School at Great Lakes.

Tailored for promotion

I was a radioman 1st class and took the exam for chief on that transport after the Wasp episode. Then I went to San Diego and received orders to report to the USS Princeton and made chief radioman. I was wearing my uniform for three days. There was a pre-commissioning detail for the Princeton and I walked into the hangar and I got a salute from one of my radiomen. I said, "What's the salute for?" He said, "You just made warrant officer." Three days after I was chief, I was notified that I was promoted to warrant officer. (In the United States military, a warrant officer is ranked as an officer above the senior-most enlisted ranks but below the officer grade of O-1.) However, the warrant officer promotion was dated before the chief. So, legally, I never was a chief radioman. It was in December 1942 that I made warrant officer. I called the tailor who made my chief's uniform. He said bring it back and he gave me 100 percent credit and made me my new officer's uniform. That's when I was sent to the radar refresher course in Washington, D.C. I stayed in school for a year. The class consisted of warrant officers, ensigns and some JGs that had never gone to electronic school. We all graduated.

I was sick of sea duty, so I took a trip to the Navy Personnel Office and said, "I've been eight years at sea now and I would like to get a little shore duty." They honored my request and assigned me to the Charleston Navy Yard, where I worked in radio and sound electronics.

Other assignment highlights

September 25, 1944—in the Service Force, on a ship repair unit until war ended (Japan surrendered); commendation from Adm. Badger, the Service Force commander.

January 5, 1945—detached to report to the ComServPac for duty on his staff (Commander Service Force, US PacFleet) as chief radio electrician; for installation and repair of electronic equipment to expedite return of battle-damaged ships to the fleet.

August 30, 1945—detached for duty with the district communications officer in connection with electronics material.

September 21, 1945—accepted appointment as ensign, for temporary service.

October 1946—transferred to Navy radio station at Wahiawa, Hawaii (had 80 huge transmitters on the air) as the electronics officer, with Japanese radio operators working for us.

June 1948—transferred to Warrant Officers Engineering School; graduated 11th in class.

June 24, 1949—graduation from U.S. Naval School Electronics Maintenance, U.S. Naval Training Center, Great Lakes, Illinois.

Late 1949—transferred to Franklin D. Roosevelt aircraft carrier (CV-42), with three-month deployment in Mediterranean Sea, shore time in Cannes and Italy.

July 15, 1955—reported for duty at the U.S. Naval Academy, assigned to Department of Seamanship and Navigation for training of midshipmen.

Retirement

I retired on October 31, 1957 after 23 years in the Navy, with full benefits. As I progressed in the Navy I made permanent chief warrant officer. However, I made temporary ensign, temporary JG, temporary lieutenant and temporary lieutenant commander. The law said any permanent officer could retire at the highest rank held. I was a permanent chief warrant officer but I retired as a lieutenant commander.

I decided to retire while the going was good and put in for a job at Hughes Aircraft, in Fullerton, California. Hughes actually hired me three months before I retired from the Navy. I left the Navy and packed up my car and two weeks later I was working at Hughes Aircraft. I bought a house in Fullerton and stayed with Hughes for about three years. It was extremely smoggy in that part of California. My wife became ill and so did I, with all the air pollution in the area. I saw a job in the paper for General Dynamics in San Diego. I arranged an interview with them and I was hired on the spot, in March 1960.

I gave Hughes two weeks' notice but I remained very friendly with my boss at Hughes. We got along fine during my tenure at Hughes. Eventually I left GD, after working for them for 10 years, and went into the brokerage business in San Diego. I started a company by the name of San Diego Securities and was with them for 10 years. When I left the brokerage business I managed the Grand Prix Restaurant and a hotel—Yacht Harbor Inn—for a year.

In 1986, when I was 70 years old, I retired from all jobs and businesses. We lived in Point Loma, California and besides a little investing and observing the financial markets, I became an avid sailor. I owned two sailboats and enjoyed participating in sailboat racing.

Sun City

I came to Sun City in 2008 to visit my daughter Lori and her husband, Steve Crabtree, for Thanksgiving and Christmas vacation. On Christmas morning I got real sick. I went to the Naval Hospital in Beaufort. They transferred me to Beaufort Memorial Hospital, where I was diagnosed with a twisted bowel. Lori told me the doctors didn't expect me to live, at my age. "He fooled everybody," she says, "but Dad developed damaged kidneys and had to go on dialysis. He is in good health except for his dialysis. Plastic tubes were inserted under his skin in his forearm to connect the dialysis mechanism."

A patriotic family

Bud also has a son, Bud. His oldest grandson, Travis, is a Marine who served two tours in Iraq and one tour in Afghanistan, in a sniper platoon. Lori has a daughter and two grandchildren. Lori's husband, Steve, served in the military with a tour of duty in Vietnam. Bud is extremely proud of his two children, four grandchildren and two great grandchildren.

He is a member of the Sun City Veterans Association and at age 93, happy to be a member of the Association's 85+ club and glad to have the opportunity to "tell his story."

Decorations, citations and medals

* Good Conduct Medal
* American Defense Service Medal (with Bronze A)
* American Area Campaign Medal
* European-African and Middle Eastern Service Ribbon (two engagement stars)
* Asiatic-Pacific Area Service Ribbon (three stars)
* World War II Victory Medal
* Navy Occupation Service Medal

Bud at home in Sun City, 2009

Sam Najarian

Sam Najarian

Sam was born on January 21, 1925 in Brooklyn, New York. He graduated from the elite Brooklyn Technical High School in June 1943. The day after he enlisted in the Army Air Corps and was sworn in as a cadet at Fort Dix, New Jersey.

In his own words

I received orders to report to Miami Beach for basic training. Yes, Miami Beach, not a bad place for a kid from Brooklyn. We slept in a small hotel right by the beach—it was heaven. Hey, imagine a poor kid from Brooklyn going down to Miami Beach. I never saw the place before.

After basic all the cadets were sent to colleges and universities across the country. I went to Kent State University in Ohio. The courses were basic academic subjects and pre-flight training. For me that was a breeze, "a piece of cake," coming from a rigorous program at Brooklyn Tech. After five months at Kent State I went to Selman Field in Monroe, Louisiana, a navigational training school. My original job choices had been pilot, first; navigator, second; and bombardier, third.

Navigation training took nine months at Selman. I received my wings at graduation with the rank of flight officer, equal to a warrant officer. I went home on leave for a couple of weeks and then reported to El Paso, Texas, where they were forming bombing crews. I met my crew members and stayed there for three weeks for training. After this stint we were shipped out to Lincoln, Nebraska, a take-off point for overseas assignment. I was assigned to New York, which I was very thankful for.

At Lincoln, we knew that our assignments would be either in the South Pacific or Europe. I was hoping and praying to be sent to Europe, because I hated to fly over long stretches of water and I knew Pacific missions would be mostly that. I never feared crashing into a mountain or parachuting onto land, but parachuting into an ocean would bother me. I pictured a bizarre scenario where I was parachuting into the ocean and a shark was waiting for me with his mouth open, poised to devour me. Plus I heard that it was a lot better if you were a POW in Europe than at a Japanese prison camp.

Shot down over Germany

I boarded a troop ship in New York Harbor, the Isle de France, and we sailed to England. I was assigned to the 8th Air Force, 305th Bomb Group, and 364th Bomb Squadron out of Chelveston, England. All told I had 26 combat missions over Germany as a navigator in a B-17. I was shot down once over Cologne, Germany. We didn't bail out until we got into Belgium. It's quite a story!

Sam (2ⁿᵈ from left) and his B-17 crew

We took off from England on January 10, 1945 and were in formation across the English Channel on a 1,000-bomber raid. Our targets were not in Cologne but specific sites in the area. As we were crossing the Channel, we lost one of our engines due to power failure. We had to give up our position in the formation but managed to keep running on three engines. Over the target, flak intensity was very severe. We got hit by anti-aircraft fire and our second engine caught fire—we were able to feather it for a while.

Author's note: If one of the engines fails in flight, the propeller on the idle engine can rotate or windmill, causing increased drag. To prevent this, the propeller can be feathered (turned to a very high pitch), with the blades almost parallel to the air stream.

Losing two engines in flight could have been disastrous, but we were lucky they were not on the same side. The problem was that nobody could drop bombs on the bomb run. Command made a decision to fly in a 360 degree turn-around and go over the target a second time. The entire formation did a complete "360" but we were lagging behind because we only had two engines. The formation went over the target and dropped their bombs; we went over by ourselves but after dropping our bombs got hit again by flak, and the third engine started sparking and windmilling. Our wing caught fire and finally the pilot gave the order to bail out.

It was mid-afternoon over the outskirts of Cologne. The plane was in bad shape. It was vibrating and the wing was on fire, but it wasn't really out of control, we weren't in a spin, just losing altitude. When the pilot gave the order to bail, I got on the intercom with him and said, "You know we're only a few minutes flying time to Allied lines (in Belgium). If we can manage to stay aloft for a few minutes to reach the Allied lines and then bail out, our chances of survival would be much better than to parachute into Germany." He agreed and rescinded his order. We chugged along westward, while the rest of the formation was on its way back to home base.

"Prepare to bail!"

It was hectic on board. The plane could have blown any minute. I was trying to navigate as best I could. When I thought we were near the lines, I radioed the pilot, "I think we're over allied territory now." He put the plane into automatic and repeated his order: "Prepare to bail!" The crew proceeded to our designated escape hatches.

My bombardier buddy was alongside me. The escape hatch we were supposed to use was under the nose of the plane. I tried to pull the release to open up the hatch—it was frozen shut. I tried to kick it open but that hatch release was frozen solid. We had to go through the bomb bay area and jump out the side waist gunner's opening after all others had jumped; we were the last left on board from a nine-man crew that day. Seven of us survived. Our engineer was shot on the ground when he landed, by retreating Germans or enemy sympathizers. The co-pilot dove out and never pulled the rip cord on his chute. They just found his body on the ground. Anything could have happened to him, but I suspect that he just froze with fright.

We landed in Belgium but to this day I never did find out which town we landed in. I don't even know the names of the people in that town that took me in—and I wish I did. They must have told me, but I was a 19-year-old kid, fighting to survive. I landed in an open field, a really barren area. The ground was covered with about three feet of snow; I noticed a farm house a quarter of a mile away. I got out of my parachute harness and cautiously made my way over to the barn. I found the barn empty and decided to hide there at least until dark and then try to find somebody to help me.

"American, American!"

I was hiding about an hour when a very elderly woman, maybe about 90 years old, came into the barn. But she was tall and strong, carrying what appeared to be buckets. She came within 25 to 30 feet from where I was hiding; I wondered whether or not to stay put. I decided to step forward and hope for the best. I stepped into view and from my pack pulled out the little American flag the Air Corps had given us to identify ourselves. I waved the flag and said, "American, American!"

On seeing me she dropped her buckets and came charging right towards me. She grabbed me under the armpits, picked me up off the ground and bounced me in unbridled joy while my feet never touched the ground. She took me into the farm house where the rest of the family lived, and they broke out some wine and cheese and called a neighbor over and started a little celebratory party on my behalf.

From a couple of younger people in the family who understood and spoke a little English I learned I was the first American that they had personal contact with. The Germans had pulled out of that area only a day earlier. I was extremely lucky! I stayed in that farm house for a couple of hours and my bombardier, who landed about a mile and a half on the other side of the farm, walked into the same farm house, dragging his parachute behind him.

"What are you doing here?!"

He saw me and said, "Sam, what the heck are you doing here?!"
"I was here first, baby!" I said.
"Where is your parachute?" he asked.
"I left it outside."
"You're going to go outside and get it, aren't you?"
"No, are you crazy? I'm not going out there and get it. What am I gonna get it for?"
"Don't you want a souvenir of your bailout?"
"Forget it!"

Later I borrowed a scissors in the farm house and cut a little sliver from his chute. While we were talking about retrieving my chute, one of the kids in the family overheard us and admitted that she ran out to the field, gathered up the chute, brought it back and hid it in the closet in her room. "You keep it!" I said.

The Allies had just entered that area and didn't have time to set up general headquarters. The civilian authorities who were notified had no good way to notify our military. Finally the Army dispatched a vehicle to pick us up and deliver my bombardier buddy and me to Brussels, where the Air Corps had set up a makeshift hotel for downed airmen until they were flown back to their base in England. I stayed in the hotel for 10 days and flew back in January 1945. They grounded me for a couple of days and gave me a couple of weeks R&R before I went back to flying with a new crew for another 13 missions. Germany surrendered in April.

The war ends

Those of us who did not complete our tour of duty were prime candidates to be shipped over to the Pacific Theater. I flew back to the States with our crew; we landed in Newfoundland, and on to Boston. I had home leave for two weeks and then orders to report to Texas, where we were expected to be shipped out to the Pacific since the war was still raging against Japan. Of course, the bombing of Hiroshima and Nagasaki quickly ended the war.

I was discharged in November 1945 and went home to Brooklyn. I was 20 years old, and took a few meaningless jobs for a while. To get ahead in life, I realized, I should pursue a college education. I enrolled in Brooklyn College for pre-engineering for two years, and then transferred to CCNY (City College of New York) School of Technology to become an engineer. I received my degree and became a professional engineer specializing in environmental engineering pertaining to dams, treatment plants and water-related projects as part of a team of consulting engineers until I retired some 40 years later.

My family

I met my wife, Helga Haberle, at Brooklyn College. After a long courtship, we wed on December 20, 1952 and lived in Fresh Meadows, Queens. After our two sons were born and my firm moved up to Westchester County, we decided to live as close to their corporate headquarters as possible. As a result, we ended up in Norwalk, Connecticut, very close to the firm's headquarters.

After I retired in 1988, one of my clients asked me to do some consulting work, which, with other consulting jobs, kept me busy for a few more years. We moved to Sun City—Hilton Head in 1997 as pioneers. Back then there was nothing between Sun City and the bridge to Hilton Head except a few other gated communities.

Wedding of Helga and Sam, December 20, 1952

Impressions of military service

I was very proud to serve in the military. Some of the positive aspects for me were gaining maturity, learning how to accept responsibilities and the opportunity to go to college under the GI Bill. Without the GI Bill, I would not have been able to attend college.

I entered military service when I was 18 years old and was discharged when I was 20. For me, this disrupted the chain of friendship that one normally develops during those years. Most of my friends I knew as a youngster went into the service. Some did not come back. Some came back, stayed a week or two and took jobs elsewhere. What I missed terribly was that chain of friendship that I could have had during my school years, and would normally be carried throughout my life.

I came home right after I was discharged. One day I overheard my sister talking to my mother, and my mother crying. Later my sister said mother told her, "Sam went into the service thinking and acting like an 18-year-old. Two years later he came home thinking and acting like a 30-year-old." When I think about it, those are the years for a normal person in normal times for fun and enjoyment. I missed all of that. My college life was not joyful either. I was six years older than most of the other students. I didn't go in for all the "rah-rah" stuff—but that was part of the fun in college life and I missed that, too.

Sam at home in Sun City, 2009

Keeping others informed

Sam has volunteered as a tour guide at the Mighty Eighth Air Force Museum in Pooler, Georgia, since 2004. He plans to do this as long as possible because he cherishes the opportunity to keep the current and future generation as well-informed as possible about people and events during World War II.

Carl Nusbaum

Carl Nusbaum in Manila, 1944

Carl was born September 17, 1922 in Chicago. After graduating from Tuley High School in 1939, he worked as an office manager for a delivery service and attended Northwestern University night school. Carl joined the U.S. Army Signal Corps in June 1942 and was sent to Spry Telephone School in Chicago. After completing school he did basic training at Camp Crowder, Missouri.

In his own words

From Camp Crowder, I jumped around from camp to camp as my unit—the 350th Anti-Aircraft Artillery Battalion (a searchlight battalion)—was sent to Camp Butner, North Carolina; Fort Eustis, Virginia; and Fort Ord, California, to prepare for overseas. We headed to New Guinea on a troop ship and stayed there for a year. It was a desolate place, with guys dying day by day—not necessarily the result of combat, but from tropical diseases characterized by infection and high fever.

Author's note: Malaria was the greatest debilitator, but dengue fever, dysentery, scrub typhus and a host of other tropical sicknesses awaited soldiers in the jungle while scattered, tiny coastal settlements dotted the flat malarial north coastline.

> *The terrain was a commander's nightmare because it fragmented the deployment of large formations. On the north shore a tangled morass of large mangrove swamps slowed overland movement. Monsoon rains of eight to ten inches a day turned torpid streams into impassable rivers. There were no roads or railways, and supply lines were often native tracks, usually dirt trails a yard or so wide tramped out over the centuries through the jungle growth. Downpours quickly dissolved such footpaths into calf-deep mud that reduced soldiers to exhausted automatons stumbling over the glue-like ground. Fed by the frequent downpours, the lush rain-forest jungle afforded excellent concealment to stubborn defenders and made coordinated overland envelopments nearly impossible. Infantrymen carrying sixty pounds of weapons, equipment, and pack staggered along in temperatures reaching the mid-90s with humidity levels to match. Thus the U.S. Army faced a determined Japanese foe on a battleground riddled with disease and whose terrain made a mockery of orthodox military deployments. (courtesy of U.S. Army Center of Military History, by Edward J. Drea)*

I was initially a radio operator and after being in New Guinea for about a year, I went on an R&R to Australia. I spent time in Sydney and was hastily called back because the Army was getting ready for the invasion of the Philippines. We traveled from Lae to Finschavin to Hollandia in New Guinea and then on to the Philippine Islands. I arrived on D plus 1. The main attack began early on the morning of December 22, 1944, as 43,110 men of the 48th Division and one regiment of the 16th Division, supported by artillery and approximately 90 tanks, landed at three points along the east coast of Lingayen Gulf.

The next day 7,000 men of the 16th Division hit the beaches at three locations along the shore of Lamon Bay in southern Luzon, where they found Gen. Parker's forces dispersed, and without artillery, protecting the eastern coast.

All equipment lost

When we were going across, we lost all of our Signal Corps equipment. When we finally landed we didn't have any of our communication/aircraft or searchlight equipment at all. As a consequence, eventually we were assigned to Gen. MacArthur's headquarters and became guards. We spent most of our time guarding ammunitions dumps and other vital military sites in Manila. Our long trek across the Philippines began when we first disembarked, marching down from Clark Field. Our sleeping quarters were cots in tents. We ate C-rations and a lot of Australian beef—"bully beef" as we used to call it.

The U.S. 8th Army then moved on April 17 to its first landing on Mindanao, followed by invasion and occupation of Panay, Cebu, Negros and several smaller islands in the Sulu Archipelago. These islands provided bases for the U.S. 5th and 13th Air Forces to attack targets throughout the Philippines and the South China Sea.

Following additional landings on Mindanao, U.S. 8th Army troops continued their steady advance against stubborn resistance. By the end of June, the enemy pockets were compressed into isolated pockets on Mindanao and Luzon, where fighting continued until the Japanese surrender on September 2, 1945.

By that time I had become a TEC/3 (technical sergeant) and when I started processing to go home, they asked me to take over as first sergeant—which I accepted. I returned to the States in April 1946.

Attuned in the Philippines

But first, after being in the jungle of New Guinea for so many months without any contact with women, I arrived in the Philippines where the women were plentiful. But I had to figure out the best way to make contact. I had been a singer since I was a kid. So one of the first things my buddy and I did was to learn some of the Filipino songs and sing them in one of the main languages, Tagalog. This worked and gave us an opportunity to meet and talk with the girls. Speaking their language gave us an upper hand, plus we had our own little singing group. We sang for the girls and also entertained our fellow GIs. When we were going over to New Guinea we had a group of guys who entertained the troops on the ship.

GI Bill

Back in the States I decided to take advantage of the GI Bill, and enrolled in Roosevelt University in hometown Chicago. I received a bachelor's degree in commerce and psychology and accepted a position at the Michael Reese Hospital in personnel administration, which would be known as human resources today. I started as an intern and a year later became the assistant director of personnel. Two years later I was promoted to executive vice president of the hospital. Thanks to my college degrees—I also earned a master's in hospital administration from Northwestern—I was able to begin a lucrative career.

In the meantime, I married Carol Greenberg from Chicago in 1947. The marriage ended in divorce in 1969. We had two boys, Cary and Bruce; Carol is now deceased. In 1969 I married my present wife, Catherine Anne Sevebeck, who also had two children, Michael and Donna. We lived in Deerfield, Illinois.

In 1951 I had become CEO of the Schwab Rehabilitation Hospital in Chicago, which later was the first rehabilitation hospital in the Midwest to be accredited by the Joint Commission on Accreditation of Hospitals. I was there for some five years.

Double CEO

In 1956 I became CEO of the Gottlieb Memorial Hospital, funded by the Gottlieb family and the community. I started from scratch, hiring the staff and doctors and building it up before leaving in1963 for another general hospital. After three years I went to Sheridan General Hospital, serving as CEO of two hospitals (Sheridan General and Doctor's Hospitals) during that period.

I left Sheridan in 1973 to become an administrator of Pritzker Children's Hospital—a small children's hospital for the developmentally disabled affiliated with the University of Chicago. We took care of autistic children and children with a wide range of emotional problems, at a time when autism was not well known. We had a team of young people who identified with kids and were wonderful caregivers. After building a solid foundation at Pritzker, I returned to Sheridan General and spent another two years there.

A theater career

Both Anne and I became involved with the North Shore Theater Company while living in Illinois. I served as president for two years, and also acted. We participated in many activities in the theater. It was sort of cross-pollination in the North Shore area, where there were a number of different theaters. We would go from one to the other. In essence, I really had two professions—as a hospital administrator and professional actor.

In 1973 I asked a former associate who had gone into the travel business to find a spot that was unique, climate-friendly and where we could play tennis. He knew just the place—Carefree, in Arizona. Anne and I flew out and booked a room at the Carefree Inn.

As we drove from the airport Anne looked at the absolutely barren landscape and said, "Carl, where are you taking me? There is nothing out here!" But as we approached Carefree we began to see beautiful outcroppings and massive rock formations, and as we looked down in the valley and saw the lights glowing from the homes in Scottsdale, it was a beautiful sight. Our stay was enjoyable and we signed an agreement to buy a house in Carefree while at the inn. We thought we would use it for vacations as a second home.

A year later we had gone to Anne's son's Michael's wedding in Colorado. While driving back with Anne's mother and father, we took a detour to visit Carefree. Anne's mother, reading the Carefree paper, noticed an ad for a hospital administrator for one of the medical facilities. We had no thought of moving away from Chicago, but I made an appointment just out of curiosity. When the interview was complete, the representative said, "Carl, your credentials are too great for the position we have open. But there is a hospital nearby looking for an administrator right now." They gave me the name and called the chairman. We set up an interview, and they asked me if I would accept the job. I agreed and in 1974 we moved from Chicago to Carefree.

We missed the theater and the love of acting, and decided to try to start a theater group. Carefree had only about 400 people at the time, but a nearby community, Cave Creek—that used to be an old stop for stagecoaches—had a large and growing population. So we put an ad in the paper to see if we could attract people interested in forming the Desert Foothills Theatre. People responded and we formed our theater company. It is now in its 35th year and still going strong.

Carl (right) stars in "Fiddler on the Roof"

As proud founders, we held workshops and put on all kinds of shows over 20 years, such as *Music Man, Oliver* and *Annie.* We brought in the kids from Cave Creek because most of the people in Carefree were adults. I also served as president of Kiwanis and on the Carefree board of directors, so we made a substantial contribution to the growth and the culture of that area.

Our wandering years continue

In 1995 we visited my brother, Jack, and sister-in-law in Sarasota, Florida. They lived in a high-rise overlooking the bay and tennis courts. My brother told me about an apartment available in his building. Anne and I took a look, fell in love with it and bought it. We returned to Carefree, packed our belongings, moved to Sarasota and formed a singing group called the Landoliers, which gave us an opportunity to entertain the residents.

Acting, singing and entertaining became an integral part of our life—an ability to reach out and touch the lives of others. After five years in Florida we were on a trip to Hilton Head, South Carolina to take advantage of our time-share in Sea Pines. We had two time-shares in two organizations—one in Scottsdale (The Scottsdale Camelback Resort) and another with an organization in Hawaii, the Kakelai in Princeville. We could trade our time-shares through a company called RCI. This allowed us to choose where and when we wanted to go. We chose a spot in Hilton Head to take a vacation. While there in 1998, we spotted a sign announcing homes in Sun City. We looked around, liked everything that we saw and decided to buy a small unit so we would have another place to go during the holidays. But after a while we decided we needed to make another change. Having lived in Florida for five years, we sold our apartment and moved to Sun City permanently, in 1999.

Sun City Community Theater

When we first moved to Sun City there was a small theater group called Act One. They had about 30 people as members. Since the theater is our "lifeblood," we became very active in this fledging group. Our first suggestion was to change the name, to better identify what they represented. I suggested Sun City Community Theatre, and it took. We also suggested instituting the "Sunny Awards" to recognize talented performers; we had "Annie" awards in Arizona for performers there.

It has been my pleasure to serve as president of the Sun City Community Theater for five years. We went from less than 200 members to 1,300 when I left office. We have wonderful people who followed me as president. At the start I had to cajole and coax people at our regular monthly meetings to get involved. We kept saying, "Take a chance, fulfill yourself; fulfill your dreams!"

While serving as president of the SCCT, I was asked to serve on a committee to plan for the expansion and improvement of the stage at Sun City's Pinckney Hall. Our recommendation was not to proceed with changes, but to use the funds to construct a new facility, as had been promised by

Del Webb to the residents when they purchased their Sun City homes. As a result, a magnificent theater was built and now Sun City residents enjoy a wonderful venue for the performing arts and other functions. The new facility, opened in January 2009, is known as Magnolia Hall.

Final thoughts on military service

It was the most positive experience that influenced my life. It taught me discipline, it taught me how to be self-sufficient and it taught me to be a man. It saddens me to think about those in today's younger generation who never had the opportunity to take on responsibility. And I say to myself that it would be great to create mandatory programs to serve our country for today's young men and women (though there would be a lot of opposition to it). I would personally be in favor of a draft, because I think that it would enhance the ability of our young people to serve this country. I strongly believe that military service prepares young people to take on the world.

Carl at home in Sun City, 2009

Earl Rogers

Earl Rogers

Earl was born on October18, 1923 in Clyde, North Carolina, the family's sixth generation in Haywood County. On graduating from high school in 1942, he was drafted into the Army and reported to Fort Jackson, South Carolina. Earl volunteered for Airborne when they offered him $50 more a month, a sum he had yet to see in his young life. After completing infantry basic and jump school at Camp Blanding, Florida, he was shipped in a convoy to Nottingham, England and the 508th Parachute Infantry Regiment. His unit jumped into Normandy at 1:30 a.m. on June 6, 1944, six hours before the Normandy beach landing. They were transported in

C-47s, 13 troopers on each side, and jumped into a pitch-black night to land at St. Mere Eglise, Normandy—the first town taken on the western front of Europe. Earl says he was one of the lucky ones who survived the assault. "Morale was high," he recalls. "Everybody wanted to get this over with and get home. We thought we'd knock them out in the first lick, but the Germans had a different idea."

Q & A: D-Day

Arnold:	You were behind the lines?
Earl:	Yes. We were about 10 miles inside. Did you see the movie, "Saving Private Ryan?" Now that's Airborne, right there. That looked just like it when I was there.
Arnold:	When you hit the ground, what did you do with your parachute?
Earl:	I left it. The Germans flooded everything. They knew we were coming and opened the dikes, flooding the fields, so we landed in the water. It was so dark; you couldn't see anything at first. A lot of the guys drowned; we were loaded down with ammo, food for three days and anti-tank mines. There were a lot of paratroopers hanging in the trees. The bullets and shells lit up the heavens, knocking planes down with the flack.
Arnold:	So you didn't hit ground, you hit water. Was it over your head?
Earl:	No, but in some places, yes.
Arnold:	What happened next?
Earl:	I just walked until I reached high ground.
Arnold:	And you left your parachute in the water?
Earl:	I left it! I didn't want to carry it anymore.
Arnold:	You just unstrapped it?
Earl:	There's a pin in that pack. You pull the pin out, take a half-turn to the right and you come right out if it. Most of the paratroops who died couldn't get out of them.
Arnold:	Did you have a back pack?
Earl:	Yes. We were walking around with a total weight of 300 pounds—your weight plus the back pack and all the other equipment. When we landed it was six hours before the beach landing occurred. The 4th Infantry Division was supposed to come in and relieve us. But they were stuck for 31 days before they came.

Arnold: So when daylight came, did you encounter German troops?

Earl: Oh yeah, there were plenty of them—behind the hedge rows.
          I was cold. In June it was cold. I was wet from the water and
          I crawled up on high ground waiting for daylight. In the dark,
          before daylight came, you couldn't recognize who was friend or
          foe. So we carried little cricket clickers. If you clicked it twice
          and if he was a buddy, he would click it back in response. The
          Germans got on to that. They would click the bolt on their rifles
          to duplicate the sound of crickets chirping. Then they would let
          you have it! I was one of the lucky ones, I reckon. We scattered
          everywhere. It was cold and damp and I got wet all over. I made
          sure to keep my ammo and rifle dry. In daylight I saw someone
          coming around the edge of the water and I clicked the safety off.
          I was gonna let him have it but then I saw his American helmet
          and I didn't shoot him. Many American soldiers lost their lives
          that way.

Did you ever see "The Longest Day?" That boy was hanging on that church
steeple. His name was John Steele and they shot him in the foot. He played
possum and hung on that steeple; didn't move a muscle, and they didn't
shoot him. Eventually they got him down and he lived. He got back home
to Wilmington, North Carolina and died of cancer.

Arnold: What happened next?

Earl: At first light we began to see each other. We stayed in Normandy
          31 days. After the 4th Infantry relieved us we went back to England.
          We got new clothing, new equipment, trained some more and
          made some more practice jumps and on September 17, 1944 we
          made a daylight jump into Nijmegen, Holland. When we flew over
          the English Channel you could have walked down on the flak. I
          thought I'd never get down. And our Intelligence didn't know that
          there were two SS divisions that moved into our jump site.
              We were supposed to capture the Nijmegen Bridge—the
          Germans were retreating back to Germany and Montgomery (the
          British general) under Eisenhower wanted to seal off the bridge
          to capture them. We thought there wasn't going to be fighting,
          but we encountered fierce resistance from the two German SS
          divisions. We took the bridge, but at a price. I was wounded and
          received a purple heart at Nijmegen.

Battle of the Bulge

On December 15, 1944, word was received that the Germans were heading into Antwerp. Their troops had successfully overrun Allied troops and scattered them all along the Belgian border. The fear was that many Allied troops would be left behind enemy lines. An all-night trip in a cattle trailer took Earl back to the front—and a brutal 16-day battle as he and 67 buddies were stuck behind enemy lines. It was zero degrees—he thought he was going to freeze to death.

Earl lost 27 pounds during his ordeal behind enemy lines and his small group of five was the only one that got out alive—and one of the group died later. Earl fought other battles; he was wounded several times, earned another cluster to his Purple Heart and had some metal pieces removed from his leg as a reminder of the day he almost froze and bled to death in the snow.

He also witnessed the aftermath of what's been called the Malmedy Massacre, where American soldiers who had been taken prisoner were lined up in a field, their hands tied with barbed wire and gunned down. After Malmedy, Earl's captain told their unit, "We fight under a black flag. We take no prisoners."

After months on the front lines, Earl's unit was finally dispatched to the Rhineland where, in the spring of 1945, the war in central Europe was coming to an end. Next assignment for the 508th Regiment: The highly decorated members were chosen as the All-American Honor Guard for Gen. Dwight D. Eisenhower. At that time Earl was in the Ruhr Valley, Germany. When the war was over Eisenhower was at Supreme headquarters in France. This was in stark contrast to yet another duty Earl was assigned to before completing his service.

Liberating Dachau and Wobbelin

Gosh, it was pitiful! The dead were lying everywhere. The ovens and everything were there, even skeletons of the people. Some had starved to death. Dysentery got others. The smell was awful. There were quite a few of them alive. The Germans had buried people alive who were supposed to go in the ovens. We made the Germans dig them up and give them a decent burial, put a white cross at each grave.

Author's note: On April 26, 1945, as American forces approached, there were 67,665 registered prisoners in Dachau and its subcamps; more than half of this number was in the main camp. Of these, 43,350 were categorized as political prisoners, while 22,100 were Jews, with the remainder falling into other categories. Starting that day, the Germans forced more than 7,000 prisoners, mostly Jews, on a death march from Dachau to Tegernsee far to the south. During the death march, the Germans shot anyone who could no longer continue; many also died of hunger, cold or exhaustion. On April 29, American forces liberated Dachau. As they neared the camp, they found more than 30 railroad cars filled with bodies brought there, all in an advanced state of decomposition. In early May, American forces liberated the remaining prisoners who had been sent on the death march. The number of prisoners incarcerated in Dachau between 1933 and 1945 exceeded 188,000. The number of prisoners who died in the camp and the subcamps between January 1940 and May 1945 was at least 28,000, to which must be added those who perished there between 1933 and the end of 1939, as well as an uncounted number of unregistered prisoners. It is unlikely that the total number of victims who died in Dachau will ever be known.

A survivor in Wöbbelin—
photo courtesy of United States Holocaust Memorial Museum

German civilians from Ludwigslust file past the corpses and graves of 200 prisoners from the nearby concentration camp of Wöbbelin. The U.S. Army ordered the townspeople to bury the corpses on the palace grounds of the Archduke of Mecklenburg. May 7, 1945. *United States Holocaust Memorial Museum*

Meeting Ruby

We returned home on the Queen Mary in November 1945, arriving in New York. I went to Camp Shanks, New York and later to Fort Bragg, North Carolina, where I was officially discharged, and returned home to Clyde, in North Carolina, on January 6.

I looked all over the world for a woman. I didn't find her until I came back to Clyde—and there she was! Ruby Thompson! (Ruby chimes in from across the room, "I lived across the river and he lived over in town.") I was a "city slicker." That little town wasn't over 500 people. We were married in 1948. After we married, I bought a little house, for $6,000, and went to work in a paper mill in Canton, four miles away. I worked 40 years at that mill as a pipefitter and steamfitter. In 1984 I retired and remained in Clyde. Ruby and I are blessed with two children, four grandchildren and one great-grandchild.

Our daughter decided that it was time for us to move. I couldn't take care of the property outside and Ruby was finding it difficult to take care of the house inside. As a result we decided to sell our land and home and come down here next to our daughter, who lives nearby in Richmond Hill, near Savannah. We moved to Sun City on May 29, 2008.

Final impressions

I figured the government got three years out of me. I'm not sorry. I grew up in the Army. I wanted to get in a good outfit if I was to serve so I volunteered for the paratroops. I made 29 jumps—two were combat jumps. The worst battle I got into was that Battle of the Bulge. I was about to freeze to death. It was 10 below zero—we didn't have a place to go. I was hoping and praying that a shell would hit and bust that frozen ground so that we could dig a hole to crawl into.

I'm glad I served my country and I am thankful that I survived the war.

Earl in Sun City, 2009

Don Shaw

Don Shaw

Don was born on June 29, 1926 in New Kensington, Pennsylvania. After graduating from high school in June 1944, Don enlisted in the Marine Corps at Pittsburgh. He took a train and bus to boot camp at Parris Island, South Carolina, and remembers going through the gate for the first time as passing recruits shouted at those on the bus, "You'll be sorry!"

Don completed basic in September 1944. His unit was moved to Camp Lejeune for infantry training, and informed they would be shipped out to Guadalcanal to replace empty slots in the 1st or the 6th Marine Division. Don became a private 1st class when Congress passed an act that raised their pay to $56 a month.

Q & A

Arnold: What was your next assignment after Lejeune?

Don: One morning our sergeant calls out about 60 names. My name
          was in that group and he said, "You guys get over here. Pack your
          gear, you're going to Quantico." They had an Officer's Candidate
          School at Quantico and we would be assigned to do the grunt
          work. The remaining guys from Lejeune went to Guadalcanal,
          where they replaced other Marine combat divisions. I was in a hut
          in North Carolina with eight guys and they were sent to Okinawa.
          Two of my buddies from that group were killed. I remained in
          Quantico and worked in the mess hall and was assigned to other
          mundane chores. I was eventually placed in a training battalion
          where I engaged in infantry training on the firing range and in
          foxholes while live ammunition was fired overhead.

Don at Quantico

Eyewitness to devastation

I shipped out to Japan in February 1946, assigned to the 2nd Division to
work in the Headquarters Battalion. Our journey began by taking the train
to San Diego, boarding a troop ship to Pearl Harbor and finally docking

at Yokohama. It was leveled as far as the eye can see. We went through Hiroshima—there was only one building standing.

Author's note: The city was heavily damaged in World War II by the first-ever nuclear weapon used in military action. The nuclear attacks on Hiroshima and Nagasaki were major factors leading to the surrender of the Japanese government several days later. The bomb exploded over Hiroshima at 8:15 on the morning of August 6, 1945. About an hour previously, the Japanese early warning radar net had detected the approach of some American aircraft headed for the southern part of Japan. The alert had been given and radio broadcasting stopped in many cities, among them Hiroshima. The planes approached the coast at a very high altitude. At nearly 8:00 a.m., the radar operator in Hiroshima determined that the number of planes coming in was very small—probably not more than three—and the air raid alert was lifted. The normal radio broadcast warning was given to the people that it might be advisable to go to shelter if B-29s were actually sighted, but no raid was expected beyond some sort of reconnaissance. At 8:16 a.m., the B-29 Enola Gay dropped the atomic bomb called "Little Boy" over the central part of the city and the bomb exploded with a blast equivalent to 12,000 tons of TNT, killing 80,000 people outright.

I traveled down to the island of Kyushu, where the Marines were stationed. I peered out the windows of the train and saw Japanese cities leveled to rubble from American bombing raids. Our destination was Fukuoka. Saturation bombing of Japanese cities had commenced on Honshu with Fukuoka one of the targets. It was leveled as well.

The Army took over the occupation of Japan. They pulled the Marines out of Japan and I returned to the States. I had an offer to enroll in the Naval Academy Preparatory School, in Bainbridge, Maryland, a six-month classroom-structured environment to review basic academic high school subjects. It was for fleet appointments to become a U.S. Navy officer. In April I took the test and passed, but decided I had enough military and opted out of the program and was discharged from the Corps in August 1947, with the rank of corporal.

Life after the military

I returned home and decided to get a college education. I enrolled in Purdue University (under the GI Bill), graduated with a degree in civil engineering and, in 1951, was offered a job in Kansas City with Owens Corning Fiber

Glass. The company taught me how to design furnaces to melt glass, which, in turn, could be processed into glass fibers. This was to be my life career. My job title was project engineer. I was with OC seven years; with PPG (Pittsburgh Plate Glass) for seven years in the fiber glass division; and with CertainTeed Products and a small company in Kansas City called Gustin Bacon. I ended up working for myself as a consultant in Toledo when I finally retired.

My family

I had a blind date with Mary Ferguson, from Purdue, in 1950 and after a memorable courtship we wed in the summer of 1952. She lived in Highland Park, Illinois. We had our first child, Cathy, in 1953 and 2½ years later we were blessed with another daughter, Carol. Mary and I lived in Kansas City about 17 years and then I changed jobs and we moved to Shelbyville, Indiana. We left Indiana and moved to Toledo. In 1999 Mary died of lung cancer. A year later I married Patty Walters (Patty and Mary were high school classmates and good friends). In 2002 Patty and I moved to Sun City. Sadly, Patty was diagnosed with cancer and passed away in the fall of 2008.

Impressions of military service

I never felt like a warrior. The Corps tried to instill that mindset into Marine recruits. Hardly any of us felt that way. I was delighted to serve and never really remembered any truly bad days in the Corps; we got treated well and I guess I could say it was "the highlight of my life." The military gave me a college education. I don't think I would have gotten one otherwise. My tour in the Marine Corps was a positive experience and I probably would feel the same way if I was in another branch serving my country during World War II.

Don and sister, Jean; back home on leave, 1946

Ray Smith

Ray Smith

Like many newborns in his time, Ray Smith did not arrive in a hospital delivery room but in his mother's bedroom, in Malden, Massachusetts, on April 13, 1922. From age five, he lived and went to school in neighboring Melrose, famous for its championship hockey teams, marathoner Clarence Demar and as the only liquor-free city in the Old Bay State.

Growing up in the Depression

To help his mother, sister and brother during the Depression, young Smith brought in money by running errands, delivering newspapers and singing as a boy soprano soloist in a church choir. Seasonally, he also caddied, picked apples, raked leaves and shoveled snow. In his teenage years, he performed janitorial work after school hours at 20 cents an hour and set up pins in a bowling alley on weekends at four cents a string.

When Ray graduated from Melrose High School in 1940, the unemployment rate was 15 percent and it took him eight months to find a job as a file clerk and office boy in a printing firm at $12 a week.

Becoming a soldier

By the time he was drafted into the Army in the summer of 1942, Ray was a print planner and estimator at the handsome salary of $25 a week. The Melrose draft board sent him to Fort Devens, Massachusetts. One lasting memory of that induction was giving up his first Army breakfast to the bushes after a night of fitful reaction following a day of indoctrination and inoculations.

Ray was assigned to the Signal Corps and received basic training at Camp Leonard Wood and specialist training as an administrative NCO at AGF (Army Ground Force) School in Fort Monmouth, both in New Jersey.

The final test of his basic training was a full-pack, 25-mile march to Fort Monmouth—seven miles of which were stumble-stepped on a railroad track. "Railroad ties," he recalls, "are not spaced for comfortable marching and the calf muscles quickly and painfully found that out."

After Monmouth Ray was shipped to Drew Field in Tampa, Florida, assigned to Signal Aircraft Warning (radar) duty and received further specialist training as a radar oscilloscope operator ("scope dope"). After 10 months of training, he was assigned to a permanent unit on the eve of heading to the mid-Pacific theater of war. All told, he served 42 months in uniform (32 months overseas) and never received a furlough or a single day's leave at home. He did get a 48-hour pass while at Fort Monmouth and visited New York City.

The soldier as sailor

To and from various island assignments, Smith spent a total of 72 days on the Pacific Ocean on everything from an APT (Attack Personnel Transport) ship to a converted Hudson River ferry boat to an LST (Landing Ship Tank) to an LCI (Landing Craft Infantry), and was seasick on every one of them. It started under the San Francisco Bay Bridge before his troop ship even left the dock because the lower hold was full of diesel fumes.

"After that," Ray said, "I slept on deck every night I could—usually on the tarpaulin cover of a cargo hold." But in a stop at Eniwetok Harbor one night, they "blew out the stacks" and he woke up the next morning covered with soot, looking like Al Jolson on the "Jazz Singer"—which called for a detested salt water shower.

Island-hopping—and Iwo Jima

The next two years with his 568th S.A.W. (Signal Aircraft Warning) Ray was on duty island-hopping between the Hawaiian and other mid-Pacific islands. In the fall of 1944, he learned his unit was to be assigned to the 5th Marine Assault Corps (VAC), headed for a small island called Iwo Jima.

He further learned that Iwo Jima was about 660 miles south of Tokyo and shaped liked a keyhole, with a 500-foot-high volcanic mountain called Suribachi at the bottom of the keyhole. The island had two airstrips and was manned by a garrison of 28,000 Japanese Royal Marines and Army. They were commanded by Gen. Tadamichi Kuribayashi, who was partly educated in America. His orders were to defend Iwo Jima to the death.

The 568th Battalion was to establish and maintain the signal aircraft warning coverage for the campaign, which included installing a unit on top of Mt. Suribachi. The first assault, landing on the morning of February 19, 1945, was spearheaded by the 4th and 5th Marine Divisions, with the 3rd Division acting as a floating reserve.

Despite many weeks of Air Force bombing and strafing—and days of pre-invasion shelling by American battleships and cruisers—the Japanese garrison, heavily fortified with their artillery dug into Mt. Suribachi on rolling tracks, was virtually undamaged.

For more than an hour the Japanese allowed the invading Marines to come ashore, unload equipment and slowly struggle up the steep volcanic beaches before they opened fired. They didn't even have to aim; the range and patterns had been pre-set. The artillery and automatic guns were zeroed in on every square yard of the five crowded beaches. Horrendous casualties were inflicted in both the 4th and 5th Divisions.

Q & A

AR: Were you actually a part of the invasion force?

RS: Not as an infantryman—but by D plus 5 all of the reserve 3rd Marine Division was on shore, fighting alongside the 4th and 5th Divisions. Our small advance unit landed shortly thereafter.

AR: Did you go into the beach on a landing ship or craft?

RS: At Saipan we were loaded onto an LST for the 750-mile sail to Iwo. During the night a most unsettling sight came into view—a brightly illuminated hospital ship with big red crosses painted on the sides, sailing south to Saipan hospitals with its precious cargo.

AR: And the LST took you right up onto the beach?

RS: Almost. We landed in the late afternoon, knee-deep in water. Wrecked American ships, vehicles and equipment were everywhere. But in front of you was a long, uphill slope of loose lava granules. It was like climbing a hill with large black Grapenuts®.

On top of the ridge there were Japanese bodies and wreckage amidst pillboxes, barricades and abandoned equipment. The ground was more solid and we got into foxholes that had been used a couple of days earlier by the Marines. They were no more than shallow ditches; eventually we piled up bags filled with lava gravel for better protection.

Wrecked Japanese bomber, from Ray's photo collection

**Dead Japanese soldier on the beach at Iwo,
from Ray's photo collection**

AR: Besides the volcanic footing and general mayhem, what's your most vivid impression of your first night on Iwo Jima?

RS: It was cold, damp and dark—except the sky and terrain would be lighted up, from time to time, by parachute flares. I would hear occasional small arms fire and loud artillery blasts to the north. I was pooped and shocked by the physical and emotional events of the day. I barely slept that night. I developed a fever and shivered constantly. It was confirmed later that I had dengue fever, a mild form of malaria. Under the circumstances it was negligible and I didn't report it.

AR: Did you see any actual combat?

RS: Not in the infantry or attack sense. We weren't combat troops but we were bivouacked in an area subject to enemy fire and reconnoiter action. The Japanese were good at determining and assaulting areas assigned to service troops or Air Force personnel, including our unit on two occasions. Even as the main battle line moved north on the island, the basic areas were subject to attacks and raids by left-behind pockets of enemy troops motivated by hunger, thirst or suicide.

AR: Did you lose any buddies?

RS: I lost three close friends—two on Iwo and one by suicide before we left for the States.

AR: Iwo Jima is considered one of the Marines' toughest battles. How long did it last?

RS: The original plan called for a 10-day campaign. It was 36 days before the island was declared "secured" and I say that cautiously because skirmishes and mopping up went on week after week.

AR: Iwo Jima created one of the greatest armadas of the war, I understand.

RS: Some 800 ships of all categories brought 70,000 Marines, Army, Air Corps and Seabee forces to Iwo Jima. Think of it, Arnold, 98,000 combatants on a 10-square mile island filled with tunneled hills, cliffs, plateaus, countless pillboxes and barricades. American casualties were predicted to be 10 percent; they reached 40 percent—nearly 7,000 deaths and 21,000 wounded, mostly in six to eight weeks. Of the 28,000 Japanese forces, more than 26,000 died there, including the Japanese commander, Gen. Kuribayashi.

Ray (right) holding a Japanese flag, from Ray's photo collection

AR: What happened to those 33,000 bodies on Iwo Jima?

RS: After the fighting moved to the high ground, north of the airstrips, cemeteries were established for each of the three Marine Divisions, the 3rd, the 4th and the 5th. Each grave was identified with a suitable marker and many also displayed touching tributes and mementos put there by their buddies.

AR: Is it still the same today?

RS: No. For two to three years after the conclusion of World War II, the remains of many of these fallen heroes were transported from all over the world—including the island of Iwo Jima—and were buried with honors in home towns all over America. At the time the 26,000 enemy dead were buried in unmarked mass graves on Iwo Jima; I don't know what happened to them after the war.

Life (and more death) on Iwo

AR: You said even after the island was secured, combat actions continued?

RS: The Marines left Iwo Jima late in March and the Army took over. It wasn't just mopping up—short but fierce battles and casualties continued on the northern heights until late spring. But remnants of enemy troops were being flushed out or sealed in caves and labyrinths of tunnels right to the end of the war in August.

AR: How long did you stay on Iwo?

RS: The rest of the war actually; a total of nine months. We settled down to S.A.W. duties with our radar unit on top of Mount Suribachi, right near the flag site and temporary memorial.

AR: What other events do you remember from your nine months on Iwo?

RS: Arnold, Iwo Jima was never dull. One day (I think it was in March) news flashed across the island that Germany had surrendered and the war in Europe was over. War-weary, island-happy troops shot off so many celebratory rounds and firearms in the air, emergency ammunition supplies had to be flown in. The news proved to be a complete hoax. In April, Japanese tracer bullets hit a Marine Engineering Depot and shook the entire island when 8,000 cases of dynamite exploded. Three weeks later, one of those ubiquitous flares misfired and came down on a primary ammunition dump—setting it on fire. The dump was located near the base of Mt. Suribachi in a series of revetments, about a quarter of a mile from our bivouac area. The fire lit up the night with frequent explosions, throwing burning objects and shrapnel into the air, spreading the fire to other revetments. Everybody jammed into Quonset huts and sheds, in and under trucks, in abandoned caves. For 3½ hours it burned and erupted.

Finally, after a seemingly long period of quiet, I made my way back to my cot in the pyramidal tent that was "home"—now shredded with many gaping holes and tears. No sooner had I laid down when a tremendous explosion shook the earth, hammered my chest, battered my ear drums and I landed against the center pole with the cot on top of me. Later we found out it was the result of 148 500-pound GP demolition bombs exploding simultaneously.

A Pacific typhoon struck the island in May and I saw a jeep go spinning like a top 15 feet up into the air. Also in May a number of Japanese soldiers escaped from a sealed cave in Suribachi and were killed and captured in our area. That was my scariest night of the war.

Island sanctuary

AR: What was the object of this terrible battle for Iwo Jima?

RS: The round-trip flight from the American bomber bases on Guam and Tinian to the target cities in Japan was a challenging round trip of some 3,000 miles. If a plane got hit over the target, it was 1,500 miles—almost five hours flying time—back to the home base. The main purpose of taking Iwo Jima was to provide an emergency landing place—a safe haven—for damaged bombers and wounded crew members halfway back to their home base. Almost daily/nightly, we'd track on our radar screens and hear with our ears, hundreds of B-29s flying overhead on the way to the target—and four-five hours later, the stricken and crippled bombers would circle and start landing on the air strip of Iwo Jima.

Occasionally, planes would be too damaged to land and you'd count the surviving crew by the number of parachutes opening—before the plane was ditched into the sea. It was reported that by the end of the war, about 2,400 B-29s had landed and some 27,000 crewman had been saved by the sanctuary of Iwo Jima and the help of their on-the-ready crash crews and medical teams.

AR: When did you leave the service?

RS: I was honorably discharged in December 1945 at Fort McPherson, in Atlanta. During the war, my mother had remarried and moved to the Savannah area; I took a Central of Georgia train from Atlanta, arriving at the railroad station (now a museum and visitor's center) on what is now Martin Luther King Boulevard. A local orthodontist repaired some of the dental damage done while I was in the service. One unforgettable incident took place during a two-week field exercise in Florida in the spring of 1943 when a technician 5th grade filled a couple of cavities using a manual dental drill he powered with a foot pedal.

Back in Boston

In January 1946, back in my native Boston area, I rented a furnished room and returned to my interrupted career in graphic arts and printing. I had left at $25 a week and during the war, the Office of Wage and Income (OWI) authorized my new salary of $29.

AR: What did your service in World War II teach you? How did it affect you in later life?

RS: I grew up poor in the Depression as the oldest of three siblings in a single-parent family. In effect, I was a teenage male head of a family. That taught me the reward of hard work and the value of money. It taught me self reliance. I think, too, it even developed, perhaps, a will for survival. My wartime service matured and reinforced those strengths and taught me the benefits of teamwork. In the Army, authority was authority! You might not agree with it but you obeyed it. But obedience is not necessarily respect; I learned that later in business.

AR: World War II has been termed "the last good war." What's your thought on that?

RS: History tells us some 67 million people died in World War II, 42 million of who were civilians. We had 16 million Americans under arms and 416,000 of them died in 45 months. To answer a question with a question: Can any war ever be "a good war"?

        Let me speak on a personal level: Only one in 16 of the Armed Forces were ever involved or witnessed personal combat at first hand. I saw enough to learn and firmly believe all of these past 64 years that war is the scourge, the shame and the ultimate flaw of mankind.

World War II did not need any other justification (for the U.S.) than Pearl Harbor but war should never be anything but the completely definitive and ultimate final resort. Back then there was a saying: "There are no atheists in foxholes," but at the same time, there are those who believe that war is de-humanizing, an eternal curse which can undermine, even destroy one's faith.

AR: How do you square those thoughts with patriotism?

RS: My patriotism is based on my service to my country and is fully dedicated to the courage, valor and sacrifice of our armed forces and citizen soldiers in the defense and preservation of our country, its values and its people, as demonstrated throughout our history.

Meeting "Mal"

I was making $50 a week when I met Edith ("Mal") Marilyn Chase from Swampscott, Massachusetts in January 1948. I married her in September and we lived two magical years in a furnished apartment on Beacon Hill in Boston, a block above historic, picturesque Louisburg Square.

Ray and Marilyn

We walked to concerts by the Pops on the Esplanade, to Sunday double-headers at Fenway Park and Braves Field, to opening nights at the Colonial, Shubert and Wilbur Theatres—and there were strolling carolers and bell-ringers at Christmastime!

When, in 1951, the first of super siblings arrived, we moved to the suburbs, bought a home and I'm proud that Mal's sole occupation from 1951 to 1969 was: mother and homemaker. We've been hanging together now some 61 years. I knew it would work!

Business career

I was an account representative in a printing firm until 1962, when I abandoned selling for production and creative management, which I enjoyed thoroughly, by joining Dickie-Raymond Inc. of Boston.

Starting in the 1920s, Leonard J. Raymond was a dynamic and innovative pioneer in the direct marketing profession. Over the years, we were merged and acquired, in turn, by John Kluge's Metromedia, Needham-Harper and, eventually, by Omnicom. I retired from Omnicom in 1988 at the age of 66 after 47 years in the graphic arts and advertising profession.

Sun City—Hilton Head

In September 1997 we moved to Sun City—Hilton Head. We had had our fill of overshoes and overcoats, of snow tires and snow blowers, of February sub-zeroes and August burned-out lawns. We wanted a "kinder climate." We also wanted to get out of our over-sized "empty nest." While loaded with 40 years of warm memories, it had too many stairs and levels. It was a house for younger people. We wanted one floor, fewer walls, more open space, with a walk-in closet and a two-person shower.

Also, though we had a great life-style in Boston, comfortable and affordable while working, after several retirement years of domestic and global travel, a more relaxed and less expensive environment, a "kinder C.O.L" (cost of living) made sense for us, at 72 and 76. Both of us were born and raised in old New England, particularly in the suburbs of Boston, and we are so grateful for that. It is one of the great cultural, intellectual, financial, educational, medical centers of the world.

Native citizens have diversity, curiosity, inventiveness, erudition, are surrounded by the energy of 250,000 college students and more than a dozen universities and colleges. It's a great sports, music and restaurant town, not to forget its colonial traditions and history.

Today, 11 years later, we enjoy our neighbors and friends here at Sun City—Hilton Head and love our home with a two-acre lagoon out back and the untamed woods on the opposite shore with the flora and fauna and occasional visit of wildlife.

Although I never gave it a thought for years, when the 50th anniversaries of World War II became prominent in the media in the 1990s, so many proud and sad forgotten memories came rushing back.

This, together with those remembrances of the years of my youth forcefully brought the realization of what a truly great family and a good life Mal and I have had. And now, at 83 and 87, we are, indeed, both blessed and grateful.

Author's note: Ray has enjoyed a life-long avocation which enhanced his journey through life. Inspired by his choir experience and his high school love of big bands and jazz music, Ray continues in his 51st year of hosting THE JAZZ DECADES program on Boston radio and for the last 36 years on WGBH and NATIONAL PUBLIC RADIO—now produced and recorded in digital sound in his home studio in Sun City—Hilton Head.

Ray at his home studio in Sun City, 2009

A self-taught drummer, Ray has played jazz concerts, festivals, cruises and tours in the United States, South America, Canada and the British Isles with his own Paramount Jazz Band as well as with other famous jazz bands and has recorded extensively since 1966.

But that's another story for another time.—Arnold Rosen

Russell Smith

Russell Smith

Russ was born on July 7, 1923 in Bellmore, New York. After graduating from W. C. Mepham High School in 1940, he attended Lafayette College and Worcester Polytechnic Institute before transferring to the Naval Academy, where he graduated in June 1944 and was commissioned as an officer in the United States Navy.

In his own words

I served aboard the USS Massachusetts from October 1944 until 1946, much of that time as a fighter director. Let me explain, to understand better the incident I am about to relate.

The Massachusetts (BB59) was one of the 10 "fast" battleships that served with the carrier task forces in one of five such groups. The task force group had the challenge to clear the way prior to an island invasion and to secure absolute air control. Radar was instrumental in allowing these groups to identify incoming enemy aircraft and guiding our own planes back to their home base, usually their home carrier. In this period radar was big and bulky. Near the end of World War II radar was just beginning to be introduced aboard naval aircraft, mainly in night fighters. Mission control was done from shipboard via radio communication. For long range search, however, the largest radar was found on the largest ships. Carriers certainly had the best but fighter directors aboard a carrier were occupied much of the time with "housekeeping" chores. In other words, keeping updates on the location, fuel status and assignments of its planes, rather than tracking enemy aircraft and potential attacks. Not that they didn't do this also, but battleships also carried large radar and could devote themselves to the external situation. Battleships were also stationed miles away from the carriers, always in position on the side of the incoming attack potential.

All this activity aboard ship was coordinated in the Combat Information Center (CIC). The captain's place was on the bridge. The executive officer was in charge of the CIC. Most information was fed directly into the CIC and the exec had the job of filtering the information stream and keeping the captain up on only what was immediately necessary for the captain to do his job. Radar information and control of search radar was from the CIC. In the CIC were radar plotting boards where petty officers kept track of all aircraft in the area. If an unknown aircraft were discovered, the group fighter director would assign, via radio, aircraft from the combat air patrol overhead to some ship, which then was responsible for investigation or attack on the unidentified aircraft, again controlling by radio. By today's standards for radar used to intercept aircraft, this system seems pitifully slow, but such was the state-of-the-art in 1945. (One of the group fighter directors for our task force was named John Connelly. I have often wondered if he was the future governor of Texas.)

Saving downed pilots at sea

So much for background! In July 1945, just prior to the atomic bombing of Hiroshima, the carrier task forces were making attacks directly on the

Japanese mainland. The B-29 raids were area attacks. Naval planes at lower altitudes could make pinpoint attacks on such targets as bridges, tunnels and railroads. This, of course, was in expectation of the invasion of the home islands proper. All such operations involving this many units were covered in an operation plan. Officers assigned to the CIC were required to know every detail of their part of the operations plan as well as the supporting cast. The attacks usually had the carriers quite far at sea. Several miles away were vessels like battleships between the carriers and the target area. Still nearer the shore line were picket destroyers (Picket destroyers were fitted with special radar communications systems which enabled the ship to act as an early warning unit when stationed ahead of a task force). These ships were there for rescue of downed returning aircraft. In addition PBY flying boats were available to land in ocean waters to rescue pilots. PBYs saved hundreds in the South Pacific, where air warfare over the main islands and the snail island mazes of the South Pacific reached its fiercest heat. The PBY's primary duty was rescue flying. Like Walt Disney's elephant with the helicopter ears, its name was DUMBO.

Lastly, often within sight of the shore line was one or more submarines (submerged), again for potential rescue of downed pilots and crew. This was the ideal plan. Each operation was set up slightly different for any one of a thousand reasons. In the case I am going to relate there were no DUMBOS, since we were too far north and out of their range. In addition, we were told to expect only slight enemy activity. I had been assigned a group of Grumman Hellcat F6F fighters. Code names are always used and this group was "Jack of Diamonds." In short, my job was to see that they all got home to the Diamond Mine (carriers).

The operation plan had the expected time for my aircraft to cross the shore line, both coming and going, and the location. Our radar could not distinguish planes from the land mass at the extreme distance at which we were working. Perhaps 15-20 minutes before the return time, one of my "chickens" (Navy slang for young fighter pilots) called in that he had been hit by anti-aircraft fire and turned back. He further reported that his engine was running rough, his wind screen was covered with oil, he had zero visibility and had caught occasional glimpses of flames under his cowl flaps. To top this, his oil pressure was slowly dropping. On the plus side all the instruments seemed to be working and his control surfaces functioned normally.

In fighter director school we had practiced analyzing information, fitting this in with the operation plan and making a decision on what to do. The most ominous thing he reported was the dropping oil pressure, which meant he had no chance of making it back to be close to the carrier. The submarine seemed the only choice. I was able to locate his Hellcat; for one thing he was early and the only aircraft in the area. Identifying planes was usually done with a radio beacon "Identification Friend or Foe" device. This plus flying box patterns was the typical way of sorting out lost aircraft one from another on a radar screen. I checked the operations plan location of the rescue sub and immediately gave the pilot a vector to the best interceptor point.

Fighter directors work in teams. I called for help and found two of my cohorts who were not in trouble. I asked one to check on the location of the submarine and to have him get ready for a rescue. I asked the other to contact the "Jack of Diamonds" squadron commander and tell him one of his pilots was in serious trouble. Meanwhile I kept the pilot in touch and reassured him that we would stay with him. Oil pressure continued to drop.

Crash landing or parachute bailout

In fighter director school we had periodic lectures on the characteristics of various types of aircraft as far as water landings (crashes) were concerned. Some were worse than others, none were very good. I was planning on having the pilot as close to the sub as his oil pressure would allow and have him bail out. If close enough, the sub might be able to catch sight of his parachute, or the aircraft itself, on the way down. A pilot in cold water has a life jacket and not much else. He has perhaps a half hour before hypothermia catches up with him. To add to the problem, a submarine, even surfaced, is not very high over the water and visibility is poor. A water landing is a better choice but this pilot could see nothing. A water landing must be timed to kill the engine at exactly the right instant. If done too soon, the plane stalls and drops its nose down into the water. If too late, the spinning propeller will probably flip the aircraft over on its side when it hits the water.

The pilot has a small rubber life raft in the plane, which in turn has a flare pistol and a dye marker. He also is good for hours of floating around.

My other partner had not only located the squadron but they in turn had located the damaged plane. He was the only casualty of the raid.

The reports confirmed that oil covered the windscreen and there were occasional flashes under the cowl. The squadron commander wasted no time. His other charges were all low on fuel. He sent them all back to the Diamond Mine but kept his wing man. He vetoed my bailout plan and said he was going to stay and coach a water landing from his plane. `The wing man was kept to watch the squadron commander to make sure that he in turn didn't go into the water. Meanwhile, he had charted a course for both the aircraft and the submarine for the shortest path. We gave this information to the aircraft involved. As I recall the planes were under oxygen level, which was 10,000 feet. I estimate that the let-down started about 8,000 feet. The rate of descent worked out to be in the 400-600 fpm (feet per minute) range. We had calculated this to give the best shot at crossing the path of the sub.

All the pieces now fit together. The let-down started; everything now hinged on the oil pressure holding up. After some 15 agonizing minutes, silent except for the squadron commander's instructions, the three planes reached the critical point. The squadron commander timed the engine cut-off and the vector into the wind perfectly. The submarine had already surfaced fully and was on course to the calculated splash point. They had seen the aircraft before splash down and had the pilot aboard in minutes.

The squadron commander and his wing man were now so low on fuel that they had to be diverted to another carrier closer in than their own.

I have often reflected that the pilot's life was saved because everyone involved was highly trained. The operations plan had been followed to the letter. When I called for help, all the others involved were senior to me and could have demanded I relinquish control. Except for the enemy damage there were no equipment failures. Possibly, best of all, no one panicked.

Back to civilian life

After discharge in 1946, Russ went back to Worcester Poly, obtained another degree in electrical engineering and was hired at General Electric to help design locomotives. He specialized in electrical control systems, earned a master's degree in electrical engineering from Penn State University and was awarded 15 U.S. patents related to electrical control systems.

These accomplishments led, after retirement from GE in 1985, to consulting work in Taiwan, Germany, Switzerland, Belgium and Austria as well as in the U.S.

Russ met Allene Beattie while working for GE in Schenectady. They married in 1948 and settled in North East, Pennsylvania (near Erie). Russ and Allene have two daughters—Penelope and Tracy.

A love of skiing

What began as a way to get outdoors with his wife and exercise a little during the winter has turned into a passion for Russ during his retirement. He didn't begin skiing until the age of 55 but ski racing has been a joy for him well into his 70s. He racked up several awards and trophies for finishing first in ski racing events for his age group, 71-79.

Russell at home displaying his ski trophies, 1996

Final thoughts

I have no regrets for having spent three years in the service. Everybody in my era bracket was involved. After the war I was transferred to the USS

Chicot (AK-170), where I was engineering officer. We decommissioned the ship—this brought me back to engine rooms, diesel engines and sundry machinery, as opposed to the functions on the USS Massachusetts. I decided right then that this is what I wanted to do, so it was back to WPI on the GI Bill. I'm proud that I served in an active combat zone, but it was just one phase of my life and I don't feel that anyone owes me anything special because of it.

Frank Stanley

Frank Stanley

Frank was born on January 25, 1924 in the rural village of Collingham, north of Nottingham, England. His full name is Sydney Frank Payne Stanley, following an English tradition of adding the mother's maiden name to a child's when it appears there will be no male offspring to carry the line. Many British hyphenate the last two names; Frank's family chose not to do so.

Frank attended Sir Thomas Magnus Grammar School, a private school near his home. He completed school at 16 in 1940, and with a friend rode their bicycles 16 miles to Lincoln and volunteered for military service. They enlisted on June 7, 1941. Frank took basic training in Yorkshire for flying with the RAF (Royal Air Force), and after graduation was sent to Rhodesia, Africa (now Zimbabwe) for advanced pilot training.

Q & A

Arnold: What kind of aircraft did you learn to fly on?
Frank: We trained on small aircraft—a Harvard. It was a two-seater.

The Harvard trainer, courtesy of North American Aviation

Author's note: The North American Harvard trainer was built in greater numbers—17,096 in all—than most combat aircraft during World War II, with over 5,000 supplied to British and Commonwealth Air Forces. To equip an ambitious Empire Air Training Scheme as conflict became inevitable, the Royal Air Force turned to the United States to acquire the trainer aircraft needed. A first contract, for 200 Harvards, was placed in June 1938, long before lend-lease arrangements began. Soon after the outbreak of war most flying training units were moved to Canada, Southern Rhodesia and the United States. This made room for operational aircraft in Great Britain and provided safer conditions for training.

Arnold: After you completed your flight training, what was your next assignment?
Frank: I was first sent to Durban, South Africa, and then by rail to Rhodesia.
Arnold: Were you in combat while in the RAF?
Frank: No, in training. We flew non-combat in Africa.

Arnold: What was your rank in the RAF?

Frank: Flight sergeant.

Arnold: In the American military pilots had to be commissioned officers to fly. But in the RAF you were able to fly with an enlisted grade rank?

Frank: Yes, I was a flight sergeant.

Arnold: Did you have any interesting stories while flying for the RAF?

Frank: I remember one incident after the RAF returned me to a base in England. My buddy and I were practicing aerobatics in bi-planes. At one point my plane came too close to his and our wings touched. The two planes locked together and went into a spin. I tried to climb out of my cockpit but could not get out of the plane. I was harnessed to my parachute and with the other plane locked on top of mine there was not enough room for me wearing my parachute to exit. While struggling, I must have hit my head and passed out momentarily. Shortly thereafter I regained consciousness and found that the planes must have shifted because I was able to lift myself out of the cockpit and jump, while the wreckage continued spinning down. Though groggy from a head injury, I was able to pull the rip cord and see my parachute open. Someone who was watching on the ground told me that I must have fallen over 1,000 feet before I pulled the cord and my parachute opened. Fortunately, I landed near a little house which was a temporary first aid station and they attended my wound. I learned at that time that the other pilot was killed in the accident. I am now a member of the *Caterpillar Club,* which is open to pilots who saved their lives by parachuting from a disabled or flaming aircraft.

In the words of Edith Anne Morgan, Frank's wife

One of the most fascinating stories Frank has told me was about an incident that happened when he was in school at the age of 14 or 15. He had taken a great interest in planes. He joined the Royal Air Force Volunteer Reserve and took extensive training in enemy aircraft identification.

One day as he bicycled home from school he looked up and saw a low-flying plane. He heard the engines erratic groaning noises, typical of the unsynchronized engines of German aircraft. Frank recognized the craft as a German Heinkel 111. *(The Heinkel HE 111 was often described as a "wolf in sheep's clothing"; masquerading as a transport aircraft, its purpose was to provide the Luftwaffe with a fast medium bomber.)* Frank was near the local train station. He could see that the plane was following the railroad tracks. He tried to run into the signalman's booth but the railroad signalman barred his entry. Frank shouted, "You have got to call Nottingham. That's where the bomber is headed." The railroad signalman grew more annoyed and told Frank again, "You get out of my station! You are not allowed in here!" Frank reluctantly complied but warned the signalman, "Okay, but you better warn Nottingham!" Frank stood outside the railroad booth. All of a sudden he heard an alarm bell go off. The signalman ran outside the booth and shouted, "Nottingham's been bombed!" Frank was trying to warn the air raid wardens at Nottingham of the approach of a German bomber, but the signalman had ignored him.

From RAF into the Army

Frank was discharged from the RAF in Harper Hill, England on April 24, 1945. That day about 100 aircrew in Frank's group were ordered to assemble on the base parade grounds, which were bordered with men armed with machine guns. A commander presented himself to the men and made a surprising announcement: "Gentlemen, you are no longer in the Royal Air Force! You are in the Army." Frank served as a clerk in the British Army's 62nd Training Regiment until his discharge on May 28, 1947.

Frank (2nd from left) and his RAF buddies, April 1945

Frank's first wife was Irene, whom he met at school when he was 16. They were married when he went off to Africa. Upon his return home the marriage disintegrated and they divorced. Shortly after his Army discharge he met Bettye Ruth Rarey, the American widow of an RAF pilot shot down over the English Channel. Frank and Bettye fell in love. She returned to the States and in 1947 he left his homeland to join her.

When Frank boarded a shipload of military wives and dependents headed from Southampton to America he was instructed to line up with a group of girls. He was sent to a large room on the ship where he saw a line of beds. The ship's steward said, "You can't get in here!" Frank asked, "Where should I go?" He said, "You have to get in line with the men. What are you doing here?" When the ship's officials had looked at his passport and saw his name was Sydney, they assumed that he was a girl. Edith laughed and said, "He probably would have stayed with them, if they would have let him. He was almost a male war bride!"

Frank arrived in America and went to Decatur, Georgia, where he married Bettye Ruth. In 1956 they adopted a baby girl, Kathleen Elise.

Frank meets Edith

Frank was divorced from Bettye Ruth in 1958. In January 1961 he met Edith Anne Morgan in Atlanta. She was working in the sales office of at a downtown Atlanta hotel. Frank was a graphic artist for the Mead Packaging Company. Regarding their first meeting, Edith recalls, "We met on a blind date. A friend of mine at the hotel arranged for us to go on a double date. She told me, 'I want you to meet this guy; he's the freelance artist for the ballet company.' I had my doubts about the blind date, but when I saw him I was pleasantly surprised. He had Tyrone Power good looks and I have always been an Anglophile. I fell for his looks and his accent." They were married on December 7, 1963.

Edith and Frank on wedding day

Frank's primary career was in art with the Mead Company for 35 years. He retired in 1990. Edith left the Henry Grady Hotel in 1963 and went to *Time* magazine's Atlanta bureau as a secretary. Edith retired in 2002 after 15 years working for the *Los Angeles Times'* Atlanta bureau.

"In early 2004," said Edith, "our younger son moved to Savannah. We drove down to Savannah to help him find a place to live. After a frustrating search we decided to make a trip to see Sun City. It only took us 24 hours to realize this was the place we wanted to live. We returned to Atlanta, put our house on the market and moved here in June 2004."

Impressions of Frank's military service

My service was a definite positive experience. I met many good friends and it was a wonderful life for me and one that evokes fond memories.

In Edith's own words

Frank tells our grandchildren all these stories about serving in the RAF and Army. His father, who served two tours of duty in World War I for England, used to tell our children stories about World War I. Our kids loved his stories; our grandsons are now 9 and 12 and they love Frank's stories. Frank has one son and we have one daughter, two sons and three grandchildren.

We've been back to England many times. Unfortunately we've lost most of Frank's family. When we visited, Frank took me around to many places where he shared his memories of growing up. I remember one place near his home where an RAF bomber flown by a Polish pilot crashed. The casualties were buried in the nearby Newark cemetery. (There are a total of 400 graves of Polish airmen in this cemetery, all killed while flying British bombers for the RAF from Newark-area bases.) Frank added, "The Polish airmen stationed at the airfield near us (RAF Swinderby) flew a plane called a Fairey Battle. Often these Polish pilots would patronize the local pubs with us and we would have a grand time exchanging stories."

Author's note: The Fairey Battle was a British single-engine light bomber built by the Fairey Aviation Company in the late 1930s for the Royal Air Force. Siren-like whistles were installed on the bottom of the fuselage between the wheels. When pilots dove they turned the siren into the wind and the device emitted a loud scream. The result was intended to scare the heck out of the Germans.

A little bit of home

Frank and Edith say they feel a "little bit of home" when they visit the Mighty Eighth Museum near their home in Sun City, South Carolina. "There are so many connections to England there," Frank said, "and the Chapel of the Fallen Angels is exquisite. It reminds me of my village church back home."

Frank and Edith in Sun City, 2009

Dana Stewart

Dana Stewart

Dana was born on January 14, 1920 in Clio, South Carolina. He grew up on his grandfather's cotton farm. After graduating in 1937 from McColl High School, where he played on the football team, Dana worked for a Railway Express Company outlet, JC Penny and repaired tractor engines and other farm machinery. (He bought a broken-down Model T Ford for $20 and restored it to road-worthy shape.) At 18 years old, he attended Mars Hill College, and then transferred to Presbyterian Junior College in

Maxton, North Carolina, where he took CPT—Civilian Pilot Training—for his love of flying.

A military pilot

After accumulating 300 hours of flight time at Maxton, Dana received his commercial flying license. Teaching several flying courses to Army Air Corps cadets convinced him to join the Army, in 1942. Sent to Fort Bragg, North Carolina, he qualified for all airborne positions—pilot, navigator, bombardier and engineer/gunner.

In June 1943 he graduated from flight school and was commissioned a 2nd lieutenant. A year later he received orders for overseas combat duty, to pilot a B-25 as part of the 7th Air Force. He met his crew at Bragg and they all took a troop train cross-country to San Francisco. They sailed on a troop ship bound for the South Pacific that docked in Hawaii.

The B-25 Mitchell (NA-62) was a twin-engine medium bomber manufactured by North American Aviation. It was used by many Allied air forces, in every theater of World War II, as well as by many other air forces after the war ended, and saw service across four decades. In WWII, it was used frequently in the Southwest Pacific theater (SWPA) on treetop-level Para-Frag (parachute-retarded strafing-fragmentation) missions. A crew included pilot, co-pilot, navigator, waist gunner, engineer/gunner and tail gunner.

The missions

Dana had two tours as a pilot in the South Pacific on several islands. In a tour you were assigned a certain number of missions to fly. At the end of that tour, you could either be selected to go home or to stay for another tour. In his two tours, Dana accumulated 113 combat missions. He feels he was lucky to survive all of them. He remembers looking out his cockpit window, to his left and right, and watching planes of his comrades hit with flack and go down in flames. "Sure," he says, "I got shot at, got holes in my aircraft and at times my engines would go out, but I never had to walk or swim home."

Dana (top row right) with his crew in Tarawa, South Pacific

On Dana's first tour of combat he flew missions to Japan and Okinawa. On his second tour he became a commander of a squadron and flew missions to Japan and Naha, Okinawa.

In Hawaii in 1944, he met a nurse, Helen Hollingshead, whom he married after the war.

Post-war decisions

When Dana returned home after the war, he saw that many of his friends were divorced and there were shortages in consumer goods. He had saved quite a bit of money in the South Pacific and was able to buy farm land for his father to build a home on. His parents wanted him to work on the farm, but he was restless and wanted to live a more challenging life. The Army offered Dana an enticing opportunity to remain in the Army Air Corps with opportunities for education and advancement. He accepted, determined to advance his career through hard work and education.

Dateline of a distinguished career

1950—Sent to Langley Air Force Base as an instructor pilot and supervised maintenance and engineering work on a B-45 aircraft (the first jet bomber of the United States Air Force). Dana performed flight test work on this new aircraft.

1952—Stationed at Royal Air Force Station Sculthorpe in England and became commander of the 47th Maintenance Squadron. Dana was a part of a top secret project that used the B-45 jet bomber in the Cold War.

1955—Graduated from the University of Maryland with a B.S. degree.

1955—Attended Air War College at Maxwell Air Force Base, Montgomery, Alabama.

1956—Sent to the Pentagon to work with the Strategic Air Command (SAC).

1962—Went to Cairo as a U.S. air attaché.

1965—Returned to the Pentagon and enrolled in a master's degree program at American University.

1971—Retired from the Air Force with the rank of full colonel.

Military service impressions

I enjoyed the military service! I left our farm with very little money and no career plans but found maturity, character-building, adventure and wonderful opportunity in the military.

Civilian life

Dana began investing in the Stock Market, where he became moderately successful. With some of his investments he bought one of his grandfather's former farms, added land adjacent to it and planned to spend his civilian life as a gentleman farmer.

Dana traveled back and forth from his home in Fairfax, Virginia to his farm in Clio, South Carolina. He enjoyed life on the farm. His mother was still living there and he supported her. He worked at home in Virginia on his investments, using the telephone to buy and sell stocks. He hired workers to tend the farm and the crops.

Dana meets Joanne

After 18 years as a bachelor—his first wife died of cancer in 1971—Dana met Joanne Smith at the Instep School of Dance Studio in Fairfax. Ballroom dancing was their favorite pastime; they loved to dance at social gatherings throughout the Washington, D.C. area. Dana told her one evening, "I could dance with you for the rest of my life!" Joanne looked into his eyes and said, "Why don't you?" They married on April 1, 1989 and continued to live in Fairfax.

Raising a child—in Dana's words

My daughter, Dona, was born at Langley in 1951. She is my pretty daughter and everything was fine until she began to have behavior problems. At first we thought she was going through a period of erratic behavior and it would pass. Then we received a definitive diagnosis that Dona had schizophrenia. At that time the disease was not well-known. When I married Joanne, Dona's episodes were continuing. She refused to take her medications; it was a rough period for all of us. Joanne helped, she was a blessing! Dona took her medicine and improved. We took her to Walter Reed Hospital and she was under the care of an excellent psychiatrist. Dona, 57 now, lives with us and is doing very well.

To Sun City—in Joanne's words

I was a school teacher and kept working until 1997. When I was about to retire, we took a trip down to the Lowcountry and visited Sun City. I said, "We are going to live here some time." It took us until 2006 to get our 'things in order'; Dana had a stroke, and fell down a flight of stairs, while Dona continued having her episodes.

"That's it!" I said. "We're moving to Sun City!" We came down again and they had just put model homes on sale. One was available. We had 30 minutes to make a decision—the positives were too tempting to pass up! The location was ideal—near the fitness center and the swimming pool (I'm a swimmer) and all the homes on one level: no more steps to climb! So we bought the home.

We enjoy life here in the Lowcountry of South Carolina. It's been fun to explore Bluffton, Savannah and Hilton Head. In the historic town of Bluffton, the Spanish moss hangs from the big oak trees and creates a beautiful setting. We attend Sunday services at the Church of the Cross nearby, on the May River.

Dana is a member of the Sun City Veterans Association and attends meetings and special patriotic events. I'm a member of the Sun City Synchronettes and enjoy the camaraderie of the group and the discipline of synchronized swimming. We have really settled down to the good life in Sun City, with its many amenities. We enjoy the mild weather and the many good friends and neighbors we've had the pleasure of meeting.

Joanne and Dana in Sun City, 2009

MILITARY SERVICE
BETWEEN THE WARS

David Kerins

David Kerins

David was born January 3, 1929 in Carbondale, Pennsylvania. David's father died in 1932 and his mother, left with three children, moved to Wilkes-Barre to live with her sister Ann, who was also a widow. David's aunt had her own three children, but she welcomed them all "with open arms." David's mother worked scrubbing floors in a local hospital while his aunt, a public school teacher, held both families together.

David went to Grand Army of the Republic High School and graduated in 1946. He enlisted in the Navy, one of 4,000 inducted in Philadelphia in one day. His mother had to sign for him because he was too young to go in. She really didn't want to do that because his brother was wounded twice in World War II. Boot camp was at Bainbridge, Maryland. David went on to radio school in Bainbridge and Newport, Rhode Island. He was assigned sea duty on a destroyer.

In his own words

I boarded a destroyer, USS Power (DD-839), and served on board for two years as a radio man. We sailed up and down the coast to Cuba, engaged in training. We slept in 3-tier racks. We had the greatest baker on our destroyer. I would kill to get his cherry pie. Leaving Pensacola in winter 1947 we had to ride out a hurricane in the Gulf of Mexico. I was saying my prayers because I thought we were going to "go down." We had 37 degree rolls—that's turning over pretty good. Fortunately I never got seasick. The ship suffered major damage to the forward gun mount. I could not believe the force of the ocean that would do that. We had tremendous swells, wind and rain. Somehow we survived the storm and headed for the Brooklyn Navy Yard to undergo repairs

End of commitment

I was scheduled to be discharged in 1948 but in the middle of the process a corpsman came into the room and announced: "Kerins and Rossi are wanted in sick bay immediately." It was April, 19, 1948, a beautiful spring day, the first day of baseball season. When I arrived at sick bay, they told me the captain wanted to see me. He said, "We think you have tuberculosis. On your discharge X-ray we spotted something on your lungs. I would advise you to call your mother and tell her you won't be going home. We're going to send you to sick bay here in Portsmouth and run some tests on you." I was shocked! The captain said, "Actually, it would be probably a year, if you have TB, before you get home."

I went back and packed my stuff and went to sick bay. The next day I looked out the window and saw guys marching out the gate with their sea bags, discharged and heading home. I called my mother. Fortunately she wasn't home; I told my cousin the bad news. The Navy ran tests on me. I didn't have a cough and I wasn't bringing up anything. I was only a little guy then—117 pounds—when I entered the Navy. I really didn't take good care of myself; I was smoking and drinking and trying to act like a macho guy at 18. The Navy conducted gastric tests on me. They placed a plastic tube up my nose through my esophagus and into my stomach to suck out fluid and test it. They conducted X-ray and fluoroscope exams and discovered something on my left lobe.

The Navy flew me up with other sailors from Portsmouth, Virginia to Floyd Bennett Naval Air Station in Brooklyn, New York. I was transferred by ambulance to the Naval Hospital at St. Albans, Queens. I was in St. Albans for 10 months where they ran tests on me continuously. At that time St. Albans took care of many WW II wounded vets and others with TB. I met a lot of guys that served on submarines who often got infected with tuberculosis as a result of working in close proximity to one another.

I was finally discharged in February 1949 but was still sick. I had temperature and night sweats which were all indications of this disease—although they never picked up positive sputum on me. I was not coughing much either. But I was still sneaking out smoking and drinking whiskey. St. Albans treated us very well. Christmas and Thanksgiving were special at St. Albans. Because New York City radio stations encouraged giving, these holidays brought an avalanche of cards and gifts for patients. The Navy offered to send us to any Navy hospital or sanitarium that we wanted but you had to stay in the sanitarium. I was going to be discharged but they were going to transfer me to a Veteran's Administration facility in Sunmount, New York. As a civilian I was 100 percent disabled and was drawing 100 percent disability pay.

On February 6, 1949, I was finally discharged and traveled to White Haven, a private sanitarium near Wilkes-Barre. At the sanitarium I met three of my high school classmates—all had tuberculosis. Was it a coincidence that we were there? They told me that a close friend of mine in high school, Bill Cook, died a month after high school graduation. He hemorrhaged on the street and died of tuberculosis in Wilkes-Barre.

I think I had TB when I went in the Navy but when 4,000 of us were sworn in on one day, they never X-rayed me. I spent a year at White Haven Sanitarium undergoing tests and treatment. One of the treatments was pneumothorax. In this procedure, gas or air is injected between the lung and thoracic wall, temporarily collapsing and resting the upper portion of the lung. I had shots every week to collapse my lung artificially in order to rest it. Lungs work all the time, the only cure was if the lungs rested. New drugs, such as streptomycin were just coming out. Discharged from White

Haven Sanitarium, I went to the VA hospital as an outpatient for my shots. At that point in my life, 19 years old, I was not a "happy camper."

I needed special treatment and told the counselors I did not want to be close to home. I was terrible to my mother. I was just a nasty person. My poor mother—I put her through the ringer. She would come to see me all the time.

Q & A

Arnold: Were you in pain?

David: No, I was just unhappy.

Arnold: Did you have trouble breathing?

David: No.

Arnold: What was your main ailment? Fatigue?

David: You were tired all the time and losing weight, although they tried to fatten me up in the sanitarium. They fed me about five times a day. I think it was mental because we were all doing things we shouldn't have. I was sneaking out to smoke.

Arnold: Do you feel that if you had stayed on a strict protocol it would have helped you?

David: Well, one of the problems when you are in a situation is not knowing whether you are going to live or die, and you not knowing whether you are going to get out of here.

Arnold: For you was it a fine line between mental and physical distress?

David: Exactly. Viktor Frankl has a great book on that. He survived the Holocaust. He compares prisoners in the Holocaust in concentration camps to tuberculosis patients, believe it or not.

Arnold: Because both are serving a sentence?

David: Yes, because you don't know when you are coming out—whether you are going to live or die. I went to the VA hospital in Tupper Lake, New York in the Adirondacks. They were treating me well. I continued to drink and was always on the lookout for girls. I made a bet with the guys in the next bed that I could get a date with the first nurse on our floor. We heard that young nurse graduates were scheduled to arrive here from Albany. Helen was one of the young nurses.

Arnold: What year was this?

David: 1950.

David meets Helen

Helen came into my room on her rounds and I made up a story that I had a Cadillac. "How would you like to go out next weekend?" I asked her. I was on a ward where I was "up and around." Helen Palmer was an RN from Philmont, New York, a small town near Albany. She graduated from the nursing program at Albany. I won the bet and did get to date her and 55 years later, she's still taking care of me. We were married June 6, 1953.

Arnold: What happened while you were married? Did you work?

David: During our marriage I was not a very nice person. The chief medical officer of the VA hospital said, "We are not going to discharge you unless you have a plan. What are you going to do?" When I got out of the sanitarium I bought a big car and bummed around about a year. I was 100 percent disabled. "I was a bum!" I thought about it for a while, returned to Wilkes-Barre, back to my mother and aunt, and enrolled in Kings College, a Catholic institution. It was a wonderful environment to be in. We started each day with a prayer and it made me feel good inside. I graduated with honors and became a teacher in Candor, New York, a small town outside of Ithaca. I taught history, English and philosophy for 30 years

Helen and David Kerins retired to Hilton Head Island 14 years ago and now live in Sun City, South Carolina. They have five children and 11 grandchildren.

David has written a book, *Through the Dark Valley: A Veterans Three year Battle against Tuberculosis,* published in 2007. By revisiting those dark days, David hopes his experiences and revelations will help others who may be going through difficult times.

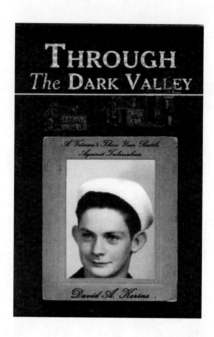

Book cover, *Through the Dark Valley*

David and Helen in Sun City, 2009

KOREAN WAR ERA

Harry "Skip" Marhoffer

Skip Marhoffer

Harry was born on December 26, 1930 in Danbury, Connecticut and lived in Wilton during his childhood years. After graduating from Staples High School in Westport in June 1948, he enlisted in the Navy for a three-year hitch for what "Old Salts" referred to as a "Kiddy Cruise" (in at 17, out at 21). The Navy had so many enlistments that year that he didn't start Boot Camp until September 12, at USNTC Great Lakes. Then came a 16-week program there to prepare recruits to operate and maintain ship engines. His rating was machinist mate fireman apprentice.

In his own words

After eight months of training I was ready to go to sea and, as the saying goes, see the world. I had no idea what kind of an interesting journey lay ahead. I was assigned sea duty aboard the USS Noble (APA218), an amphibious attack transport homeported in Newport News, Virginia. We were attached to COMPHIBLANT, which is headquartered in Little Creek, Virginia, a large amphibious training base. The Noble had 22 LCVP Higgins boats also called Peter boats and 2 LCMs most commonly called mike boats. We had troop berthing space to accommodate 1,500 troops. I was assigned to the M-B division and whenever the boats were lowered and we made landings I was one of the three crewmen on a Peter boat as the engineer. The boat was P-24.

USS Noble

We spent the summer of 1949 training West Point cadets, Annapolis midshipman and Marines from Camp Lejeune who we took on a large scale amphibious training exercise on Vieques, Puerto Rico. When we returned to Virginia, we got word that our home port was being changed to San Diego, as part of the COMPHIBPAC fleet. Because we had lots of berthing and cargo space the Navy agreed to allow dependents to come aboard ship with their furniture, autos and other belongings. Various compartments were converted to living spaces, nurseries and lounges. It turned out to be an interesting two week cruise. The crew called it "Operation Pin-Up" because there were lots of children still in diapers. As we went through the Panama Canal and passed ships going the opposite way, especially the cruise ships, passengers didn't believe they were seeing a Naval vessel with women sunning and kids running around on deck.

We arrived in San Diego Sept 12, 1949, almost to the day of being in the Navy one year.

In October we received orders to go to Hunters Point Naval Shipyard in San Francisco and go into dry dock there to have our hull inspected. It was the first of many times to go under the Golden Gate Bridge but the first time was overwhelming for a New England country boy. It's always a very special experience.

After our Yard period in early 1950, we were given orders to take part in a very large amphibious training exercise in Hawaii with the U.S. Army, called Operation MIKI. We were assigned to transport elements of the 3rd Infantry Division, at the time at Fort Lewis in Olympia, Washington at the end of Puget Sound. It's a long trip to navigate the sea lanes on the south end so our captain decided to stop in Seattle overnight and gave us Cinderella liberty—be back to the ship by midnight.

On to Hawaii and Pearl Harbor

The operation was good training because our coxswains and boat crews had never experienced swells and surf like we did landing at an unknown black sand beach. We ended up losing eight boats that broached and were torn apart by the surf and beyond repair except for the engines. My P-24 boat survived but required major repair.

After MIKI, the 3rd Infantry Division contingent we had aboard was transferring to Fort Stewart in Savannah, and it was decided it would be more expedient and less costly for us to take them so we went back through the Panama Canal and then turned around and headed back to San Diego. I was a throttle man at the time, standing 4 on and 8 off watches, and was so exhausted from all the steaming we did that I slept during the offloading and until we got underway early the following morning. I didn't see much of Savannah.

War breaks out

In June, when the Korean War broke out, we were at Mare Island Naval Shipyard in Vallejo, California. Suddenly the tempo of activity to get us operational took on a new dimension. The yard went to 24/7 shifts.

Vallejo is at the north end of San Francisco Bay, with a big anchorage of pickled ships put there four or five years earlier. After the war broke out the Yard brought in a hospital ship that had been mothballed and moored it next to us. The U.S. Maritime Service operates hospital ships so the first contingent of the civilian crew along with some yard workers came aboard to take it out for sea trials. It was a foggy, rainy day—and they never came back. Out in the Bay around Alcatraz it collided with a freighter and both ships sunk with large loss of life. As I remember it was the USS Benevolence.

When the Noble completed sea trials and passed in all respects we headed south to San Diego and the Navy Pier at the foot of Broadway to pick up a contingent of 1st Marine Division Marines led by Col. Chesty Puller, their regimental commander, and all their equipment. We fueled and took on provisions and on August 17 went to sea bound for Japan, arriving at Kobe September 2. It was clear that we were headed for combat because of all the Navy and merchant ships in the harbor. Kobe was one of Japan's biggest deep water ports and the remnants left by our World War II bombardments were still there. We hadn't combat-loaded, I think because the Inchon landing hadn't been firmed up yet due to objection to Gen. MacArthur's plan. Because of the 32-foot tides, the powers in Washington thought he was crazy and would lead to a major defeat. The disagreement was finally resolved and we got orders to tie up at a pier and offload and reload for combat.

Typhoon Jane—and Inchon

The USS Noble was tied up by a pier in Kobe when we were hit by Typhoon Jane on June 3, 1950. Corrugated steel roofs from rundown shacks near the pier blew away and became flying missiles. We broke our mooring lines and the wind pushed us to the other side of the pier into a safer zone. Our captain lowered three P-boats (landing crafts) but the 100-mph winds pushed us into the opposite pier, which crushed our P-boats.

On to Inchon

We sailed out of Kobe on September 9 and didn't know for a few days that we were headed to Inchon for the landing. We steamed up Flying Fish Channel and dropped anchor on September 13 about 1 p.m. and General Quarters was piped, meaning we were going to war and to man and lower all boats. "AWAY ALL BOATS!" is the official word. There were over 100 ships dropping anchor and the destroyers and cruisers were bombarding the port and beaches where we were going to land.

We were lowered into the water and the Marines started coming down the cargo nets. When loaded we circled while the boat group commander gave us a beach assignment and a signal to join up. We were told to go to RED beach, which had a seawall which even at high tide is difficult to climb. We were receiving some fire but it was passing over our heads. Some of the Marines were hit when they went over the top of the seawall but none fatally. After going back to the Noble to get more troops they sent us to BLUE beach and there was some resistance but lots of NKPA (North Korean People's Army) bodies. This was the last time we would go to the Noble for four days. The beach master would tell us what ship to go to, to unload cargo and take it into the boat basin for unloading. It got cold at night and we didn't have foul weather gear so we used bonfires to keep warm and heat up our C-rations. Each boat had a .45 pistol and a carbine for protection in case a boat got stuck in the mud or got sniped at.

After Inchon we went to Wonson but the Soviets had helped the North Koreans mine the harbor so we never made a landing there. The Navy lost two minesweepers as they were sweeping the harbor. Our advancing U.S. Army came up the coast and by the time the harbor was free of mines it made no sense to land troops invasion-style. We just disembarked the Marines that were aboard at a pier and we learned later that they were headed to Chosin Reservoir.

Our forces were retreating toward the Sea of Japan. The Chinese had 300,000 men and temporarily overwhelmed our forces. We were ordered to Hungnam post haste and started evacuating troops and equipment not necessarily going to the Noble—U.S. flag merchant vessels and ships that didn't have small boats. As we left Hungnam, the battleship Missouri was in the process of leveling the city and anything we left behind that would be of value to the enemy. We had two men killed and about a dozen wounded that Christmas Eve.

San Diego, ahoy

Finally our tour of duty came to an end. We left Yokosuka on April 13, 1951 and arrived in San Diego April 29. My hitch would be up in September so I started researching colleges and any requirements for testing. On or about July 1, President Truman extended all enlistments for a year and I found out we were going back to Korea and Japan. In September we sailed for Sasebo, Japan, which would be our base or temporary home port. We were close to Korea and could respond to any crisis if needed.

At Christmas time we went to Hong Kong and that's where I celebrated my 21st birthday. We spent almost two weeks there. I had advanced to 2nd class petty officer and 2nd class POs got overnight liberty so it was a special two weeks—party time.

On the way back to Japan we stopped for about four days at Okinawa to pick up some new Marines and a lot of vehicles that were needed in Korea. When we got back to Korea in late January (1952) my division officer had recommended me for R&R, so for six days I skied at Shiga Heights, in Nagano, the northernmost island in Japan, where the winter 1998 Olympics were held.

It was early May when we finally got back to the West Coast. We didn't do much except make mock landings on Coronado Island and do maintenance on the ship. On Labor Day weekend the ship was back at Hunters Point Shipyard and I was sent to the Naval Base at Treasure Island in San Francisco for discharge. It was September 9, 1952.

Finding a college

I went home to Connecticut and started to look for a college—going to a testing agency in Bridgeport to take the college boards and entrance exams. The first semester had already started but West Virginia Wesleyan College, in the town of Buckhannon—I needed an atlas to find it—agreed to let me start late as long as I made up the work, with a reduced course load of 12 hours. My plan was to transfer to a school closer to Connecticut after freshman year but Wesleyan was a perfect fit for me. I lettered in golf and football, got very involved in fraternity and social events, and in 1956 received my Bachelor's of Science degree in business.

When I returned to Connecticut I had several job offers but the one that jumped out at me was with Burndy Corporation in Norwalk specializing in electronic components. I was placed in the management training program—the first 18 months working for stretches in each department, including a few days in the foundry.

Gearing up for Gitmo

One of the people at work that I became friends with was an engineer and ex-Naval officer who was in the ready reserve at a Navy training Center in Stamford, Connecticut. In fact, he was the executive officer. One day he mentioned the he'd seen a directive about the shipboard USNR needing engineering people for ready reserve training ships. The Navy had 26 DEs (destroyer escorts) located in major ports on both coasts and in the Great Lakes. He got me more info and I ended up applying. After some very tough testing, both physical and mental, I received a commission as an ensign in the Naval Reserve, effective April 1958. I was then given a billet aboard the USS DeLong (DE 684) that was tied up at the New York State Maritime Academy in Fort Schuyler, New York. We would take the DeLong out one weekend a month and usually go up to New London and do exercises with submarines. We were part of Escort Squadron 8, made up of ships from Chicago, Cleveland, Connecticut, Boston and New York, though we usually operated independently.

When the Cuban Missile crisis and the Berlin Wall problem occurred, President Kennedy saw it necessary to activate many ready reserve units. On October 1, 1961 we were activated, and the DeLong commissioned as a regular USN ship of the destroyer Navy. We were assigned to Newport, Rhode Island as our new home port and soon headed for Guantanamo Bay, Cuba for underway training and then patrol in the Windward Passage.

We spent seven months on patrol—10 days out, 5 days in "rigging" (identifying) all the ships that came through the Passage, with a special interest in Soviet ships. We had counts on things like missiles and other deck cargo that was too large to fit in a ship's hold. I was a conning officer and normally when other ships show up and get too close you take great caution to avoid them. On patrol we would get contacts on our radar and plot collision courses to intercept them.

In September we returned to Fort Schuyler and turned the ship over to a new reserve crew. I had been promoted to lieutenant in January, and that ended my Naval career—five years active, four years ready reserve.

Lt. Skip Marhoffer

In 1961 I was discharged (again), this time with the rank of a full lieutenant. I went back to my old civilian job at Burndy as a sales manager. Eventually I went into business for myself as a manufacturer representative selling products to utilities.

I retired in 1995 and moved into Sun City in 2005 from Northbrook, Illinois. In addition to the Veterans Association, I am a member of the Computer Club, the Community Theatre and keep fit by playing softball and bicycle riding.

VIETNAM WAR ERA

Frank Ambrosino

Frank Ambrosino

Frank was born on July 2, 1950 in Queens, New York. His family moved to Central Islip on Long Island, where he attended St. John of God Catholic School until his family returned to Queens.

In his own words

I went right into the Marine Corps in 1967, before graduating high school. The Vietnam War was going on and I wanted to be part of it. Prior to enlisting in the Corps I tried to enlist in the Army, Navy and Air Force but they wouldn't accept me because I did not complete high school. At the Marine enlistment booth on Main Street in Flushing, New York, next to Shea Stadium, the recruiter assured me that if I passed a series of tests, the Marine Corps would accept me. I passed the tests and was accepted. My mother signed the necessary papers, though my father was a little leery about my joining because he fought in World War II, and knew firsthand about the risks of combat.

Q & A: Parris Island

Arnold: Tell me about Parris Island, in South Carolina. When did you arrive?
Frank: In the winter of 1967.
Arnold: How long did you stay there?
Frank: At that time they needed replacements for the war in Vietnam and I believe it was 10 weeks of training.
Arnold: Did you go through "the crucible" as part of your training?
Frank: "The crucible?" I don't know what that is.
Arnold: I take it that's a no . . . How did you survive boot camp?
Frank: Well, it was easy for me. I was a gymnast so I was pretty well fit. I was on the high school baseball, football and swimming teams. I only weighed about 124 pounds when I joined.
Arnold: You saw your buddies struggling?
Frank: Oh yeah, everybody else was struggling except me and I thought it was a joke.
Arnold: So you didn't have the DIs picking on you as much?
Frank: Well, they picked on me because I was the smallest guy. They used to call me "Mouse." The drill instructors wanted to protect me. I told them, "Don't worry, I'll protect myself." "But you're so damn small," they said. I assured them that I could take care of myself.

Vietnam coming up

Frank was sent to Camp Lejeune in North Carolina, where he had infantry training in a variety of weaponry and then specialized in mortars. (Camp Lejeune is the largest Marine Corps base on the East Coast, where about 40,000 Marines and sailors engage in advanced training.) He then returned home on leave for 21 days and went to Camp Pendleton in California for survival training. He received orders for Vietnam and flew there to Da Nang Air Base where he was sent to Hill 41 and was attached to Delta One Seven, 1st Marine Division.

Their unit was called "Delta's Death Dealers," which had a priority and objective of "getting kills" (killing the enemy). Their icon was the ace of spades, the highest card in the deck, which symbolizes the end of one's life. Their missions were to patrol the area near the Cambodian border in the middle of a valley for rockets, mines and ambushes.

Q & A

Arnold: Where did you sleep?

Frank: Any place you could.

Arnold: Did you have sleeping bags?

Frank: There was no such thing as sleeping bags for us.

Arnold: When you went on patrol, what did you carry?

Frank: We had C-rations, ponchos, dry socks and extra ammo. I was a rifleman and at that time a squad leader. I carried a number of weapons such as an M-16, M-14 and the last year I was there an M-79—a grenade launcher.

Arnold: What was the terrain like?

Frank: We were always in the jungle.

Arnold: Besides encounters with the enemy, what other hardships did you endure?

Frank: When we shook out our ponchos in the morning, spiders and leeches and some snakes would drop out. We slept on the ground against the trees. When it rained, you tried to sleep under a banana tree with large leaves that provided a thick canopy.

On patrol in Vietnam, USMC photo

An unforgettable mission

I had one mission that I will never forget. The Corps gave me a medal for it that I did not want to accept. We were on an escort patrol for the Army Corps of Engineers while they were conducting a mine sweep on a road. Our patrol was in front of a tank as part of the escort. I was a point man (squad leader) for our patrol of 15 Marines. We had guys on each side of the road and the Army guy with the mine sweeper was just a short distance in front of us. As we were walking down the road, there was water on both sides of us. At one o'clock (directional) there was a large tree line across the rice paddies. I turned around and told everyone, "This is the perfect place to get ambushed or pick up mines." I cautioned them to be careful: "Whatever you do, walk in my footsteps and on the hard ground. Don't turn around; don't step off into the soft ground on the shoulders of the road, because it would most likely be a booby trap or mine. The hard ground has already been stepped on so you should know better." I told the guy on the tank, "Keep your gun facing the tree line because if we're going to get hit, we're going to get hit from that area."

We walked down the road about a hundred yards in front of the tank and I passed over the mine, the next guy in back of me passed over the mine and the third followed without incident. The fourth guy in line happened to be a very good friend of mine. He was an orphan, a quiet type and not too bright. I kept him "under my wing" on other patrols. I told him, "Don't look back at the tank. Keep your eyes forward and never stray off the hard ground." Sure enough, he drifted off the path that I was taking and hit the mine. I looked back and all I could see was . . . (At this point in the interview, Frank breaks down in tears and is unable to continue. He mumbles, "You'd think after 43 years . . . I . . . I would . . . Excuse me . . ." and he walks out of the room, returning a minute later, apologizing.)

All I could see was a flight jacket and a head of the person going off about 30 yards into the water. Then I saw him flying into the water, one of his arms gone. I turned around and everyone hit the dirt and then we starting taking incoming fire from the tree line. The tank opened up on the tree line position. I turned around, dropped all my gear and ran through the mine field and jumped into the water to try to find my guy. I only could find his jacket. When I pulled it up I found him and I wanted to reach for his legs but found that they were gone. He was submerged under water; I pulled him up and over my head out of the water. Again I tried to reach for his legs and there were no legs. He had no legs, no arm and his second arm was shredded. I remember his ear was gone. Amazingly, he was still alive!

I managed to get him out of the water and laid him on the shore. I started yelling for somebody to help me. The sergeant that was on the tank jumped off and he grabbed my friend and pulled him off to the side; a corpsman came over and he helped me out. I just looked at the mutilated body of my friend and got sick. I didn't have enough time to say much to him. Another soldier, who was behind my friend, also got hit—shrapnel in his arm and he also lost part of his ear from the mine blast. I picked up my weapon and just started firing into the tree line. I heard the rotors overhead of an evac helicopter land and pick up my wounded friend. I have never seen him again after that day. I don't know if he is dead or alive.

The Marines sent a letter of commendation to my home in New York stating what I did and awarding me the Naval Commendation Medal with the Combat V. I wouldn't accept it because I had told my mother I was working in the warehouse and she didn't know I was doing any kind of fighting. I didn't want to worry her. The sergeant told me he wanted me to attend the promotion ceremony to present me with the medal. I refused to attend. The guys in my tent advised the sergeant to stay away from me. They told him, "You can't talk to him at this point. He doesn't want any medals." They did give me the medal but did not promote me. The Navy sent the letter (see below) to my home to my mother and she was very upset because she was not supposed to know that I was in combat in Vietnam.

A few weeks after my mother received the letter and the medal, I was on patrol in the middle of a firefight when my mother called me on the radio. How she got through on the unit's patrol radio, I have no clue. The radio man handed me the phone and my mother asked me what the medal was all about and what I was doing. "Why did you do this?" she asked. That hurt me, to have her find out that I was in combat because I knew it would worry her. I sucked it up and continued my tour going out on missions.

On March 20, 1969 the Commanding General of the Fleet Marine Force in the Pacific sent the letter below:

The Secretary of the Navy takes pleasure in presenting the NAVY COMMENDATION MEDAL to:

PRIVATE FIRST CLASS FRANK AMBROSINO

UNITED STATES MARINE CORPS

For service as set forth in the following

CITATION

"For heroic achievement while serving as a motor man with company D, First Battalion, Seventh Marines, First Marine Division in connection with operations against the enemy in the Republic of Vietnam. On June 16, 1969, Private First Class Ambrosino's platoon was deployed to provide security for an engineer unit conducting a mine clearing operation on Liberty Road north of An Hoa, when a Marine detonated a large mine and the concussion traumatically amputated three of his major limbs and threw him into a rice paddy. Ignoring the possibility of other mines in the vicinity, Private First Class Ambrosino unhesitatingly ran 100 meters across the hazardous terrain to assist his wounded comrade. Rapidly assessing the situation, he lifted the injured man from the deep water and comforted him until a corpsman arrived. His heroic and timely actions inspired all who observed him and undoubtedly saved the seriously wounded Marine from drowning or succumbing to his wounds. By his courage, bold initiative and steadfast devotion to duty at in the face of grave personal danger, Private First Class Ambrosino upheld the finest tradition of the Marine Corps and of the United States Naval Service."

Private First Class Ambrosino is authorized to wear the Combat "V."

FOR THE SECRETARY OF THE NAVY

H. W. BUSE, JR.
LIETENANT GENERAL, U.S. MARINE CORPS
COMMANDING GENERAL FLEET MARINE FORCE, PACIFIC

Another close call

I was on this mission with my patrol along the Da Nang area in the valley. It was nicknamed the "Arizona territory," and there were nine of us. I had three guys in front of me including the point man. As he was going around the tree bank he walks up on a Viet Cong soldier. The soldier turns around and shoots him in the head. Now we are getting fire from the other side of the bank and all hell breaks loose. Five men in my patrol are hit.

I had the M-79, and called in for ReAct (for another platoon to help us) because we were taking all kinds of incoming hits. They could hear the firefight because we were only 500 yards away from our outpost. I placed a shotgun round into my tube in my weapon and I fired into where my point man was wounded. I killed the Viet Cong soldier. My shotgun round had large ball bearings in it and it sprayed out when fired. When I fired my weapon again, it jammed. I no longer had any weapon except my .45. I took a rifle from one of my men who got hit and fired on the opposite side of the bank. The ReAct squad arrived and corpsman attended to the wounded. An evac helicopter landed and picked up the wounded. Five out of nine in our patrol were hit. I was one of the lucky ones who survived.

My tour in Vietnam was almost two years, into 1969 and including the Tet offensive (a major military campaign conducted between from January into September 1968, by forces of the Viet Cong and the North Vietnamese Army against the forces of South Vietnam, the United States and their allies, hoping to end the war).

Malaria

At the end of my tour I contracted malaria. I was in a MASH unit hospital in Da Nang and I almost died. While on patrol, an evacuation helicopter transported me out. I was on a hill during a mission and became overwhelmed with sickness. I had the shakes, sweating, with high fever, dysentery and severe stomach cramps. They brought me into the hospital and found I was completely dehydrated—weighing about 90 pounds. My temperature was 106 and I was starting to convulse. They covered my body with rubber bathtub mats connected to a machine to "ice me down." They really didn't have ice at the hospital because the temperature outside was over 100 degrees. The machine was connected to a generator to create a "freezing effect." I was laid up for two months. After recovering I was sent back to my unit in Hill 41 and resumed my patrols until my tour ended and was finally sent home in September 1969.

My flight landed in Camp Pendleton, I changed flights and arrived at the Newark, New Jersey airport. I hailed a cab to Manhattan, and then took the subway home to Queens Village, New York. It was great! I walked up to the house, rang the bell and said, "Hi, Ma!" She was surprised but delighted to see me.

After my discharge from the (active duty) Marines became effective that September, I signed up for four years in the inactive reserve.

Civilian life

I was hired by Metromedia, a visual communications company specializing in billboard printing, banners and building wraps, stadium and arena graphics. I worked there as an electrician for seven years, all over the city.

I didn't get married until 1973, when I was 22 years old. My first wife, Beverly Broad, and I lived in Queens, where we raised our three children. We bought a home in Levittown, Long Island in 1980. My main job after Metromedia was as a longshoreman for 14 years for the Atlantic Container Lines and Maersk Lines, a world-class outfit specializing in shipping cargo.

My next job was at BOCES (Board of Cooperative Educational Services) for the Rosemary Kennedy Center in Wantagh, Long Island as a custodian. I helped the Down syndrome and autistic kids, retiring after 12 years there.

My first wife and I were divorced; I was basically a workaholic and stuck on shifts and didn't come home for three or four days at a time. In 1997 I met my present wife, Chris Errante, at a dance at Oz's in Franklin Square, New York. We built a wonderful relationship. Our courtship was adventurous and we both enjoy life to the fullest. I introduced Chris to hiking and camping in the beautiful mountains in upstate New York. In fact, we held our wedding ceremony—on June 17, 2000—standing on a cliff in North Ridge, North Lake, New York, near Hunter Mountain.

Frank and Chris Errante

Sun City

After the wedding we moved into our home in Commack, Long Island and stayed there until we decided to move to Sun City, South Carolina in 2008. We were fortunate to sell our home in Commack and were able to buy a beautiful resale home here in Sun City. Both Chris and I are gainfully employed. I work full-time as a security officer for Sun City and Chris works for the International Junior Golf Academy in Hilton Head.

Final impressions

Let's put it this way—if you were having problems with your life and you wanted to get your head straight, the Marine Corps will set you straight! I found the Corps tough, but very disciplined. They turn young immature kids into mature individuals with responsibility and build good moral character. For me, joining the Marine Corps was one of the best decisions that I ever made. It has changed my life in so many positive ways that trying to list every detail wouldn't be possible. Anything that I look back on in my civilian days as being negative has been improved by my experiences in the Corps.

The Corps has made me different in several ways. I'm much more focused, I have a much stronger desire to be successful and I find hard work rewarding.

Physical fitness has been an additional benefit. Not only am I in pretty good shape, but I saw other young men join the Corps and become transformed into top physical shape.

It's not an easy life, but it's not supposed to be. It is, however, a very rewarding life on a personal level. I left the Corps with many qualities that employers value, such as discipline, dedication, initiative, integrity and a strong desire to win. I'll always remember what my father would say to me: "Common sense is a virtue. It should be your guiding light throughout your life."

Frank as Sun City security guard, 2009

Ray Clifford

Ray Clifford

Ray was born on August 5, 1935 in Stamford, Connecticut. He graduated from Greenwich High School in 1953 and enlisted in the Navy. Ray took boot camp at U. S. Naval Training Station, Bainbridge, Maryland, and was assigned to an amphibious ship out of Norfolk, the USS Fort Mandan (LSD 21), a Casa Grande Class Dock Landing Ship. His job was in supply.

Q & A

Arnold: Where did you sail on the LSD?
Ray: The ship was used to carry troops and supplies. We went to the North Pole and re-supplied the DEW line (Distant Early

Warning), a line of radar stations near the 70th parallel across the North American continent.

Arnold: What other sea duty did you have after leaving the LSD?

Ray: I was assigned to the USS John Paul Jones (DD932), a destroyer.

Arnold: What was your job on board?

Ray: I handled incoming supplies, mostly food and provisions.

Arnold: How long were you on the destroyer?

Ray: Eighteen months. It was a great ship. We went to Gitmo (Guantanamo Bay Naval Base in Cuba). After leaving Gitmo in 1959, we sailed to Scotland, Norway, Denmark and the cities along the Mediterranean. We slept in a compartment with other sailors on 3-tier racks. The food was excellent. On the first ship, the Fort Mandan, we went to the North Pole (in 1954) for six months and saw the same movie 40 times. Boll weevils were in our cereal. All we saw were polar bears and ice. We followed an ice breaker in the North Atlantic with stops at Thule, Greenland and St. John's, Newfoundland.

Arnold: Did you ever get seasick?

Ray: Yes.

Arnold: On which ship?

Ray: Both—the Fort Mandan and the USS John Paul Jones. In the North Atlantic it was rough.

Arnold: You worked outside on deck during the cold and the storms?

Ray: Yes, loading and unloading supplies. On the LSD we had cranes to move the crates of supplies onto the ship. On the destroyer we had to lug the supplies on board. On my next tour of duty I was on the USS Goodrich, a destroyer out of Newport, Rhode Island, which cruised the Mediterranean. Back in the States I was transferred to Mayport Naval Air Station in Jacksonville, Florida. Next stop: Portsmouth, New Hampshire where the Navy offered me what would be a "dream tour of duty"—Italy!

Bella Italia

My father died when I was a year old. My mother had to go to work and we moved into an Italian neighborhood and became friendly with many Italian families. I'm not Italian but I feel I'm more Italian than many native-born Italians, because thanks to the Navy I lived in the country for many years.

I went to Capodichino at the airport in Naples in 1960. When I first signed up with the Navy my commitment was for four years. Then I reenlisted for another four. After several re-enlistments my service with the Navy totaled 26 years. At the Naval Overseas Air Cargo Terminal in Capodichino, I loaded all the planes with PMCs (Packs Mail Cargo). Periodically I sailed out with the 6th Fleet for sea duty. I slept on the base until I married my wife, Adriana Di Concetto, in 1961. She was a local girl whom I met in the PX and was chaperoned for nine months—more on that later.

We had to fly out when a ship pulled in. My job was to check the incoming cargo that arrived at the airport. There were times when I flew to Wheelus Air Force Base in Libya for several weeks, from midnight until 5 in the morning because it was too hot during the day. I also went to Tangiers, Casablanca, Turkey, Cyprus and many Greek islands.

Then I was contacted by Washington. The Navy was looking for an experienced cargo specialist to coordinate cargo for the Commander Service Port 6th Fleet. My name came up. I went to Naples for an interview and they selected me. I got transferred from Gaega to Naples aboard the Cascade, which is a destroyer tender. The staff on the ship was the Navy elite. My job was to brief the personnel of the 6th Fleet when they came from sea. When new ships came in I had to go to the ward room of the carrier with the commander and brief staff officers about the port cities along the Mediterranean—where to get beans, bullets, gas and anything else. I had that job for two years.

Managing Navy clubs

I had orders to go to NATO Headquarters in Naples but the Navy really didn't need me there. I was placed on TDY (temporary duty) at the base chief petty officer's club. An E-6 sailor managed the club and the master chiefs felt that they needed a chief to manage the club so they recommended me for the position. They sent me to the Navy's Club, Messes and Slot Machines School at Naval Air Station Patuxent River, Maryland. I returned to Naples and worked another three years in the club managing the slot machines, the restaurants and the floor shows. I was the host and master of ceremonies for the shows and manager at the club.

I worked the room and schmoozed with the guests. I did such an excellent job they sent me to Naval Air Station Sigonella, Sicily ("The Hub of the Med"), a U.S. Navy installation at a NATO base. I was assigned to the club as the senior person on "sea duty" and ran the chief's club, with extra pay for the long hours I put in, but it was prime duty. I never wore a uniform. As a host I dressed immaculately in civilian attire. My tour was for 18 months and the captain approached me and said, "I need you to take over the officer's club and the package store." My job duties expanded to include the officer's club, the package store, the chief's club and the slot machines.

At a crossroad

In 1969 I had a choice to return to the States for shore duty. I should have taken it, but didn't. They offered to extend my service for four more years and return to Naples to take the same club and extend my tour to 30 years. When you add up the amount of money you make and your age, I had to decide if this would be worth it at this point of my life. My three girls (two were born in Italy and one in upstate New York) would ask me, "Poppa, are we American or are we Italians? All we go to are American schools all these years." At that time, I decided to retire and return home. The clubs wanted me, but I decided not to take their offer. I told my wife, "I'm getting out!" You know what made me bitter? A stipulation that essentially said: "*Once you retire from the military overseas, your rights cease. You have no benefits to utilize the base services in Italy. You cannot use the commissary or purchase items in the PX.*" I was disappointed. We even had to pay for schooling. I had to put my young daughter in an Italian school and drive her there every day. Now she said to me, "Poppa, why did you take me out of American school?" I was filled with emotion and very happy to return to the States with my family.

It was a turning point in my career. I was offered jobs at three officers or chiefs clubs—in Jacksonville, Memphis and New London, Connecticut. I interviewed at the submarine base in New London and took the chief's club job there—while our first daughter started school in the third grade. I began a new job in the auto industry. We lived in Connecticut for 20 years.

Meeting Adriana

I first saw my wife-to-be when she came on base with her best friend, who was married to my friend Tony Mazzaferro, an Italian-American sailor. I was working on that Sunday in Capodichino and they went for ice cream in the PX, where I was, too, on my break. I was struck by how attractive she looked. The next day I asked Tony to introduce me to the lovely lady, Adriana Di Concetta. He hesitated, and suggested that it might not work out. He reminded me that Americans were not too well liked in Italy because they had a reputation for drinking and bad behavior. I assured him that my intentions were honorable. He finally agreed to introduce me, and on our first date I waited for her on a Sunday outside the main gate, with flowers in hand, for three hours. When she finally arrived she apologized for being late. We talked for hours and "hit it off" on our first date. A courtship ensued and we dated for several months. Then, with my buddy Tony scheduled to return to the States, we were both invited to dinner at Adriana's home.

Her home was huge. At dinner we were seated at a large round table where 25-30 relatives were looking me over pretty good. My intentions were to ask Adrianna's father permission to marry his daughter. He only spoke Italian and I asked Tony, who was fluent in Italian, to act as my interpreter. After dinner I went into another room with the father and Tony and told Tony, "Tell Mr. Di Concetto that his daughter is very beautiful, very lovely. I don't love her, but we'll see what happens in a couple of months more." The next thing I know the father says, "Bravo!"

I got a ring and about a week later we had another big party with her family with a band and I looked at her and she was crying from happiness. I really started falling in love with her right then and there. I was chaperoned for nine months, and never kissed her. I didn't care, I was madly in love with her. I submitted the marriage papers, saw the priest and was converted from Protestant to Catholic. I never went to church anyway. We finally got married on August 27, 1961.

Wedding of Ray and Adriana, August 27, 1961

Years later, while stationed on recruiting duty in Albany New York, I reconnected with Tony, who was in Massachusetts. He said, "You know what I told Mr. Di Concetto the night you asked me to interpret? I told him that you loved her. You were going to submit the paperwork and you were going to get married." I said, "What? Why didn't you tell him what I asked you to say to him?" "He would have killed you!" Tony said. "Could you imagine if I told him 'Ray doesn't love her, but he wants to hang out with her?'"

We were in Capodichino Napoli Italia Airport for four years. We lived in our own home and I reported to work at the airport every day. Our first baby was born in Capodichino. In 1964 the Navy transferred me to Albany, where I was assigned to recruiting duty for three years. My rank then was E-6 and I made chief while on recruiting duty. I enjoyed my tour in Albany. I was home every night. Adriana had a good job as head seamstress in the alterations department at Macy's. We were blessed with another baby and life was good. In 1967 I got orders to go to Pearl Harbor and report on board the USS Walker, a destroyer. I thought it was the worst ship I was on in my life. It was a World War II rust bucket.

Vietnam—and Italy again

I volunteered for Vietnam to get away from the ship, and was attached to the Naval Support Activity at Da Nang Air Base. My job was to take care of the killed in action, missing in action and personal effects of the deceased. I worked in downtown Da Nang with three other chiefs and 140 Vietnamese. We also did customs inspections for the troops. They were allowed to ship 2,000 pounds of company baggage (mainly gifts and personal items). I worked with 10 customs inspectors (American sailors). Our job was to track items that soldiers and seamen would try to smuggle, such as weapons, narcotics and other illegal items.

After my Vietnam tour ended in 1969, I received orders to report to Gaeta, in central Italy, to the 6th Fleet flagship, the USS Little Rock, a heavy cruiser. Commanding officer of the 6th Fleet was Adm. Elmo Zumwalt, who rode on board our ship. After a year we came back to the States, but when I heard about one sailor who didn't want to transfer to Italy, I wrote him a letter and we swapped assignments. I stayed on his ship for three years. Italy was the best choice of duty I ever had. Adriana lived in Naples, where she had bought a home. When I was in Vietnam, I sent her every dollar I made and reenlisted in Vietnam tax-free.

We had wonderful cruises in the Navy during my tour in Italy. I remember we would sail to Spain, Greece and Italy. Adriana would fly in to meet me in those beautiful cities along the Mediterranean.

Retirement

Retirement ceremony, Sigonella, Italy

I retired from the Navy on October 31, 1979 and our family returned to Connecticut, where Adriana owned a successful bridal shop and I managed the chief's club as a civilian employee at the New London Submarine Base. My title was a GS-12 club manager. I eventually left the job at the base and entered a car dealership position and traveled throughout the state.

I was putting in a lot of hours in and enjoying a nice income from my military pension and my civilian pay—enough to support a large home on the water with our own dock and paying college tuition for our kids. But the long hours and stress of two jobs (plus helping Adriana in the bridal shop) was beginning to take its toll on me. Working 12 hours a day, often seven days a week was wearing me down. It was time for me to make a change in life style. We sold our home and moved into an apartment and I started to slow my pace. Believe it or not, I got a job driving a school bus to get away from the turmoil. It was a welcome change of pace, and a change of scenery.

Sun City

I remember in 1960 I took a train ride with a Southern friend down to the Lowcountry of South Carolina and we went fishing in Ridgeland. It was mostly dirt roads and barren, but I remember the food, the friendly people and the beautiful whispering pines that provided a shady canopy for the quaint roads. I just loved it!

Flash forward to 2001. A friend invited us to visit them here in the Lowcountry. During our visit we had an opportunity to explore the area and we liked what we saw. My lifestyle used to be, "Life in the fast lane!" Adrianna doesn't like me to say that. I love it here. I found it to be such a welcome change from my previous fast-paced life. We returned to visit Sun City and toured the model homes. Adrianna grabbed me by the arm, and she whispered, in Italian, "This is paradise!! ("Este es paradise!!") I want to talk it over with the children." "No way," I said. "Let's just do it! We will give Sun City a deposit and return to Connecticut." We told our daughters, "We're leaving before you!"

A final salute to the Navy

I had absolutely no regrets about serving in the Navy. It was a great experience and a fabulous opportunity to truly see the great cities and ports of the world. You name it! I saw it! Actually I only spent three years in the States.

Notwithstanding the disappointment of the stipulation of excluding me from the base stores upon retiring, there were so many wonderful and positive occasions where the Navy "took care" of its men and women. When I was aboard the Springfield, we were in Malta. I got sick and the ship was scheduled to leave. The doctor said it was appendicitis. He gave me my records, put me in a taxi and sent a corpsman to accompany me. The taxi pulls up at the Royal Naval Hospital and they're waiting for me—doctors and nurses. They operated just in time. This is just one of many stories that exemplify the Navy going above and beyond for me.

Yes, civilian life is good, but I do miss the rapport and camaraderie of the Navy!!

Family portrait of Ray, Adriana and the children

Ken Copley

Ken Copley

Ken was born January 19, 1942 in Weston, West Virginia. His family moved to Portsmouth, Virginia when he was 13. Ken graduated from St. Paul's High School in 1960 and went to St. Bernard's College in Cullman, Alabama for four years, to become a Catholic priest. After graduation he studied for 18 months at Mt. Savior Monastery in Elmira, New York and then at Old Dominion University in Virginia, where he was told, as the Vietnam War neared, that if he didn't volunteer he would be drafted into the Army.

Ken volunteered for the U.S. Army in March 1967. He went through basic training at Fort Dix, New Jersey and then on to OCS (Officer Candidate School) at Fort Belvoir, Virginia. Commissioned a 2nd lieutenant in May 1968, Ken went to flight school in Fort Walters, Texas and from there to

Fort Rucker, Alabama for Chinook CH-47 (helicopter) training. Next stop: Fort Eustis in Newport News, Virginia for aircraft maintenance training, then off to Vietnam for a year tour of duty.

In his own words

In Vietnam my job was as an Army helicopter maintenance test pilot and combat missions pilot in a Chinook (CH-47) line unit assigned to Bravo Company, 101st Aviation Battalion Airborne Division.

Chinook helicopter, courtesy of Boeing Aircraft Corp

On promotion to captain, I was made the Brigade Aviation Maintenance Officer and shortly thereafter asked to assume the position of 101st Division Aviation Maintenance Officer (a junior captain in a major's position), where I had to brief Division Commander Gen. Henessey, on the daily maintenance activities of the division's aircraft. I was also flying periodically (usually an OH-6 helicopter by myself or taking a staff officer with me), mostly to check out a unit's aircraft and posture—while doing my best to not get shot at and get back in time to brief the general.

Close calls

Memories creep back of a series of close calls and highly challenging incidents during my yearlong tour in Vietnam.

I remember the night I could hear the gravel bounce off the tin roof of our hut as incoming shells were exploding "too close for comfort." After being assigned to B Company I actually heard the first incoming missile before it hit near my hootch (hut) as I was almost into the bunker.

I remember the night I and two other company maintenance officers were playing cards when the enemy hit us with rockets and our big test pilot ran and got wedged in the doorway with his chair. I was able to rescue him by snatching his chair out of the way so he could pop out the door and make it safely to the bunker. This event was a later cause for laughter.

I remember the closest time I came to being shot—by an unannounced South Vietnamese artillery barrage that exploded right in front of our windscreen on our Chinook at 2,000 feet.

I still have flashbacks of having to go from Camp Eagle to Phu Bie as unit Graves Registration Officer arranging for some deceased unit members' proper identification and follow-through paperwork.

I remember flying and listening to a young trooper being yelled at to stop before he walked into a helicopter rotor blade—to no avail. He was walking face down and couldn't hear our warning screams because of the loud sound of the rotor blades. He was killed immediately.

I remember having to stay away from my landing pad because the unit I needed to visit was catching incoming fire and after landing, learning that an incoming round had literally made a trooper disappear (blown away) beside the mess hall where I was supposed to be.

I remember bringing my large Chinook to a hover at a fire base just as all six 155's (howitzers) fired and lifting my aircraft more than 10 feet to escape unharmed.

I remember the hard time I had keeping my load of lumber stable, hanging from the hook beneath the belly of the Chinook flying along at 50 to 60 knots way up to a high fire base.

And I remember how I struggled to keep a .50 caliber machine gun dangling from the hook stabilized enough to allow the South Vietnamese to position it on a cliff overlooking the DMZ.

Back to the States

When my tour was over I reported to Fort Eustis, Virginia and stayed there until 1975. I kept my options open about making the Army a career. As I progressed I kept getting good assignments and enjoyed what I was doing. At about my 18th year, I decided to make this a career. At the 20-year level, the Army dangled a little "carrot" at me and offered me an assignment in Germany. My wife happened to love the Army. She didn't want me to get out.

I met my wife, Brenda Gohagan, at Fort Stewart/Hunter Army Air Field in Georgia in 1977 at the Officer's Club. We were wed in 1978; this was the second marriage for both of us. Shortly after the wedding I went directly to Korea for a tour. My job was in aviation maintenance, which was my primary job in the Army for 25 years. I arranged to have Brenda and her daughter, Christie, come to Korea and join me.

Ken, Brenda and Christy, Korea, 1979

I returned to Hunter Army Air Field and spent all my time there with the exception of two tours in Korea ('78-'79 and '83-'84). My final tour of duty was at Manheim, Germany for three years. I (and Brenda) really enjoyed it. We lived in Studernheim, a small German village, and were the only Americans there. Brenda and my little daughter, Rebecca, attended school in the town. We wanted her to go to a German school, but she had to learn the language first—which she did. It was a wonderful tour of duty.

I was involved in three rear-end collisions in Germany. So that along with my having flown helicopters and all that bouncing in helicopters I developed severe back problems. When I returned to the States I underwent surgery in Fort Gordon, Georgia where the surgeons replaced one vertebrate. This was the end of my flying career and I decided to leave the Army. I was discharged in October 1991 at Hunter with the rank of captain.

Ken was awarded the following decorations, medals and campaign ribbons:

* National Defense Service Medal
* Good Conduct Medal
* Vietnam Service Medal
* Army Commendation Medal
* Bronze Star Medal
* Civil Actions Medal
* Overseas Bar (two)
* Vietnam Cross of Gallantry with Palm Vietnam Campaign Medal
* Army Aviator Badge

Back to civilian life

I received a master's degree in counseling at Old Dominion University and found a job as a counselor in Effingham County, Georgia, where we bought a home. I spent my first five years as a high school guidance counselor and my last 11 years as a middle school counselor. I retired in September 2007. Brenda and I moved to Sun City in May 2007.

Final thoughts

My thoughts about military service center on my tour in Vietnam. People ask me, "Were you worried or scared about going into a war environment?" I was not scared or fearful because I have a strong faith in God and I felt that He was going to take care of me. The reason I went to Vietnam was because it was my job; it was for my country and I felt that we were fighting communism on their turf. I wanted to do that to protect our territory.

It was back to what my parents always told me—"God, country and family." It reinforced and defined my priorities of life: God—I was instilled in a strong belief in the seminary and the monastery; Country—serving my country in the military; and taking care of my family. My Catholic background served me well.

Brenda and Ken in Sun City, 2009

Alvin J. Doublet

Al Doublet

Alvin Doublet was born on September 29, 1928 in Pittsburgh, Pennsylvania, one of five children. His father passed away when he was 10 and his mother joined forces with her mother, two sisters and two brothers for a household of 11 people. Al graduated from St. Basil's High School in 1947. "The good nuns," he says, "knew how to rap you in the fingers when you were bad."

In his own words

I got off the streets of Pittsburgh in 1948 and joined the Corps that September; it was one of the best blessings I ever had. The Corps instilled pride, discipline and character in me. I would advise any young person who is deprived of good spiritual or parental guidance that they could certainly find it in the Marine Corps.

I went to boot camp in Parris Island, South Carolina. At that time there were 75,000 active duty Marines. I entered with the idea of having an aviation option specializing in aircraft mechanics. My older brother was an aircraft mechanic at Pearl Harbor during World War II. But the Corps had other ideas for me. They sent me to Cherry Point, North Carolina for the better part of a year waiting for an opening to enter a school—which never happened. The Corps was turbulent in moving me around and I ended up at the Naval Gun Factory in Washington, D.C., where I remained until the Korean War started.

We had about 250 marines at the Gun Factory. It included a detachment that provided security on Connecticut Avenue, where the Navy had vital communications sites and at the Vice President's residence. We went from 250 Marines down to 65 because they became a core unit that went out to the West Coast to form the 1st Marine Brigade. I stayed in Washington for another three months and returned to Parris Island in August 1950, to become a drill instructor.

Eventually I was promoted to corporal and assigned a platoon with another corporal. We trained a great bunch of recruits and were proud to become an honor platoon. After my Parris Island stint I became a drill instructor for college students who came to Parris Island from Quantico, Virginia because it was overcrowded. I received a nomination for a temporary commission and reported to Houston, Texas in 1952 to help rebuild a reserve organization.

Moving on

Al married Mary Alice Frisch, who was a year ahead of him in high school, the day after Christmas in 1949 in Pittsburgh. Their first child was born in Texas in 1951.

Al's commission was approved and he was sent back to Quantico to go through the 23rd special basic training class. He graduated as a 2nd lieutenant in October 1953 and received orders to ship out to Korea. By the time he arrived, the war was over (July 27, 1953). His next assignment sent him to Okinawa, where he was away from his family for 18 months. He became company commander in the 3rd Marines of the 2nd Battalion The Corps redeployed Al back to Korea for a second tour of duty and he became the company commander of "*Baker's Bad-Ass Bastards*" in the 1st Battalion. When Al was ordered home his unit was the last battalion out of Korea in 1955.

Al in Korea, 1954

His unit arrived in Camp Pendleton, California in April. Next assignment: at the Naval Ammunition Depot in Fallbrook, California, near Camp Pendleton. The unit consisted of two officers and some 20 marines. Their objective was to patrol and secure the munitions stockpile. This was to be a three-year tour, with Al as an executive officer. During that stint, he began his off-duty education program with extension courses at the University of Maryland.

While spending three years at the Basic School at Quantico as an instructor, Al continued to pursue his education at the Pentagon, enrolling in evening courses at the Pentagon. After his tour of duty at Quantico, Basic School

CO Lou Wilson, (later Marine Corps commandant) helped Al receive an assignment at Headquarters Marine Corps for six months so that he could go to school in the afternoon—his new assignment was as a funeral director for Headquarters Marine Corps. His job involved presenting the flag to next of kin at Arlington National Cemetery.

In his own words

I had my introduction to Vietnam in what they called the OJT program—on the job training. The Corps sent company commanders to Vietnam and we were attached to Vietnamese Marine Battalions. That was my first two months in Vietnam. I came back to lead a company and when I came back to the United States we became 2nd Battalion, 9th Marines. I had 18 months back in the States and our "two seven" was fortunate to have a super leader by the name of Lt. Col. Leon Utter, my battalion commander. I was proud to serve as his operations officer. We went back to Vietnam for a year as a part of the Marine brigade commanded by Oscar Petross; the present Parade Deck at Parris Island is named for him. We had about 12 significant operations and I am proud to say I earned my Silver Star and a couple of Bronze Stars during my tour in Vietnam.

Bronze Star presentation with family

After my second tour in Vietnam I returned to the States, did a three-year tour in Quantico under another great leader, Col. Walter Gall, and went back to Vietnam for a third time in 1969 as operations officer for MACV (Military Assistance Command Vietnam) and remained there until 1970.

In those days living quarters for dependents weren't available. When I was overseas, Mary Alice lived in Quantico. During my final tour in Vietnam, I bought a house in Oceanside, California where I lived for only eight months while my family lived there for four years. Mary Alice was a wonderful mother for our three children; I was away for long periods of separation, including five Christmases away from my family.

Al Doublet at home in Sun City, 2009

Back to civilian life

After retiring in 1982, we bought a home in North Carolina. Our son was a student at Georgia Tech and our younger daughter was completing her school as a dental hygienist. My older daughter, Debbie, had completed her program as a physician's assistant and now works with her orthopedic surgeon husband in Pine Bluff, Arkansas. They returned to North Carolina and lived with us for a while.

I received a call from my Marine buddy, Gen. George Bartlett, who worked for the Marine Corps Association. I accepted his offer to join him at Association headquarters at Quantico as to be his deputy. My job was to travel around Marine Corps bases to tell Marines about our Association's services, benefits and programs and to encourage them to submit articles for our publications—*Marine Corps Gazette* and *Leatherneck*. I worked there for about two years. Unfortunately I had a heart attack—first of two—which limited my activities.

I did receive a Master's Degree in education from American University before I got out of the Corps, which enabled me to teach at a junior college in Beaufort, North Carolina. I also obtained a real estate broker's license and sold real estate for a very short time. I retired again for the last time in 1989.

Reflections

I spent 34 years in the Marine Corps—I enlisted in 1948 and got out in 1982, retiring as a colonel in Yokosuka, Japan. I have some interesting memories about my years as a DI (drill instructor) at Parris Island, and a few letters from parents of kids that I "have taken through" boot camp. One letter said, "We don't recognize our son. He is so disciplined now." Others express gratitude to the Corps for what happened to their son. It's the Corps! I just can't say enough about how proud I was to be a Marine. The Corps and its leaders gave me the drive, motivation and confidence to succeed in life. They became my surrogate father.

You know it's a shame we don't have the draft. I can understand the ramifications but today there are so many kids living in single parent homes.

Sun City

We lived for 10 years in Washington, North Carolina. We made several trips down to the Lowcountry in South Carolina. On a trip in 1999, we saw Sun City, bought a home and moved in 2002. I enjoy my retirement life here in Sun City and stay active volunteering at the Department of Social Services and at the local Catholic school.

Dr. Peter Frank

Peter Frank

Peter was born on March 24, 1944 in Vineland, New Jersey. His dad was in the military and the family moved around quite a bit before the father was discharged, pursuing a career as an engineer for major corporations as well as NASA and Aberdeen Proving Grounds. Peter's mother was a teacher, and lives in Pennsylvania.

After graduating from high school in Yardley, Pennsylvania in 1960, Peter worked in a camp for retarded children in upstate New York and then enrolled in Temple University that September. He received a BS degree in psychology, worked as a substitute teacher in Philadelphia public schools during the day and drove a taxi at night. In 1964 he enrolled in the Chicago

College of Osteopathic Medicine and interned at Lakeview Hospital in Milwaukee.

Peter married when he started med school, but got divorced at school's end. His present wife, Patty O'Brien, was the chief nurse at Lakeview Hospital; later she joined Peter in Vietnam when he was serving as a medical doctor there and she found work, too.

After medical school Peter received his draft notice while on his rotating internship in Lakeview. It basically said, "After you are done, Peter, you are joining us in Vietnam." He was assigned to the U.S. Army Medical Corps, his second paying job as a doctor, and was commissioned a captain. This rank was given to doctors as credit while in medical school.

In his own words

It was kind of funny—I was 25 years old and was one punk captain. I had guys twice my age saluting me. It was part of what the Army did for me. We had no basic training; instead, all Medical Corps personnel, including medics, do six weeks at Fort Sam Houston, San Antonio, Texas. We stayed off base in a motel. Most of our time was spent in classroom courses and some tropical medicine—malaria and other indigenous diseases that one might find in the jungles of Vietnam—which we really didn't have in medical school.

Within a few days after our stay at Sam Houston, I was off to Oakland, California. I got on the plane, landed in Long Binh and began what I thought would be a 13-month tour in Vietnam. At the end of my tour I opted to extend my stay there for another six months.

Q & A

Arnold: Tell me about your medical duties.
Peter: I was assigned to the 3rd Field Hospital in Saigon. My MOS (military occupation specialty) was 3100, which is a general medical officer.

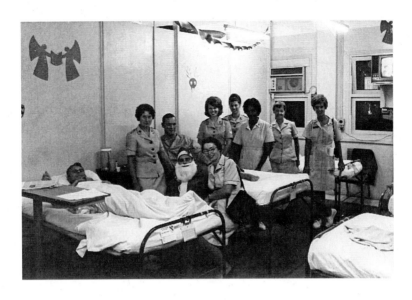

3ʳᵈ Field Hospital, Saigon, Christmas 1968

Arnold: When was this?

Peter: October 1969. It was after the high point of the March 1968 Tet offensive.

Arnold: In Saigon, was the city stable or dangerous?

Peter: Relatively safe during the day. Occasionally there would be bombings at night. I was in no hand-to-hand combat.

Arnold: What kind of a facility was your hospital?

Peter: The 3ʳᵈ Field Hospital was a beautiful full-service hospital facility. It was a school or hotel before the war. We had air-conditioning, kidney dialysis and a full array of medical equipment and services. We mainly stabilized serious cases to be put on planes to the Philippines or Tokyo. My initial assignment was with the 673ʳᵈ Medical Detachment at Camp Davies, which was on the Saigon River, on the outskirts of Saigon. I was a general practice physician, sort of like what I am now. I was known as the world expert in gonorrhea, a common sexually transmitted infection.

Arnold: Did you ever perform surgery?

Peter: No.

Arnold: Your patients were all military? Any civilians?

Peter: All military patients. I also worked part-time at Tan Son Nhut
            Air Base as a GP. When Patty came over it sort of irritated the
            powers that be and they transferred me to DiAn, Vietnam, home
            of the 1st Cavalry, where I practiced general medicine.
Arnold: Peter, any unusual medical cases that come to mind?
Peter: The most heartbreaking was when I had to pronounce a guy
            dead. He was taking some Momasans (housekeepers, civilian
            employees) home and flipped his Jeep and was killed instantly.
            And I thought, "How tragic is this?" He survives all the rest of
            Vietnam but through his own fault, basically showing off, he
            killed himself.

Patty

Patty's influence on Peter's career was significant in that she worked for
the Salvation Army, contracted by USAID (U.S. Aid to International
Development). Many of her cases involved children with arms or legs blown
off. She made many attempts to have these poor kids treated at Army medical
facilities and Peter tried to help her with this task. She successfully brought
many children under the care of the U.S. military doctors and hospitals.
Those cases were memorable for her.

In her own words

We had clinics in the refugee camps around Peter's base. When we had
unusual cases we appealed to the Army and the American physicians to
treat them. We would go to the Army medical facility nearby and request
their help. I had a Vietnamese counterpart. The whole set-up in Vietnam
was that I was hired as a medical social worker. I was an RN and doubled
as a nurse helping out in the clinics. In cases that were difficult, we would
bring the patients to Army physicians. Any time the Army accepted these
critical patients it provided a grand opportunity for the doctors and staff
to nurture, care and treat these innocent Vietnamese citizens caught up in
the ravages of war. Peter said, "The whole mission in Vietnam was to win
the hearts and minds of the Vietnamese people. You saved someone's life,
or fixed a cleft palate, they were your friends." He helped me with that
because he would tell me who to go to and get me an entree to key people
in the Army Medical system.

Collage of Vietnamese images created by Peter Frank

In his own words

The standard tour of duty was 13 months. But if you extended six months you got a 30-day leave any place in the world as an additional R & R. You could get a reassignment. So by then I was all the way up in the base camp of the 101st Airborne Division. I was eager to leave and parlayed the 30-day leave into an "around the world" trip. It was a fabulous experience.

In mid-1970 I flew back to Oakland. I still had two years of commitment to military service. I became the chief medical officer at the Induction Center in Philadelphia on North Broad Street. I was 26 years old, had an apartment in downtown Philadelphia and bicycled to work every day. Our staff—me and five or six other doctors—did about 400 medical physicals a day. Obviously this was not a very comprehensive physical exam. *"If the inductees could walk in and hold a pen, they're in!"*

A love of racing

I started motorcycle racing before I left for Vietnam, and raced motorcycles over there. When I was working at the Induction Center in Philadelphia I was racing bikes one weekend and had a real bad crash in Danville, Virginia, fracturing my spine. I remained in U.S. Kenner Army Hospital, in Petersburg for over a month. I was almost paralyzed but thankfully recovered and was discharged from the Army in October 1971.

I started a medical practice in downtown Philadelphia in the ghetto in a Quaker neighborhood medical center. I worked there until 1979.

Building a foundation together

When I was an intern, I was divorced and dating and had the good fortune to meet Patty. When I received news that I was bound for Vietnam, I bid Patty goodbye and thought we would not see each other again. While in Vietnam, my thoughts returned to memories of Patty and I said to myself, "Boy, I miss that girl!" I bought her an "around-the-world" plane ticket on a commercial airliner and mailed her the ticket without really telling her. I called her up—Patty chimes in: "A day before I got it!"—and I told her, "You are going to get this 'around-the-world' ticket. I'd really like you to visit me. Stay as long as you want and 'no strings attached!'"

When she arrived she was able to rent an ideal apartment. (Patty adds, "All the bureaucrats had an apartment; I had a driver, a maid, a cook, a furnished apartment.") Patty remained in Vietnam for 13 months and we went to Hong Kong together, we went to Thailand together, we went everywhere together. Patty returned to the States and moved in with me in Philadelphia—I was still terrified of marriage.

Patty and Peter in Vietnam, 1969

We eventually got into the medical and motorcycling-sanctioning body business together. We wed in 1974 and bought a home on the same street where we once shared an apartment together—Addison Street. We were blessed with the birth of a wonderful son and have lived happily ever after.

On to the Lowcountry

Said Peter: "The move down here in South Carolina was mainly motivated by the understanding of racing that people have here. In Philadelphia, people thought I was a little weird. Here I found that racing was appreciated. Furthermore, I knew that I wasn't going to be a motorcycle racer forever because I was running out of bones to break. I gravitated toward car racing and chose Hardeeville because the mayor of Hardeeville, Thorton Butler, was himself a car racer—he's still alive and well." Peter became very active as a car racer while practicing medicine full-time.

Both Peter and Patty love living here. They find the weather ideal, with beautiful lakes, beaches and waterways, and love their home on the May River. To them, America is a great country—in spite of all its problems.

Impressions of military service

It was an informative part of my life. As a first-generation American, I never really understood how the government and the Army functioned. I studied medicine, liberal arts, but to be in Vietnam in the military and to see how these agencies of government came together was fascinating. And coming back home to the States it gave me a better understanding of how the government works. I developed a measure of maturity in my tour of duty—big time—by meeting a diverse cross-section of people and by having the privilege of serving in the military, especially coming from parents who were both born in Germany. When you get shot at a few times it sort of changes your value of life. The military was one of the greatest experiences of my life!

The first American-born Frank

My parents escaped being sent to a concentration camp by "the skin of their teeth." Some of my relatives still have numbers tattooed on their arms, but survived. But many did not get out of the camps alive; I am the first American-born Frank. We are distant relatives of the Anne Frank family.

Anne Frank was a Jewish girl who was born in the city of Frankfurt-am-Main in Weimar Germany, and who lived most of her life in or near Amsterdam, in the Netherlands. She gained international renown posthumously following the publication of her diary, which documents her family's experiences hiding during the German occupation of the Netherlands in World War II.

Anne Frank, courtesy of the American Jewish Congress

My parents were both Jewish and my mother lived through Kristallnacht and was in her father's business when it was trashed. My father's father was a physician and I realized that that part of serving in the Army was very dear to me. I'm grateful to have had the opportunity to do my part for this wonderful country. I got the privilege of growing up here and for that I will always be thankful. By the hand of fate, I could have been over in Germany during that era.

Kristallnacht, literally "crystal night" or the night of broken glass or night of shattered crystal, was a pogrom in Nazi Germany on November 9-10, 1938. Jewish-owned stores were smashed and on one night, 91 Jews were murdered while 25,000 to 30,000 were arrested and deported to concentration camps.

Dr. Frank, a physician in Bluffton, South Carolina

Bob Goldberg

Bob Goldberg

Bob was born on July 17, 1937 in Pittston, Pennsylvania. His family moved to New York City when Bob was three years old. After he graduated from the High School of Music and Art in New York (where he was a member of the Civil Air Patrol), Bob, with his brother Hal, enrolled in the Academy of Aeronautics at LaGuardia Airport and graduated in 1957 with a mechanic's license (aircraft and power plant specialist). Bob, who always wanted to fly, went to work for Sikorsky Aircraft in Bridgeport, Connecticut.

In his own words

At the Academy I took the test for pilot training, which I passed, but my mother wouldn't allow me to join the Navy until I was 21. She was deathly afraid of flying. When I reached 21, I took an aptitude test for pilot training and enlisted in the U.S. Navy at Floyd Bennett Field Naval Air Station in Brooklyn, New York. I was sworn in after a two-day physical and entered the NAVCAD (Naval Cadet) program for pilot training.

Boot camp was at NAS (Naval Air Station) Pensacola. The estimated time to finish the pilot school was 18 months. The first part was called Preflight and was similar to what was portrayed in the movie, "An Officer and a Gentleman." From there, I graduated to primary flight training at Saufley Field, about 10 miles north of NAS Pensacola. We learned how to fly in a T-34 trainer.

T-34 trainer, courtesy of Beechcraft Corp.

I was at the wrong place at the wrong time. The government did not need all the pilots they had planned to commission and since I was having difficulty making carrier approaches, in May 1959 I was dropped from the program. I finished boot camp, was designated an aviation machinist mate and my career path was changed to an aircraft mechanic. I was sent to Norfolk, Virginia and assigned sea duty aboard the USS Lake Champlain (CVS-39). The ship was designated as an ASW (Anti-Submarine Warfare) aircraft carrier. She was part of an ASW task force consisting of one aircraft carrier, six destroyers and a hunter-killer sub which we never saw.

USS Lake Champlain

Sea duty on "The Champ"

Because of my mechanical background and administrative abilities I was put in charge of all the aircraft maintenance tools aboard the ship. An aircraft carrier is considered a floating air base. When squadrons came aboard with their aircraft, we were supposed to provide all the large tools for the maintenance personnel to repair and maintain the aircraft, including changing the engines. After the mechanics used the tools they returned them to the maintenance shop. Unfortunately, the maintenance shop personnel stored the tools arbitrarily—anywhere they could (i.e. hanging large tools on rafters above the hangar deck). It was sheer clutter, almost like a teenager's room. So the ship had to reorder the same tools again. This caused some of the maintenance jobs to be delayed or not done. Because of this the squadrons would bring their own heavy tools with them when they were deployed. The aircraft mechanics were assigned carriers on a temporary basis and took their own tools when they left.

On the hangar deck there were tools for jet aircraft but the carrier didn't have jets onboard anymore. During the Korean War the carrier was designated as an attack carrier and carried jet planes. After Korea, the older carriers could not accommodate the newer, complex, high tech-jets. I planned and implemented a system of storage and indexing the tools. As a result, the squadrons were more confident in the ship's ability to supply them with the correct tools when needed. Aircraft mechanics stopped bringing their own tools. This was a big savings of time and money for everyone concerned.

Returning from a Mediterranean cruise after 14 months on the Champlain, we entered New York Harbor. That is a sight to see and every sailor that I spoke with had the same feeling of pride on seeing the Statue of Liberty. To save the government money, I was discharged from the ship in New York Harbor, at the foot of 35th Street—the same place where the retired carrier Intrepid is berthed today as the Intrepid Sea-Air-Space Museum, located at North River Pier 86 at 46th Street on the west side of Manhattan. Also showcased are the submarine USS Growler and a Lockheed A-12 supersonic reconnaissance plane (often mistaken for the later SR-71 Blackbird).

With an obligation of four years reserve time, I transferred to the Navy Reserves at Floyd Bennett Field in Brooklyn, attached to VP 833 (V stands for "heavier than air," P for Patrol), a squadron that did anti-submarine warfare patrols. After a reorganization of the Navy reserve system, VP 833 was re-designated and merged into a new squadron, VP 66. We were moved to NAS Willow Grove, Pennsylvania.

When Floyd Bennett closed down, I would drive down from New York on weekends to put in my reserve time. The base upgraded from P-2 to P-3 turboprop aircraft. To me this was like going from a Volkswagen to a Cadillac. The P-3 was a vast improvement in terms of speed, roominess and performance. During this time I flew as a plane captain and flight engineer aboard both P-2V Neptunes and P-3 Orions.

I waited until the last three years of my enlistment to stay on flight status and continue the joy of flying—which I did for 17 years in the Navy. At that time I made chief and was discharged from the reserves in December 1978.

Impressions of Navy service

I thoroughly enjoyed serving in the U.S. Navy. I would have stayed in longer but made a promise to my wife, Judy, to end my tour at 20 years. I met Judy at a party, and over a year later, on March 19, 1966, we were married.

Even though I was in the reserves and had weekend activities, I felt we were part of the regular Navy, because we were qualified to do actual patrols over the ocean doing surveillance and other intelligence missions. During the Cuban missile crisis on one of our flight patrols we sighted a Russian freighter approaching Cuba. We did flyovers photographing the ship and during a second pass we spotted crewmen covering something on board that looked suspicious. It turned out to be a propeller. We found out two years later that it was a propeller for a submarine that ultimately proved that the Russians had a form of a "silent propeller." This and other incidents made me feel like I was "doing something."

Journey to Sun City

In 2006 on the way to Florida to visit an uncle, a friend suggested that we visit him in Sun City—Hilton Head. On our way back from Florida, my wife and I spent three days in Savannah and then visited Sun City. When we returned home, I told Judy that the place seemed too good to be true, especially compared to some of the retirement communities we visited in Florida. I researched other Sun City communities on the Internet and found that Hilton Head had the most activities. That was exactly what I was looking for. We purchased a home and moved in August 2008. The hardest part of that was moving away from our grandchildren. Judy and I have three children and four grandchildren.

Dave Harrelson

Dave Harrelson

Dave was born on October 2, 1941 in a railroad car in Hadden, Alabama. His father worked for the railroad on the bridge gang, whose families lived in railroad cars that were set up like rolling apartments. Dave attended school in Jacksonville, Alabama and then the family moved to Anniston, Alabama. Dave's mother died when he was 8 years old and his father remarried. Dave quit school when he was 15 and joined a carnival. He traveled with Miller Amusements out of LaGrange, Illinois for two years, working on the amusement rides.

In his own words

I joined the Navy when I was 17 years old on January 19, 1959. The Navy sent me to boot camp at Recruit Training NTC, San Diego and I completed training with the rank of airman apprentice (E-2). My brother was on the USS Lexington (CVA-16) as a photographer's mate. I was assigned to the Lexington, which in March got underway for a nine-month WestPac (Western Pacific) cruise. I returned in December and I took Christmas leave back to Alabama, returning for duty to San Diego. We sailed up to Bremerton, Washington, where I was transferred to the USS Shangri-La (CVA 38), one of 24 Essex-class aircraft carriers completed during or shortly after World War II.

The Shangri-La was scheduled to sail around Cape Horn and to be homeported to Mayport, Florida. My job was in aviation fuels. When I first went on the Lexington, they asked me if I wanted to push airplanes or fuel them. There was no doubt about what I wanted. I figured, "A fuel hose is a lot lighter than an airplane."

Q & A

Arnold: On the flight deck did you wear one of the special-colored shirts?
Dave: I wore a red shirt and we had the skull cap. The hearing protection was simply ear plugs to cut down the loud engine noise. The flight deck boots were a desert-type boot that had a non-slip sole. The decks were wood. They haven't developed non-skids at that point.
Arnold: Describe your sleeping quarters.
Dave: Our racks were three deep.
Arnold: How was the food?
Dave: No one starves in the Navy.

Underway replenishments

Underway replenishment (UNREP) or replenishment at sea (RAS) is a method of transferring fuel, munitions, and stores from one ship to another while under way.

During UNREP the crew would organize big working parties and the food would be passed hand to hand down into the hole It would travel past some of our spaces and our guys would always try to be located close to the space (and if it was something good) they would open the door and throw the package in.

I remained on the Shangri-La from January 1960 to October 1962, when my enlistment was up. I chose to leave the Navy. I told my division officer, "I wouldn't stay in this Navy if I had my backyard as a duty station and my mother for a commanding officer. I'm *gone!*" This lasted 55 days before I returned to the Navy. Jobs were hard to find. I was a civilian—broke and jobless and missed the Navy. I reenlisted for six years, and decided to put forth the effort and make the Navy a career

I went to the Navy Transit Barracks in Charleston, South Carolina for a month doing mess cooking. My next orders were to report to the USS Hancock (CVA-19). We were in the Western Pacific when President Kennedy was shot, in November 1963.

Aircraft on board

On the Lexington we had FJ Furys, swept-wing carrier-capable fighters, and the F-11 Tigers—all jets were catapult-launched. We had the old prop planes as well; they just lumbered off the deck on their own. It was line them up, wind them up and send them off.

On the Shangri-La we had the old F-8 Crusader and F-4D Phantom. The F-4 was the Delta wing aircraft fighter. We had three elevators on the hangar deck—two on the sides and one on the forward deck. Our crew size aboard the two carriers totaled 3,000. The ship's company was one part permanent crew and when the air wing would move onboard our carrier population increased.

Meanwhile, I married my first wife in 1964 when I returned from sea duty on the Hancock. Our first son, David, was born in 1966 and another son, Craig, in 1970.

Survival training

Along the way survival school came up big. First, in San Diego at Warner Springs I took SERE (Survival, Evasion, Resistance, Escape), for personnel who risk capture during combat. My next duty station was at SERE Naval Air Station, Whidbey Island, Washington, where I taught cold weather survival. I attended another survival school at Stead Air Force Base in Reno. It was set in the Sierra Nevada; we had to trek across the mountains wearing snow shoes and carrying a heavy backpack. Next they sent me to Canadian Air Force Survival School north of Edmonton, Alberta, where we stayed out in the bush for 10 days living in lean-tos. A night of sleep in the wilderness, sheltered from the elements in a log lean-to, was part of our training; I also dug fire pits and did ice fishing in preparation for my new MOS—SERE. Before you can teach a student how to survive, you need to be taught. I advanced in rank to E-5 and achieved full qualifications to instruct every phase of the SERE course.

In 1971 I reported to Guantanamo Bay, Cuba. I worked at the fuel farm for three years refueling aircraft on the leeward side. We couldn't go out the gate. There was about 40 miles of paved road. No stop lights.

Tours of duty

From November 1971 to July 1972 I was assigned to the USS Saratoga (CV-60) in Mayport as the division leading petty officer. This was my most challenging assignment. Vietnam was at its peak; unrest in the civilian population spread to the military. I have no fond memories of this tumultuous period.

From August 1972 to February 1975 I was stationed at Naval Air Station Cecil Field, Jacksonville as the Fuel Farm section leader. My job was to issue fuel, oil and lubricants to aircraft from 5,000-gallon tank trucks and fuel pits.

My next assignment (March 1975 to April 1977) was in Argentia, Newfoundland, at a Naval facility. I served as the command career counselor, educational services officer and cargo handling supervisor. I was promoted to E-7. It seemed like I was in the middle of nowhere.

After Argentia I transferred to the USS Tripoli LPH (Landing Platform Helicopter). The Tripoli carried troops and a platform for landing helicopters. I found it to be a good ship with a good crew. After the big deck carriers the slower pace allowed more time to work with our team people and maintain our system. I advanced to E-8 during this tour.

From there I went to the Naval Air Technical Training Center in San Diego. I taught the aviation fuel system to shipboard sailors in a classroom setting from 1978 to 1980.

My next duty station, January 1981 to October 1982, was at NAS Whiting Field, Milton, Florida as command senior chief in a primary flight training squadron with about 200 enlisted members.

From Milton I went to the USS Eisenhower in 1986 (USS Dwight D. Eisenhower CVN-69), to be division leading chief petty officer and air department lead chief petty officer. I found the "Ike" to be a great ship with a great crew and a strong chain of command. I was promoted to master chief (E-9).

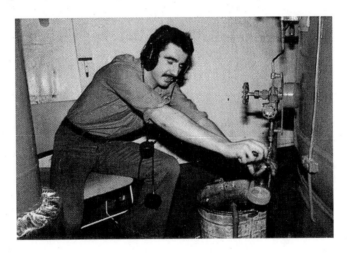

Delivery of fuel to aircraft aboard the "Ike,"
U.S. Navy photo

Life on board

Once you get into the chief's mess the food is "pick and choose"—whatever you want. They had food of every variety prepared fresh and delicious. Our sleeping quarters from E-7 and above were excellent. The E-3 to E-6 sailors usually slept in berthing compartments where the racks were aluminum and each person had a bunk light, curtains and adequate locker space. The newer ships provided larger lockers and storage facilities. I had a berthing with only nine in a compartment.

After leaving the USS Eisenhower, I returned to Naval Air Technical Center in Norfolk. At that time I divorced my first wife and met my second wife-to-be, Betsy Gilliam, when she visited our chief's club with a group of ladies from Yorktown. We married in 1985. Betsy had a home in Yorktown and I was living on the ship. She had two daughters and I had two sons.

Impressions of military service

I had very little education. It took me a long time to recognize the difference between uneducated and stupid. There is a big difference! I was able to obtain my GED (high school equivalency) while in the Navy. I realized that having a GED diploma could make a world of difference in my life: a promotion, a better job, more money and a higher standard of living, to name a few. I found that if you have leadership skills, your chances of promotion are increased. The Navy will recognize those skills.

Discharge

I served 30 years in the Navy, from January 1959 to April 1, 1989. I was discharged in Norfolk, Virginia with the rank of master chief. A master chief petty officer is the ninth and highest enlisted rank (E-9) in the U.S. Navy.

I got out still a young guy at 47 years old. The Navy opened a position in San Diego where they wanted someone with aviation fuel background. I applied and got accepted. I reported to work at the Commander of Naval Air Forces, Pacific. I was a government employee in the Department of Defense as a GS-9 and I stayed with them for 16 years. I retired as a GS-12 (equivalent to an O-4 or O-5, a Navy rank of lieutenant commander) when I turned 62 in 2003. Betsy and I had a home in Oceanside, California but our financial advisor advised us to move to a more economically friendly environment. We sold our house and looked for a 55-plus age community—"I'm too old to have skateboarders outside my door." We wanted a location near the water, close to military bases (for the benefits of medical and PX facilities) and a location in the southeast because I'm from Alabama, Betsy is from Virginia and we have kids in Florida and Virginia and Tennessee—so Sun City, Hilton Head suited us well. We purchased a resale and moved in October 2005.

Betsy and Dave in Sun City, 2009

Mary Houser

Mary Houser

Mary was born on March 27, 1945 in Pittsburgh, Pennsylvania. She graduated from Sacred Heart High School in 1963 and from the Pittsburgh Hospital School of Nursing in 1966. After working at the hospital for a couple of years, she entered a degree program in nursing at Duquesne University in Pittsburgh part-time, then switched to full-time in 1969 and received a BSN degree in May 1971.

Two months later, Mary decided to join the Navy. She enlisted in Pittsburgh and went to Newport, Rhode Island for Officer Indoctrination School (OIS).

Why I joined the Navy

I had worked for several years at local hospitals in Pittsburgh and I wanted to see and experience a more diversified nursing practice. I had met two friends at Duquesne University who were already in the Nurse Candidate Program. We were able to join together on the "Buddy Program."

I was always very impressed with the Navy nurses and had met several when they came and spoke at a Pittsburgh Hospital where I was working.

Q & A

AR: What was your rank upon joining?

MH: Lieutenant jg. The Navy gave me this rank because I worked three full years in nursing prior to joining. It was a nice jump start, because you normally enter as an ensign. I was at Newport for six weeks for indoctrination. We learned how to salute, stand inspections and partake in physical training.

AR: Did that include swimming?

MH: Believe it or not I am not a swimmer. From June to August of 1971 for some reason the Navy did not require you to be able to swim to get through OIS. I was able to get through and still not able to swim. But after September, they made swimming a requirement.

In her own words

When I look back at my career in the Navy there were many experiences that I thought were quite memorable. My first duty station was Portsmouth Naval Hospital in Portsmouth, Virginia. In 1973, when prisoners of war—POWs—were coming home from Vietnam, I was selected to work with them. That was quite an experience! After release from prison camps POWs were sent to the Philippines and then to Naval hospitals stateside. Eleven men came to Portsmouth—Jeremiah Denton, Red McDaniel and Mike Christenson were some of my patients.

Author's note: While serving as Naval aviator during the Vietnam War, Denton was commanding officer of Attack Squadron Seventy-Five (VA-75) aboard the aircraft carrier USS Independence (CVA 62). On July 18, 1965, then-Cmdr. Denton was flying an A-6A Intruder from the Independence with his bombardier/

navigator, Lt. jg Bill Tschudy, to take part in a bombing mission over Thanh Hoa. Both men were shot down and captured.

Denton was held as a prisoner of war for almost eight years, four of them in solitary confinement. Denton is known for the 1966 North Vietnamese television interview he was forced to give as a prisoner, in which he blinked his eyes in Morse code to spell out the word "T-O-R-T-U-R-E," to communicate that his captors were torturing him and fellow POWs. Questioned about his support for the U.S. war in Vietnam, he replied: "I don't know what is happening now in Vietnam, because the only news sources I have are Vietnamese. But whatever the position of my government is, I believe in it, I support it, and I will support it as long as I live." For his continuous resistance and leadership, even in the face of torture and inhumane conditions, he would be awarded the Navy Cross. While imprisoned, Denton was promoted to the rank of captain.

On May 19, 1967 Lt. Cmdr Eugene "Red" McDaniel was the pilot and Lt. James Patterson the backseater aboard an A6A on a mission to bomb a truck repair facility at Van Dien, Hai Duong Province, North Vietnam. The aircraft was shot down, but both crew members ejected safely and made voice radio contact with other aircraft in the area. Lt. Patterson broke his leg badly on landing, but maintained radio contact with rescue forces for four days. On May 21, he reported that enemy forces had taken a recovery kit which had been dropped to him and that he had moved up a hill for safety. McDaniel was taken prisoner by the North Vietnamese sent to Hanoi and never saw or heard of Patterson. He finally came to the belief that his backseater and friend had not been captured, but was dead.

McDaniel is noted for three things as a prisoner—his honor, his optimism and faith in his country, and also for having been the prisoner who received the most brutal torture at the hands of the Vietnamese. He was released March 4, 1973.

Our POW patients were active duty Navy fighter pilots who got released from Hanoi. Their treatment at the military hospital in the Philippines was very limited. They had injuries from torture to their arms and legs and suffered broken limbs. Many had injuries when they had parachuted out of their jets. They needed surgery to repair many body parts. They were all gentlemen and I found it interesting talking with them about their ordeal. At night (at the hospital) it was very hard for them to sleep because they remembered their torture, which occurred at night in the prison camps. Many nights they would get out of their beds and sit and talk and tell us the stories of torture. And you're talking how the enemy guards would place them in the worst positions and tie them up and bend their bones and limbs and place them in cages—it was just incredible the things they told us.

I remember my first visit with Lt. Cmdr. McDaniel, in the morning. At bedside I asked him what he would like for breakfast. Our policy was: anything the guys wanted, they got! If they wanted a lobster for breakfast, they got it! Red McDaniel looked at me rather funny, like I wasn't really connecting. I asked him again, "What would you like for breakfast?" Then it dawned on me that he had been in prison for so long (for eight years) he didn't know what to ask for breakfast. I said "Okay, how about I bring you a tray?!" And I brought him a tray of steak, eggs, potatoes and fruit. The next morning when another nurse went around asking him what he wanted for breakfast, he asked, "Where is Nurse Mary? I need Nurse Mary to get my breakfast. She knows how to make a breakfast!"

I remember Red McDaniel in particular. When he left for Vietnam his two boys were young toddlers. When he returned his boys were 10 and 12. After such a long period of separation, Red McDaniel was having a tough time to adjust to the kids' looks and habits.

Q & A

AR: What was your rank at Portsmouth when you cared for the POWs? And what were your specific duties?

MH: We dealt only with pilots that were shot down. When I took care of the POWs at Portsmouth I was a JG and then I became a lieutenant. The early part of your nursing career in the Navy is staff nursing. You do "hands-on" patient care. As you go up through the ranks, your fast track toward promotion is through administrative jobs. When I was promoted to captain at Portsmouth, I was director of nursing, a totally administrative job.

Now, over time, careers have changed and people do get promoted to senior ranks while remaining more clinical.

I remember a funny story about my first day on the job, working with the newly-arrived POWs. My chief nurse called to say I was to report at 11 p.m. for night duty. We all had to have security badges because the Navy was very careful in protecting the POW patients from intruders.

They did not want the press around until the Navy had time to debrief them. My badge was supposed to be waiting for me on the 10th floor when I reported for duty. I got on the elevator and was met by Marine guards who escorted me up and wanted to know where my badge was. I told them it was in the narcotics locker on the floor. We arrived on the floor and were met by two more Marine guards. They too asked me where my badge was. I told them it was down at the end of the hall in the narcotics locker: "I'll just go down and get it!" And I started to walk down the hall.

The Marine guard says, "Lieutenant, come back here!" I told him, "I can't come back; I have to get you the badge!" I turned around again and started walking. The guard repeated in a stronger tone, "Lieutenant, come back here!" I kept going and then heard this click. I turned around and he had pulled out his revolver and he said again, "Come back here!" I finally said, "No problem, sir! You've got that gun in your hand, I'll come back!" It turned out they didn't have my badge in the narcotics locker after all. The CO of the hospital was called. My boss was woken up and told the guards, "Lt. Houser has to work with these gentlemen. Please find her badge!" They finally found it, and later we shared a laugh or two about the incident.

AR: Where these POWs dispersed to other hospitals in the States?
MH: Yes, they were usually sent to Navy hospitals close to their home. Many of these guys were pilots from Oceana—the large Navy Air Station in Virginia.

Cuba, hands-on

Following Portsmouth, in 1975 Mary was assigned to Naval Hospital Guantanamo Bay, Cuba as a staff nurse and worked "hands-on" patient care. It was a general hospital that served the active duty, their dependents and the crew of ships. Mary found Guantanamo to be a nice tour of duty. It was safe, secure and they had their own schools for dependent children. Although Navy personnel were restricted to the base, her nursing quarters were excellent. Mary had a private apartment and she ate her meals at the officer's club or at the hospital.

In her own words

We took care of the Cubans that came over and worked on the base, too. Every day there was a contingent of people that came from "Castroland" through the gate. At the end of the day, they would return to their homes in Cuba. One day a worker came over and had a serious heart attack. We put him in our ICU and inserted IV lines and hooked him up to monitors, medicines and oxygen. When it got to be close to 4 p.m., he looked up at the clock and said, "I got to go!" I told him, "No, you can't go home. The doctor said you are too sick!" 'I've got to go home!" he pleaded. Finally we understood that if he did not go back, his family would be in danger. We placed him in an ambulance, drove him out to the fence line, took off the oxygen and removed the IVs and medicine lines. He got out of the ambulance and walked across and through the gate. He told us before he left, "My family would be tortured if I do not go home." And we never saw him again.

We had some folks that tried to get out of "Castroland" by coming through the mine fields (there was one near our base). For one couple, the man was blown up—he was killed—the woman made it through. We secretly held her in the hospital, gave her a false name and had her stay in one of our rooms. The story was that we had 24 hours to fly her to the States. She arrived with nothing except her dress. I remember telling my corpsman, "Go to the exchange and buy a pair of shoes." He returned with a pair and we put it on her and she was so excited. Actually they were too tight but she wouldn't take them off. We did come back with another pair of shoes in a larger size and she finally relented to swap the shoes she had on for the larger size. Incidents like these make you realize what freedom means. These people were so desperate to be free that they risked even death.

Master's degree

At the end of Mary's tour in Cuba she applied and was selected to attend the University of Maryland to get a master's degree—on Navy time; they paid all tuition, all books and even her salary. Mary had her own apartment in Columbia and attended classes at the downtown Baltimore campus.

She received her master's of science in nursing in 1978, and was assigned to the Naval Hospital in Jacksonville, Florida, where she served as the Information Systems Project Officer. The Navy was starting to put computers in the hospitals and looking to automate medical records and computerize nursing care and medications. Mary received orders to Naval Medical Data Services Center for Nursing, Bethesda, Maryland, also as the hospital Information Systems Project Officer. Her rank at that time was commander (O-5). Basically she worked on the development of hospital information systems for patient care from a nursing perspective. She remained on the Bethesda campus in a second tour as a department head for in-patient nursing and ambulatory care at the National Naval Medical Center. Mary was there when President Reagan was brought in after being shot in Washington, D.C. when coming out of his car.

In her own words

President Reagan had his bowel surgery on a Saturday morning. I had general duty at the hospital that day. The President was in a special secured unit. They needed some supplies and called me. I got them and headed for the President's room. I had to pass security dogs that sniffed what I was carrying. I never did get to meet the President. I got to the door and that was as close as I got! I always laugh about my sniffing adventure.

From Bethesda I went to Charleston, South Carolina, where I served as Department Head for Ambulatory Nursing and then as Assistant Director for Nursing Services. Charleston was to become one of the prime receiving sites for casualties from the Gulf War—thankfully there were no casualties. We were prepared to accept up to 300 patients a day, the official estimate.

I was promoted to captain in Charleston in 1991 and then was asked to become the senior detailer [an assignment officer] for the Nurse Corps, which had about 3,200 officers. I had a staff of three other detailers and a couple of enlisted sailors to help send the nurses all over the world. In 1995 I went back to Portsmouth, Virginia when I transferred to the Naval Medical Services Center as the Director of Nursing. I was there for five years and retired on August 4, 2000.

Mary and her mom, 1994

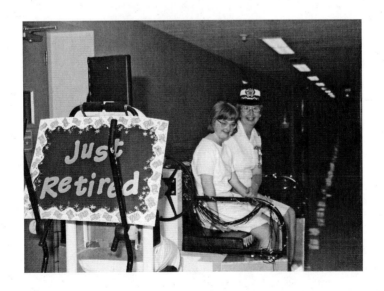

**Mary and her niece, Allyson, at Retirement Day,
August 4, 2000**

Impressions of service

The Navy rewarded Mary with a ceremony in appreciation of her service. Here is the "Welcome" in the event program:

> *Welcome to the Retirement for Captain Mary L. Houser*
>
> *The retirement ceremony you witness today is a time-honored tradition of our rich naval heritage and the nation's expression of appreciation for a job well done. The officer to be retired reads the order of retirement, thus culminating a career of unselfish dedication, devotion to duty and unswerving service to one's country.*
>
> *It is a day of great significance, marking the end of a rewarding life within the medical community that supports men, women and the families of the United States Navy and Marine Corps.*

I absolutely loved my 30 years in the Navy. I had so many wonderful opportunities to do exciting and innovative things, to see the world and to meet and work with so many loyal, skilled and dedicated nurses and corpsmen. I am grateful to all the people that helped and mentored me throughout my career. It was fabulous experience.

Awards

Mary retired as a captain (O-6). Her awards include:

* Legion of Merit
* Meritorious Service Medal
* Joint Service Commendation Medal
* Navy Commendation Medal
* Navy Achievement Medal

Civilian life

As a civilian, Mary remained in Chesapeake, Virginia for a while. She had always wanted to travel and now used the military transport system to visit Italy and other countries. At home she volunteered in medical facilities and often helped and cared for friends who became ill.

She often visited her brother at his condo in Hilton Head, South Carolina and became fascinated with the Lowcountry. She discovered Sun City, was able to sell her home in Virginia and moved to this active adult community in fall 2007. She is delighted to be living in Sun City and has many new friends and enjoys clubs and amenities that the community offers. Mary really liked the idea that there was an active veterans group down here. She joined the Veterans Association and especially likes participating in the veterans march contingent during special veteran's day events.

Mary and Millie at home in Sun City, 2009

Tom Jones

Tom Jones

Tom was born on June 30, 1940 in Cleveland, Ohio. He graduated from John Adams High School in 1958 and enrolled in Kent State University as, he says, "a *very* unmotivated 18-year old." His father, a city fireman in Cleveland, had an engineering degree he was unable to use after the Depression and instead went for one in elementary education. He told Tom, "You could always get a job teaching." At Kent, Tom took his father's advice to become a teacher, and on graduating in June 1962—having joined the school's ROTC program earlier—was commissioned a 2nd lieutenant in the Transportation Corps in the Army Reserves. During an earlier six-week ROTC summer camp at Ft. Knox, Kentucky Tom met a platoon tactical infantry officer (and Korean War veteran) who inspired him and gave him an excellent write-up. The report later influenced a priority selection of duties and assignment in the military.

In his own words

The day after graduating from Kent State I married Linda Coreno. She was from Cleveland as well, and we had met at Kent State. We moved back to Cleveland and I took a job teaching school that September at the 5th grade level. A month later, I received a letter that said, "Congratulations 2nd Lieutenant Tom Jones, you are now an infantry officer in the U.S Army. You will report to Ft. Benning, Georgia no later than 4 November, 1962." That was probably the shortest teaching career of anyone in the world. I left Linda behind in Cleveland and took off for Benning. The three-month basic officer course was followed by Ranger, jungle, mountain and airborne training at various off-site military camps.

My next assignment, which I had selected when I applied for the Regular Army commission, was with the 25th Infantry Division in Schofield Barracks, Hawaii. I returned to Cleveland, picked up Linda and we drove out to the West Coast and shipped our car to Hawaii. I served three years in Hawaii and was thinking of leaving the service—I wasn't really sure if this was the thing for me. It was a lot of down time, a lot of "looking busy, when you were not really busy," though the 25th Infantry Division was called the Rapid Reaction Force for the Pacific. We were constantly training. We trained on ships; we worked with tanks on various sites within the Hawaiian Island chain. We conducted specialized training exercises for one month every year and then returned to Schofield Barracks.

In the end, I decided to stay in the Army because I started hearing rumors, early in 1965, that the 25th would soon be deployed; President Johnson was getting ready to send troops to Vietnam. After a soldier has trained with a group it becomes close-knit and friendship and loyalties emerge. I didn't want to miss that. If they went, I felt that I had to go, too. My orders arrived shortly. Our unit was deployed to Vietnam at the end of 1965.

In Vietnam

I was the second in command of an infantry rifle company, executive officer of B Company, 1ˢᵗ Battalion, 14ᵗʰ Infantry. I went in the advance party, leaving Hawaii on January 2, 1966. We flew to Pleiku, Vietnam as the 3ʳᵈ Brigade Task Force of the 25ᵗʰ Infantry Division. We were deployed to Pleiku because just prior to that Gen. Westmoreland ordered the 1ˢᵗ Air Cavalry to the central highlands where they engaged in a fierce battle in the Ia Drang River valley. During this action, the division conducted 35 days of continuous airmobile operations. This was the first major battle involving heavy use of helicopters. The 1ˢᵗ Cav suffered numerous casualties and deaths among the troops. We were sent to Pleiku to reinforce the 1ˢᵗ Cav. I spent a year just west of Pleiku near the Cambodian border in the Ia Drang River valley.

Capt. Tom Jones, Montagnard Village, Vietnam

After my one-year tour I returned home on December 15, 1966. For my next duty assignment I filled out my "dream sheet" and requested to teach ROTC. At that point I had been promoted to captain. The Army sent me to Pennsylvania Military College in Chester, Pennsylvania. I put in my resignation papers to leave the Army in late 1967, but they wouldn't let me out. They had an involuntary retention because of the Vietnam War. By teaching ROTC, I was lucky. I feel I was blessed in many ways in my life. I was in the public eye, speaking about the Vietnam War to the veterans and civic groups. I was finally discharged in 1969 after seven years of active duty. I couldn't go back to teaching school at that point.

The dark side of military service

I had a lot of reasons for getting out. In my three years at Pennsylvania Military College, during the worst part of the Vietnam War, I had the heavy-hearted duty of confronting the families of dead soldiers. During the period of 1967 and 1968 and the Tet offensive, a lot of GIs were being killed in Vietnam. We had a duty roster for "Notification of Next of Kin," "Survivor Assistance" and for graveside duty—attending the funeral of dead soldiers. For three years I saw the other end of the spectrum. I raced off to war at 26 years old, left a wife and a 10-month-old baby daughter at home and thought nothing of it because I was invincible. When I returned home from Vietnam I saw the other end of the war and witnessed firsthand the grief that families endured. I realized that at my point in life, I was an infantry officer and just didn't want to go back to Vietnam and expose my family to that. By then we had a second daughter. I said to myself, "For the good of my family I want to resign."

Back to civilian life

I didn't want to go back to teaching school because I had been teaching college men and secondly, I was thinking about a $5,000 a year pay-cut compared to being an Army captain. I started sending out some resumes. A friend of mine from Kent State, a journalist, was doing the internal communication for a trucking company called Roadway Express. He told me, "I know you're sending out a lot of resumes, but don't overlook the trucking industry as a career choice. Roadway Express is a wonderful company and if you like, I would be glad to arrange an interview for you." I took the interview in Harrisburg, Pennsylvania and they offered me a job as a terminal manager. I moved to Akron and it was the start of a trucking career that lasted 35 years. I worked for some four different trucking companies in the first 15 years, got tired of working for other people and decided, at age 44, to exercise my entrepreneurial spirit and start my own trucking company business. It sure kept us busy, and by 1996 Linda and I were ready to retire.

Retirement

Five of my Army buddies visited Hilton Head, South Carolina for a vacation, rented a house in Sea Pines and marveled at how beautiful the area was. When I was in Ranger school, we trained near Fort Walton Beach, Florida and I remembered the beautiful beaches there, too. We also visited other Gulf Coast areas, looking for retirement spots. When we drove down to Hilton Head on our first trip in 1995 we noticed a big sign near a large construction site that read, "Future home of Del Webb Sun City—Hilton Head." My dad retired from Cleveland in 1974 to Sun City, Arizona and they stayed out there for 28 years. I was familiar with the life style and I was "sold." Our Sun City sales rep showed us a lot with a premium price that for us was an ideal location. I walked out in the middle of the lot, looked at those woods and onto that first green and plunked down a deposit and announced, "Sold." We bought in 2001 and moved in 2002.

Impressions of military service

In a word, excellent! I loved it! There was a lot of boredom involved, but the people were of excellent caliber. We bonded, especially in combat. The military changed me because I never considered myself athletic. I grew four inches after high school. My self-perception was that I would always be a short, fat kid. I got into the Army and the best thing that ever happened to me in my life was Ranger training. The first thing they do is give you a lot of physical training. They put you through psychological challenges, like jumping into a swimming pool with all your equipment and holding your rifle. You are required to jump off the diving board, in February, in freezing water and you have to make it to the end of the pool. You're watching guys that are nearly drowning and watch as drill instructors (DIs) hook them out of the pool and you never see them again. Or you spend a whole day of training and the last thing of the day they make you engage in is "hand-to-gland" combat in a sawdust pit. You are all sweaty, hot and exhausted. If you don't hit each other for real the DIs would hit you both. So you think training is over and they order you to fall out and just when you think you are going to get a shower and dinner, they shout, "Double time march!" and run you 10 miles. I learned two things: first, that I could do things physically that I never thought I could do and second, and probably the most important thing, is the power of the human mind over the body. They would wear your body down to where you are so tired and vulnerable and don't think you could ever keep going. But somehow some inner power tells you to put the left foot in front of the right—and you do! You keep going!

Tom at home in Sun City, 2009

Marvin Melsha

Marvin Melsha

Marvin was born on December 3, 1945 in Long Beach, California. His dad was just exiting the Navy after a tour of duty served on the carrier Lexington and the battleship Alabama. The Melsha family moved to Cedar Rapids, Iowa where Marvin graduated from high school in 1963 and enrolled at Iowa State University.

After two years in college, knowing he would be drafted and not wanting to become a foot soldier, Marvin enlisted in the Army and took the test for Army aviator at Fort Leonard Wood, Missouri. He passed and was sent to basic training followed by a year of Army aviation/helicopter flight school training at Fort Walters, Texas and Fort Rucker, Alabama. On August 15, 1966 Marvin was commissioned a warrant officer and sent to a new unit at Fort Lewis, Washington. New helicopters were provided and these birds were flown up to Seattle, where Marv and his unit were shipped out to Vietnam in January 1967 on a C-141 from McCord AFB. They joined the 4th Infantry Division stationed at Pleiku, capital of the Gia Lai Province and inhabited chiefly by the Bahnar and Jarai ethnic groups, sometimes known as the Montagnards or Degar.

In his own words

We established our new unit at Pleiku in the highlands, in the north central part of South Vietnam. About a month after arriving, the main unit's supplies and helicopters arrived. In January 1967 U.S. forces were in the midst of a big offensive. I served with the 4th Infantry Division for about five months and then the Army had a process of taking experienced aviators with six months in country and transferring them to other units. I went to the 170th Assault Helicopter Company at Camp Holloway.

Pleiku, Vietnam, 1967

The first six months at Dragon Mountain I lived in a GP medium tent and we used rocket tubes to raise our plywood off the ground about eight to 10 inches. I had a cot and an air mattress, a sleeping bag and four sticks about three feet tall on each corner of the cot that had mosquito netting. I would tuck the netting underneath the sleeping bag to keep the mosquitoes out. I slept with my machine gun lying alongside my mosquito netting and had a Colt .38 which I kept in a shoulder holster near my pillow. If you went to the bathroom at night, you would take your weapon with you while you walked through the dark to the latrine.

The missions

My missions varied widely. I could be hauling new people in to replace guys going home or hauling food, ammo, all hours of the day. The helicopters were parked on the strip. The night before our missions, we assembled for a briefing to learn who we would be working with, radio frequencies and map coordinates. We would receive new assignments in-flight via radio: a combat assault, going into a landing zone under fire or hauling mail, hot food or extracting wounded out of the zones. The missions changed throughout 13-hour days as a helicopter pilot.

Our crew consisted of me as pilot, a co-pilot, a crew chief who doubled as left-side door gunner and another gunner on the right side. Our bird was a UH-1D "Huey" helicopter, which to me was extremely smooth, powerful, reliable and roomy on the inside. Bell manufactured and shipped about 10,000 helicopters during the Vietnam War. They refurbished them in Corpus Christi, Texas and rebuilt them to like-new condition. It wasn't unusual to go out to the flight line and have a tail number assigned to you and have a "nearly-new fresh bird" there—along with birds which had logged high air mileage. There was plenty of room inside the cockpit; if you took some hits you really didn't worry about going down. Most of the time, I flew at 100 knots at tree-top level. What's interesting about that was that you got to know your area at tree-top level. You would see, for example, a tree with a funny-looking branch and you'd see some hills behind it and you would form a mental picture of your area at low level.

Huey helicopter

This gave me an opportunity to navigate far and wide low-level using the mental images I remembered on previous flyovers. But that's not to say that we did not fly at higher altitudes. There were times when I thought it was safe to climb up to 4,000 or 5,000 feet. At that altitude I found a measure of peace and tranquility. Up there, above the clouds, I wasn't worried about small arms fire. In fact, on one foggy morning I flew down a ravine to try to find a way towards better weather—there were hills on either side of me and I ended up boxed in by the weather so I just turned the helicopter to the left and started climbing. I climbed to 8,500 feet of clouds before I broke out of cloud cover. My radio contact in flight was with other helicopters and ground headquarters. On one occasion, out of Cameron Bay, I flew up to 15,500 feet. There was a lot of cloud cover. We were light on fuel, light on passengers and I just kept on climbing to the top of the cloud cover over these mountains. But I was running out of air speed and running out of power so I went around the highest clouds off to the right and started a long descent back to the base.

Author's note: The most widely used military helicopter, the Bell UH-1 series Iroquois, better known as the "Huey," began arriving in Vietnam in 1963. Before the end of the conflict, more than 5,000 of these versatile aircraft were introduced into Southeast Asia. "Hueys" were used for Medivac, command and control and air assault; to transport personnel and materiel; and as gunships. Considered to be the most widely-used helicopter in the world, with more than 9,000 produced from the 1950s to the present, the Huey is flown today by about 40 countries.

A harrowing experience

On one of my scariest missions, I picked up a four-man, long-range recon patrol that was being chased back by the enemy to the drop-off point where we'd left them earlier. Normally during a troop insertion we were accompanied by a command-and-control helicopter watching everything from up high, telling us how to get into the zone. A couple of gunships also watched us on the right and left sides. In this case about 30 minutes after we'd dropped off the patrol they called and said they needed to be extracted because they were being chased and under fire. When we arrived back at the landing zone we found them hunkered down in a bomb crater, firing back toward the tree line. Occasionally we could see a flash of gunfire from the tree line directed our way; quickly, one by one, our soldiers on the ground jumped out of the crater and scampered into the left side of the helicopter while our gunners were firing back at the enemy to cover their buddies. When the last guy was on board we took off. And all the time this was happening I had gunships flying down the left and right sides peeling off and coming back to strafe these enemy positions.

I expected the windshield of my bird to shatter and all the yellow lights in the cockpit to light up. I really expected to get killed that day! Thankfully we were able to lift off and get out of there to fly another day.

In other missions we flew in all kinds of weather. Some days we would see a wall of rain coming but we knew it was really going to be brief so I would slow our air speed and drop down to treetop level so that we could see the trees and just penetrate the curtain of rain.

Q & A

Arnold: What did you carry on board for missions?

Marv: I would take an M-16 machine gun and hang it on my seat and I would carry a sidearm—a Smith & Wesson .38 police special that I had in a shoulder holster in case I ever got thrown out of the helicopter and I couldn't get to my machine gun. This served as my "backup weapon." Inside that Smith and Wesson .38 every other round was a flare round, so I not only could have protection from the enemy, but I also could fire a flare if somebody was looking for me.

Arnold: Did you carry C-rations or food?

Marv: No food. I think somewhere on the bird we had a small first aid kit. We did have a portable emergency radio in case we were shot down and the main radios were dead. I could take this little survival radio out, flip out its antennae and talk to somebody.

Arnold: What was the average flight time for missions?

Marv: Our flight time averaged about 100 hours a month and I logged 1,102 for the year.

Arnold: How many missions would you say you flew?

Marv: Many times I would preflight my bird before dawn and postflight after dark. During the day our crew flew many sorties, often working 13 to 14 hour days. Let's say you come back to a resupply area, pick up C-rations, ammunitions and mail and fly 10 to 15 miles out to an artillery base, drop off your cargo, turn around and come back and then maybe do six of those trips and then leave them and do several others during the span of a day. I could do 10 to 15 missions a day.

Arnold: What was your tour of duty in Vietnam?

Marv: A year.

Arnold: Your Huey is quite different than a Medivac helicopter, right?

Marv: That's right. We did not have a red cross painted on our side, but that did not preclude us from taking out dead and wounded and going into extremely tight areas, where we would fly through dense jungle and sometimes between trees or on riverbanks to extract wounded and hurt. I had an instance where I had to take out, as quickly as possible, as many dead as I could. They put the bodies in a rope cargo net because there were so many of them. I hauled the bodies back to the grave registration area. Another time they stacked bodies like logs in the back of my helicopter and it smelled so bad I had to fly the helicopter with the windows opened slightly sideways because of the offensive order. We never left our dead. We always brought them back to keep them from falling into enemy hands. I hauled out plenty of wounded who were alive and enemy wounded that were alive. We interrogated the wounded enemy.

Arnold: Did you ever extract any civilians or children?

Marv: No.

Arnold: So winding down your tour, you were still in the 4th Infantry Division 170th Assault Helicopter Company? Tell me about your orders after your Vietnam tour.

On to Germany

My journey home began with a helicopter flight down to Cameron Bay. Then I boarded a commercial flight on Northwest Airlines to Tokyo, where we stopped to refuel, and flew direct to Seattle. I arrived home New Year's Eve 1967 in time to welcome 1968. My orders were to go back to the States as an instructor pilot for the new guys at Fort Rucker or Fort Walters. In turn, I tried to get a transfer to West Germany. To my delight, my request was granted. My commitment to serve was for three years after flight school and basic training, which amounted to a year. I served a total of four years. I spent about 18 months in Frankfurt at a small World War II air base on the north side of the city. I had an apartment there and I'd fly all over Germany in small helicopters and a variety of other aircraft. Approaching discharge, I could have gone back to Vietnam for another tour of duty, but I decided to get out for my brother's wedding and was discharged in August 1969.

Back to civilian life

In 1971, already married, I returned to Iowa State University, under the GI Bill, as a third-year student. During the spring semester, I received a job offer from the Federal Aviation Agency (FAA) for an air traffic control position in Chicago at the air traffic control center at a salary that was too good to pass up. So here I am, on a Saturday looking at going to summer school and then on to college for my last year or do I take a good job offer as an air traffic controller in Chicago. My starting salary as a controller would have been much better than if I were to graduate in another year with a degree. The decision was easy to make and I took my family and went to Chicago to begin a promising career path.

Air traffic control was to be my primary career for the next 32 years. I was a supervisor for 26 years in air traffic control; I worked in Detroit and Cedar Rapids before we moved to Green Bay, Wisconsin, where I finished my career and retired in 2004.

Marvin meets Mary

Earlier, after discharge, I went to Des Moines to get my airplane instrument rating/airplane commercial rating and airplane twin-engine rating. I needed to take a physical exam, and went downtown to a doctor's office. Taking my application was a pretty little nurse, but I didn't want to make a pass right there in the doctor's office. Maybe, I thought, I'd go back sometime and ask her to lunch. Two days later my cousin and I were at a sports bar on Ladies Night and there was that little nurse sitting there with a bunch of her girl friends. I walked up and said, "Don't I know you?" The rest is history. That was 38 years ago. Her name was Mary Swain—a long-time resident of Des Moines. We married in 1970. We are blessed with two grown sons and one grandson.

On to Sun City

When my oldest son was discharged from the military he moved to Florida. When I decided to retire I had a choice of going to Seattle or Florida. We looked at a retirement community in Florida and purchased a home—a gated retirement community with the usual amenities an hour and half from my son. A short time thereafter my both sons decided to move to Charlotte and that prompted me to put my house up for sale and explore Charlotte. We lived there with my son for about six months and decided against it. We found it had too much traffic, it was too expensive, too crowded and had a shortage of one-story homes. We discovered Sun City-Hilton Head, found it to be very desirable and purchased a resale and moved in 2008.

I have a very nice radio-controlled sailboat, 39 inches long and about five feet high and I thoroughly enjoy this pastime out on Somerset Lake. We are here almost a year and enjoy our retired life here in Sun City.

Impressions of military service

My positive impression of my years in the military prompted me to encourage my sons to enter military service. Both served in the Air Force; one was stationed in Seattle and the other in Germany. Both loved their tours of duty.

My tour of duty as an army aviator was of high adventure. I don't like getting shot at, and don't get me wrong, I don't like war—no clear-minded soldier likes war. But I entered the service as a young man and wanted to do something for my country. I wanted to help other people just like me who were "in the same boat" and were just trying to get by and be safe. To me the military was extreme adventure—especially as an Army aviator—flying in all kinds of situations, seeing all kinds of action. At the end of my tour in Vietnam, I was fortunate to spend my remaining time in Germany. It was 18 months of blissful duty. I even enjoyed my military training. The variety of what I saw and experienced in four years makes all other life experiences pretty boring. The only thing that really approaches the military as high adventure for me was being out on our sailboat in a big storm at night or in near-tornado conditions out on Green Bay.

I used to keep a little camera next to me while in flight—I took about 500 slides—they all tell a story of my tree-top view of flying over the countryside of Vietnam. There are other vignettes that I will always remember:

- I hauled around Nancy Sinatra when she appeared for a USO show for the troops. We talked while in flight and she complained about generators keeping her up at night.
- I saw Bob Hope and Raquel Welsh at a typical World War II USO show.
- I saw Gen. Westmoreland in a field awarding battle citations for troops.
- On the ground back at the base I watched an ammo dump explode at the far end of the air field—you could see a parabolic arc of yellow flame lighting up the sky and shaking up our base as stacks of ordinance exploded while my buddies and I dove into a bunker out of harm's way.

Commendations

Marvin was awarded the following commendations for his military service:

* Distinguished Flying Cross, for rescuing long-range recon patrols while under fire
* A second Distinguished Flying Cross, for flying replacements and ammunition into a beleaguered unit at night under fire and extracting dead and wounded on the way out
* Air Medal with 29 Oak Leaf clusters
* Vietnamese Cross for Gallantry

Mary and Marv Melsha

Dave Mitchell

Dave Mitchell

Dave was born on March 16, 1948 in Columbus, Ohio. After graduating from Bishop Watterson Catholic High School in 1966, he enrolled at the University of Denver but left after freshman year to return to Columbus and work for his dad, a physician—and the head of the Allergy Clinic at Ohio State University Hospital—for the summer of 1967. His draft status was 4-A, he was in good health and keenly aware of what was happening in the world. He knew that he wanted to fly and had declared to himself and his family that he wanted to join the Marines. His father, a World War II veteran, was furious. He wanted him to "slow down" and think about his decision. Dave realized that he couldn't fly in the Marines, Navy or Air Force without a college degree, but he learned that the Army's Warrant Officer Helicopter Program accepted high school graduates. Dave was sold on this the minute he heard about it.

In his own words

My road to Army aviation started at a recruiting station in Columbus. I lucked into an honest recruiting sergeant who told me the straight story about what to do to get into the program. There were three other recruits with me and we became a group of four going through a series of tests together at Fort Hayes in Columbus. I passed all the tests and was sworn in that December. I did, however, take a delayed enlistment so that I could spend Christmas at home.

I reported to Fort Polk, Louisiana in January 1968 for basic training. After basic we were sent to primary flight school at Fort Wolters, Texas. We spent five months in training and I flew Hughes TH-55 helicopters. I had a brutal tactical officer who drove us to the point where we almost quit at times, en masse. We were always up an hour earlier than any other class. It turned out at the end of the training that he was a real human being and a darn nice guy—but he was "pushing us to the edge!"

After a graduation ceremony we had a choice of going to Fort Rucker, Alabama or Hunter Field in Georgia. I talked a few of my buddies into Hunter because I thought Savannah would be a more interesting town. We spent four months at Hunter, training with Bell and Huey helicopters, and graduated in December 1968. My mother and father were there. The day I received my aviator's wings was the proudest day of my life! I look back and I think in all these years of the left and the right and the polarization of this country, I just knew that I was pretty lucky to have the privilege of wearing United States Army Aviator's wings—and to get paid for it. It was like a bonus because I loved flying. I also received orders to report to Oakland Naval Yard and on to Travis Air Force Base and departure to Vietnam.

Q & A: Vietnam

AR: Where were you stationed?

DM: I was stationed in Vinh Long.

AR: What unit were you in?

DM: The squadron was the 7th of the 1st Air Cavalry. We were a unit under our own supervision, somehow related to the 1st Aviation Brigade up in Saigon.

AR: How many squadrons?

DM: There was one squadron. It was four companies, an administrative company and three air cavalry troops (company means troop in the air cavalry). I was in Comanche Troop, which included 200 men and 30 pilots. These units were top-heavy with officers. It was a good way to drive a first sergeant who is used to the infantry nuts!

AR: What was the aircraft?

DM: We flew a mixture of aircraft. We had Hueys (we called them "slicks"). We had Cobra gunships; we had something I flew called a scout or a "loach"—a single pilot, two-passenger helicopter. In my left seat was an enlisted man, an "observer." He carried a "car 15," which was a chopped off M-16 with no stock, or a sawed-off shotgun or a grenade launcher. He sat literally leaning out the door holding colored smoke bombs and various grenades to toss out.

AR: Basically what did your missions consist of?

DM: Well, we were what some people call a "hunter/killer" team. We would be in the air with one Huey, whose pilot and co-pilot were the "C & C" (Command and Control) at 400 feet, circling loosely and directing everything. At 1,500 feet in a broader circle, were a pair of Cobra gunships watching and waiting. And we—a pair of loaches—would be at about six to eight feet above the rice paddies at very slow speeds to try to lure them, the enemy, to shoot at us.

AR: You always had an observer with you?

DM: Yes, but he was not a pilot. Quite often he would be my crew chief who also took care of the aircraft on the ground.

AR: What did your equipment consist of inside the copter?

DM: I had a trigger control of a mini gun mounted on the left side of the aircraft. The mini gun is a very rapid fire. If I squeezed the trigger, I would get a burst of 2,200 rounds a minute. And it would throw the aircraft out of trim so you had to learn to coordinate your left pedal exactly.

An undeclared war

AR: What was your objective on missions?

DM: You may recall that this was not a declared war. I couldn't shoot first.

        We were trying to find Viet Cong in their locations. We were scouts. Our goal was to find them, to fix their location on a map (we were in constant radio communication with other aircraft nearby). I was doing most of the talking and C & C is listening and advising and the gunships were quiet—just waiting. The Viet Cong would not give up their positions for anything. They would wait and wait and wait, and sometimes they would finally fire on us. There would be a moment of panic. I would squeeze the microphone and transmit, "Receiving fire!" My observer would drop colored smoke and we'd get out of there. The Cobra gunships would move in and fire some rockets and they had a mini nose gun that could fire 6,600 rounds per minute.

The gun ships would hit these bunkers or bushes, wherever the enemy was. The enemy used the rice paddies to burrow into little holes and cover themselves with palm tree leaves and camouflage. They had incredibly good camouflage. So we were basically "hanging out the bait!" That was our scout mission. It was dangerous. It was a voluntary job and only for six months but I and a number of men in my platoon served for 12 months and others for 18 months.

AR: How long was your tour in Vietnam?

DM: Originally for 12 months, but I extended it another six months for a total of 18 months.

AR: Did you wear armor or a flak jacket?

DM: Yes. That's called a "chicken plate." It Velcros around and it's about that thick (Dave gestures with his fingers about 2 inches). They were made of either boron carbide, silicon carbide or aluminum oxide and were issued to all pilots in our unit.

Body vest for protection, Vinh Long, 1968

AR: What other items did you carry with you?

DM: We had a plate under out seat and another behind our back. My observer would grab a smoke flare—he would literally hang by the door holding the D-rings. The gunship pilots could see that and fix on that visually. The interesting part of these missions was that once we got the enemy to fire and they gave away their positions, they knew that you knew that they were there and visa versa. After the first pass or two by the gunships, the C & C would say, "Go back and check it out!" That's where the nervousness got intense. Now there was no more hiding and they (the enemy) were ready for you with their finger on the trigger. We would fly out of the zone about 100 yards while the gunships swooped down and fired. We would fly over for a second pass or even make four or five more passes.

AR: How many missions did you have in a day? What was a typical mission be like?

DM: We would trade off. We would leave Vinh Long and fly off to these little air fields and be assigned to a local unit for the day. We would leave with two sets of scouts (four overall), two sets of guns (four Cobras), one C & C Huey, and four Hueys ("slicks") that would just sit down and wait until we called them and needed troop insertions. Many days we didn't engage the enemy and they would fly out and sit all day and fly back without doing anything.

**Cobra over the Delta,
photo by Dave Mitchell flying alongside**

But one day we were flying from a little field called Vi Than down south in the Delta. During our flyover, we observed a little grove of trees where a platoon of 20 VCs was spotted. As we approached overhead all hell broke loose on the ground. They were scrambling for their weapons and diving into holes and we were expecting them and they weren't expecting us and that wasn't our objective. We got into quite an aerial firefight. We had our gunships with us—but immediately we realized that this was going to be trouble. We could contain this but not by ourselves so we called in ground troops.

Shot down

I was shot down on the second to the last day of my tour. After many missions one got careless. You thought you were invincible. We could track people; we could smell people; we could follow a fishing line; we could recognize the freshness of camouflage; and the difference between fresh and not fresh—I came over this little grove of trees off the edge of some rice paddies and said over the mike: "I think we got something fresh down here!" Just then one of the VC opened up with an AK and I knew the first round was right in my main transmission and our onboard instruments went out. I cursed, jerked power and yelled, "Receiving fire! May Day!" We were above the trees, with about 40 feet of altitude; I climbed to about 80 feet before my engines began to fail. I could auto-rotate, which is a helicopter version of gliding, and was able to get about 200 feet out in the rice paddies. I landed upright in a hard landing. No injuries, smoke billowing out the back and we were picked up in less than a minute.

My first arrival in Vietnam was in December 1968. I returned home on leave before Christmas 1969 and was back in Nam in January 1970 and home again in July. I returned to Vietnam for another six-month tour. By then I opted out of scouts and flew as co-pilot in a C & C helicopter. Looking back, my last six-month tour was more dangerous than earlier. At the end of the tour I flew home on a commercial airliner and was discharged with rank of chief warrant officer (CW2).

Civilian life

I went to the University of Denver with a renewed sense of motivation. I was getting married and needed to find a stable career. I had known my bride-to-be prior to entering the service and reconnected with her during my 30-day home leave in Columbus. Her name is Mary Hughes. We were married for 31 years, have three children and are divorced.

I majored in real estate at the University of Denver and graduated with a BS degree. I went into real estate sales and hated it for 20 years. Unfortunately, I didn't have the courage to admit that I was wrong and I bounced around in several companies while living in Denver. I left Denver and returned to Columbus. I talked with one of my Vietnam buddies who owned a construction firm in Hilton Head, South Carolina. He suggested I visit him, and offered me a job with his firm. I arrived there in 2002 and worked for him for four years. His firm built large luxury homes and was building in nearby Bluffton. I was given the opportunity to supervise and plan a small, historic home.

Due to the housing market slowdown, I left the construction firm and went to work for the facilities maintenance of Sun City as a project manager.

Impressions of military service

I'm proud of my military service. I'm not, however, without criticism. I was brought up with the idea of service, was thrilled to be a pilot and even prouder to be an Army aviator. I wanted to give it all and take risks—maybe it was my "rite of passage."

In the Army (as in any organization) I met a wide range of people with diverse personalities—good guys and jerks! I was fortunate to have a terrific commanding officer while in Vietnam. He had the best combination of a being a perfect leader and a great pilot and still could be your friend—and that is a tough line to walk in the military. I remember one morning I was scheduled to fly with him. The day before our flight, a young captain, just out of West Point, asked if I would be willing to switch aircraft with him because he needed more time flying with "the old man" to learn aspects of C & C missions. He was originally assigned to fly in a Cobra gunship; I didn't want to change. He kept bugging me until he drew two strands of grass and asked me if I would draw straws to decide to make the switch. I said, "Eddie, if you accept the results would you buzz off?" He agreed and to my dismay I drew the short straw. I was furious. I lost and I was upset to give up my seat to him in a flight with our commanding officer. I had to settle for the front seat of a gunship that morning.

It appeared to be a quiet morning and we completed our morning flight without incident. We refueled after lunch and headed back up the Mekong River into Cambodia. The copter of our commanding officer, Maj. Smith, was a mile or two ahead of us. I watched as he circled in the air. I could see clearly in the front seat of my gunship as Maj. Smith flew in a real tight circle and then when I looked down and suddenly to my horror I heard over my radio, "Six is down!" (Six is the call sign for the commanding officer.) They had dropped like a rock—ironically in a walled cemetery in the back of an old French convent and school along the Mekong River. I could see black smoke billowing up. I was called on to finish the day flying another "slick." They were all dead—all in the helicopter I was supposed to fly that day. It never occurred to me until that night, when I laid down in my cot that when I drew straws with Eddie, fate had spared my life that day.

Dave Mitchell, 2009

Harry Price

Harry Price

Harry was born on August 7, 1943 in Reading, Pennsylvania. After graduating from high school, he earned a bachelor of science degree in secondary education at Penn State University, where he joined the Naval Reserve Officer Training Corps. Harry was commissioned an ensign on December 11, 1965.

On to Vietnam

His initial duty assignment was aboard the destroyer USS O'Hare (DD-889), homeported in Norfolk, Virginia, where, a 1st lieutenant, he served as gunnery officer. The O'Hare conducted gunfire support missions and plane guard duties for U.S. aircraft carriers in the Gulf of Tonkin. In February 1968, Harry joined the San Diego-based, forward-deployed USS Page County (LST-1076) as executive officer and navigator, conducting various support missions in Vietnam including offshore "mothership" duties for Swift class off-shore patrol boats. The ship was heavily engaged in I Corps re-supply runs during the 1968 North Vietnamese Tet offensive. He was awarded his first Navy Achievement Medal for navigation skills in maneuvering a 327-foot-long vessel in uncharted river and estuarine waters. Returning stateside, he spent four months at the Naval Inshore Operations Training Center at Mare Island, California.

In February 1970 he assumed command of River Division Five Fifty Four at Song Ong Doc, bordering the U-Minh forest in the IV Corps area of South Vietnam. Harry led 94 combat patrols in rivers and canals, coming under direct hostile fire. He was awarded the Silver Star and Bronze Star for gallantry and heroism during these actions. Command of River Division Five Nine Four began in August 1970 during operation Giant Slingshot on the Vam Co Ta and Vam Co Dong rivers. He was awarded the Navy Commendation Medal and the Vietnamese Staff Service Medal for river escort duties during the final re-supply of Phnom Phenh, Cambodia. Harry was medevaced out of Vietnam to the Philadelphia Naval Hospital. He wears the Vietnam Service Medal with seven campaign stars.

In February 1971 Harry was assigned to the staff, Commander-in-Chief, U.S. Pacific Fleet, Ocean Surveillance Information Center. In a first exposure to Naval Intelligence, he was awarded a second Navy Achievement Medal for duties as assistant Soviet Naval analyst and became an intelligence sub-specialist. In July 1974, he joined the USS Lucet (DD-38) in Mayport, Florida as weapons officer and deployed to the Mediterranean Sea several times. He received a third Navy Achievement Medal for supervising the deep water salvage of a crashed SH-3 helicopter with live ordinance aboard.

More medals

Harry reported to the Naval Ocean Surveillance Information Center in April 1976 as a Soviet maritime analyst. He became a full-time intelligence specialist in August 1978, and in September 1979 was assigned as an intelligence assistant to Chief of Naval Operations, Command and Control Planning and Program Division. Next duty was at the Naval Intelligence

Support Center between May 1981 and August 1983, as officer-in-charge of the Naval Foreign Material Facility, Chesapeake Beach, Maryland. He was awarded three Meritorious Service medals for the development of innovative fleet support procedures; helping write the Ocean Surveillance Master Plan; and establishing a comprehensive reverse engineering capability against foreign naval threat hardware.

From August 1983 to February 1990, Harry was involved with numerous special projects under the Chief of Naval Operations and the Commander, Naval Intelligence command. For efforts leading to new intelligence collection techniques, to acquire foreign threat hardware and actual hands-on collection, he was awarded the Legion of Merit medal.

Capt. Price reported to the National Security Agency in February 1990. For his efforts in security, communications and human intelligence, he received the Defense Superior Meritorious Service Medal in September 1983.

The captain's awards also include:

* Combat Action ribbon
* Presidential Unit citation
* Navy Unit commendation
* Meritorious Unit commendation with Bronze Star
* National Defense Service Medal with Bronze Star
* Sea Service Deployment ribbon
* Expert Rifle Medal
* Republic of Vietnam Gallantry Cross Unit citation
* Republic of Vietnam Civil Actions Unit citation
* Republic of Vietnam Campaign Medal
* U.S. Distinguished Service Medal

Harry served in the Navy for 31 years and retired in 1996 with the rank of captain (O-6).

In his own words

After retirement, I designed and built wireless video systems from 1996 for about four years. The systems allow police to stake out and place a camera, then control it remotely and have its video transmitted back to headquarters.

I built the equipment in conjunction with a fellow in the United Kingdom. I did sales, design, marketing. I had a background in electronics. The company was L M W Electronics, in the UK. I met my UK associate—Chris Smith—while in the Navy. He asked me if I would like to help introduce his product into the U.S. I did and it became very successful. I turned it over to someone who could do full-time marketing. I had set up an office in my home in Reading, Pennsylvania but the U.S. marketing got to be too much for one person to deal with, so eventually I hired a full-time person to handle the operation and I was able to retire.

In the mid- to late-1980s I began to develop breathing and related pulmonary problems. The doctors traced it back to a service-related ailment, Agent Orange. I remember being exposed to Agent Orange in the canals and waterways in Vietnam. It was so thick it used to run off my hat. The dioxins were very intense. I also was on board ships that burned at sea and might have inhaled some of the charred residue and fumes.

Q & A

Arnold: When did these health problems occur?

Harry: They were building, and really didn't start to manifest themselves until the late 1980s. When I retired, it was a concern. It really got bad about 2000.

Arnold: Did you see a VA doctor?

Harry: Yes, a VA doctor and a private doctor.

Arnold: Did the government grant you health benefits?

Harry: Yes. I have 100 percent disability. I go to the Naval Hospital in Beaufort and the VA clinic, both in South Carolina. Plus I have Medicare. I see a civilian pulmonologist primarily, and the VA doctor once a year because I have other ailments such as Post Traumatic Stress Disorder.

This is something that I realize will not get any better but what I have to do is keep myself busy mentally and physically to the extent that I can. My oxygen lady says that she has never seen anybody like me—always doing something. I still do electronics and am a ham radio operator.

Author's note: PTSD is an emotional illness that develops as a result of terribly frightening, life-threatening or otherwise highly unsafe experiences. Many who fought in Vietnam who had symptoms of what is now called PTSD were assessed as having "Post-Vietnam Syndrome."

> *Agent Orange is the code name for an herbicide and defoliant used by the U.S. military in its Herbicidal Warfare program during the Vietnam War, when an estimated 21,136,000 gallons of Agent Orange were sprayed across South Vietnam. Some 4.8 million Vietnamese people alone were exposed to Agent Orange, resulting in 400,000 deaths and disabilities, and 500,000 children born with birth defects. From 1961 to 1971, Agent Orange was by far the most widely used of the so-called "rainbow herbicides" employed in the Herbicidal Warfare program.*

Sun City—and keeping active

I met Mary Margaret Wells, my second wife, in Washington, D.C. We wed in 1990, and liked to vacation in our RV, often driving down to Hilton Head, South Carolina, where her father lived. I was fascinated with the area. On one of our trips down here we visited Sun City. At the time we were living in Reading, Pennsylvania, and my pulmonary ailment was becoming more of a problem. The cold weather in the north and the snow was not the best environment for my health. I couldn't use the snow blower, with a two-cycle engine, anymore because when I breathed in the fumes, it brought me to my knees. As I result we sold our home in Pennsylvania and moved to Sun City in 2005. (Harry has two daughters, Alicyn Claire and Jennifer Lee, by his first marriage, and is stepfather to John Charles Powers and Wendy Elizabeth Powers.)

Recently I placed a classified ad in an amateur radio magazine to sell a ham radio receiver. A guy from Florida responded. He said he was handicapped and I said the receiver was too valuable to ship. He agreed to drive up from Orlando with the help of a friend. During his visit he had to have oxygen—but less oxygen than I used. What he had done was to "hang it up" and become a "couch potato." He couldn't go anywhere unless someone drove him. Basically he had given up!

That left an impression on me. I am not about to do that. I don't really mix with people much but there is a reason for that. If I get a cold, it's like someone getting the flu. My immune system is compromised. I try to avoid crowds. I do a lot of reading and I often go out to my trailer and work on my equipment. That's basically how I keep myself busy. The primary thing is—I keep busy!

Impressions of Navy service

When I think about your question, I think about a very good friend of mine whose son just graduated from the Naval Academy (May 2009). I plan on writing him a letter and in the letter I intend to include things that are important to be cognizant of as a Navy officer. What has the Navy given me? Focus and tenacity! A stick-to-it attitude! When others say "It can't be done" or "It's too hard" or "We need more people," I like the challenge to take on any task and show that it can be done. When I write the letter, I'll ask myself what are the points I want to make: Initiative; let's not stand around; let's get it done! And finally, loyalty! Loyalty to the people who work for you! One cannot accomplish any of the above without their help.

Harry at home in Sun City, 2009

Jim Quirk

Jim Quirk

A son of Irish immigrants, Jim Quirk was born on October 26, 1941 in Boston and grew up in its Charlestown neighborhood with four sisters and an older brother. His father died when Jim was eight; after graduating from St. Mary's Catholic School, he went to a missionary seminary for five years. He worked in Boston for two years as a file and shipping clerk, and then enlisted in the Navy in September 1962 in anticipation of being draft eligible. His brother John had joined the Army in 1948 and served in Korea and Vietnam, eventually retiring as a sergeant major.

In his own words

I guess I joined the Navy because as a kid my friends and I hung around the USS Constitution, which was berthed at the Charlestown Navy Yard. I lived just down the street from the Bunker Hill monument. These were our playgrounds before they came under the National Park Service. Enlist or be drafted, was my thinking in 1962. In fact, my mother mailed my draft card to me at my first duty station.

Boot camp, at Great Lakes, Illinois, was not that hard for me since I was used to taking orders from Mom, the Catholic nuns and the seminary priests. Maybe that is why my company commander, Yeoman 1st Class Bragg, made me the religion petty officer for Company 439. We learned how to march, how to fight fires on board ship, how to store all our clothes in a small locker or sea bag and how to make up our rack the Navy way. Plus we learned lots of nautical terms and practices as well as military decorum.

We had a lot of intelligent men in our ranks who didn't complete college before they were drafted. After a battery of tests, a training center classifier said my skills were more suited to administration and talked me into signing away the recruiter's "guarantee" for "Class A" Electrician School. He was probably right. So I was off to Quonset Point, Rhode Island as a Navy yeoman. I hitched many a ride back to Boston for weekends with family. I was skin and bones; to begin with, the weight I lost in boot camp wasn't just from the haircut. I remember feeling that my Navy dress blues with pea coat did not make me feel warm when I left from cold and windy Chicago O'Hare Airport. Mom thought I looked like a scarecrow.

My first hitch

After home leave, I began my first four-year Navy hitch at Quonset Point, earning my first petty officer rank, a red chevron below a perched white eagle. Then came orders to report to the pre-commissioning crew of a new guided missile destroyer being built in Bremerton, Washington. Another petty officer and I traveled across country to the West Coast. I reported first to San Diego for training and then to Bremerton, Washington. Commissioned in March 1964, the USS Richard E. Byrd (DDG-23) headed down the West Coast, stopping at Long Beach, California and Acapulco, Mexico before transiting the Panama Canal. Upon completing crew shakedown training at Guantanamo Bay, Cuba, the ship joined the Atlantic Fleet and set out on a five-month training cruise in the Mediterranean.

One day while sailing in the western Med, the Byrd was tested by a Soviet destroyer that threatened to ram us. We lowered our large bumpers and at the last minute, the Soviet destroyer made a 90-degree turn, bumping us before steaming away. Fortunately, our skipper, Cmdr. Walt Lessman, maintained his "cool" and the ship's course, thereby avoiding an international incident. My station on the bridge during general quarters gave me a front seat during the action. I was the "bridge talker" for Combat Information Center, relaying commands from the bridge during critical periods of ship maneuvering.

Next I received orders to the USS Boston (CAG-1), a heavy cruiser homeported in—where else?—Boston. But instead of an expected North Atlantic cruise, the Boston sailed to the Mediterranean. Both of those trips to the Mediterranean were great experiences. With a small ship you get to go to smaller ports that the larger ship can't. But with the larger ship, the port stay is longer so I got to travel to Rome and Venice by train.

Jim (on right) and his sister, Margie, on USS Boston, 1965

Life was never dull in the Navy, even while at sea. One night during night operations involving a fleet of ships, a commercial ship steamed through our task force, cut in front of the carrier and struck and damaged one of the plane elevators. A Navy ship was sent to escort the badly damaged freighter to port and the Boston high-lined the admiral to the carrier to conduct a board of inquiry. Given the many naval operations, we could always expect something out of the ordinary while on deployment.

Then, when the Boston was about to leave the Med and return to homeport, it was diverted to become the command ship of Task Force 65. CTF 65 was tasked with finding one of four H-bombs that were scattered over Palomares, Spain after a U.S. Air Force B-52 collided with a KC-135 while fueling. Three of the unexploded nuclear devices were found on land and the Navy found the fourth using the deep-sea explorer vessel ALVIN.

Jim (left) in photo lab of ship while anchored off the coast of Palomares, Spain, searching for the wreckage of bombs

Four more

I shipped over—re-enlisted—for another four years, receiving a $2,000 bonus and orders to Class B School at Bainbridge, Maryland. I invested all but $500 of the bonus in RCA, General Dynamics and Tri-Continental, a mutual fund. The last was a big winner and taught me the value of compound interest. While attending school in Bainbridge, I met my future wife, Cheryl Hartman, at the NCO club in Aberdeen. At the time, she was visiting home in nearby Havre de Grace—having moved to Boston to work. We wouldn't marry, though, until I returned from my overseas assignment.

As I looked at the list of assignments drawn by me and my classmates at Bainbridge, I had to find a map to locate Ras Tanura, Saudi Arabia. Several classmates were assigned to Vietnam, one to a riverine patrol. I remember getting off the plane in Dhahran, Saudi Arabia. It was a grand-looking airport but truly a foreign place to me. I don't recall seeing any women and the men wore long white gowns and colored cloths around their heads and walked arm-in-arm.

I was assigned to a small detachment a.k.a. INSMATPET, 50 miles up the road from Dhahran. We worked and lived in a gated community with other Americans and Europeans just across from the local village. Ras Tanura is the major refinery and oil shipment port of Saudi Arabia in the Arabian Gulf. (Iran prefers to call it the Persian Gulf.) The Navy unit consisted of six officers and two enlisted men. Our main office was on Bahrain Island; we maintained radio contact. In 1967, you had to fly to Bahrain, which is independent of Saudi Arabia; today there is a bridge connecting to the mainland.

Our unit inspected petroleum bought for the military for quality and quantity in both countries. Bahrain had different rules and you could drink at the local British club. Alcohol was banned in Saudi Arabia, but I learned how to run the home-made still to produce our own booze. I could write a book on just my experiences in Saudi Arabia. It was quite an education for a kid from Boston with only a high school education to that point.

Six-Day War lockdown

On June 5, 1967, we were loading a large ship with Navy special fuel when we were notified that a threat to blow the ship up was rumored. We immediately departed the ship and directed the ship's master to depart. As we headed toward the residential area, we saw a large crowd outside the gate. When we turned to enter the compound, the crowd began lobbing rocks and bottles when they saw the U.S. Navy truck. Thus began a lockdown as the Six-Day War raged. Elements of the kingdom's Royal Guard and the National Guard arrived on the seventh day and removed all suspected protestors from the nearby neighborhood and ARAMCO property. If the compound had been attacked, we had no weapons to defend ourselves.

My next duty station took me for admin duties at the office of Deputy Supreme Allied Commander, North Atlantic Treaty Organization in Norfolk, Virginia. I worked with the greatest officer I ever met. Adm. Marmaduke Gresham Bayne was a true gentleman and great leader. I also worked with Lt. Col. Lyman Hammond, a Ranger paratrooper, who was the executive assistant, and Senior Chief Ed White. The admiral wanted me to reenlist and recommended me for the warrant officer program, but I decided to go to college full time.

New challenges

Meanwhile, Cheryl and I got married in September 1968 and spent two great years in Norfolk before heading back to Boston and college in October 1970. After graduating from Boston University in 1974 with a major in journalism, I worked on several newspapers in Massachusetts, in Fitchburg, Cape Cod and New Bedford. I returned to the military reserve, first in the Massachusetts Army National Guard in 1978—which gave me the chance to travel to Friedberg, Germany for a REFORGER exercise pegged to a possible attack by Soviet forces. Then, with my good friend Ron Harrison, a former sailor, I found a billet in the Navy Reserve and transferred into a public affairs unit in Boston.

Jim and Cheryl on wedding day, September 21, 1968

As our family grew, I took a job with more regular hours at the U.S. Postal Service in 1984. Also, joining the Post Office allowed us to remain in Assonet, Massachusetts. After working at the local post office in Middleboro for eight years, I applied for a communications job at postal headquarters in Washington, D.C. and was selected in 1992. I was able to transfer from my Navy Reserve unit in Boston to a unit at the Pentagon. When they instituted "high year tenure," which forced senior enlisted to retire, it opened up promotions and I made chief the first time I submitted my record to the chief's board. Being initiated into the ranks of the Navy's chief petty officers has been one of the highlights of my life. Since our four daughters were growing up fast, I retired from military service in 1996, having reached 23 years and eight months' service.

Impressions of service

This son of poor immigrants was blessed with a lot of good sense and made a great decision to serve in the United States Naval Service. The Navy allowed me to mature in a disciplined environment and to travel and learn about the world and meet some truly wonderful people both in and outside the service. Every day I think about our military and would gladly join if called again to serve. I cry at certain songs and moments reflecting on our country and our military. My heart beats red, white and blue.

On to Sun City

Cheryl and I checked out Sun City in South Carolina after hearing about it from a former colleague. We toured Florida and North Carolina but felt this area was less crowded and that Sun City offered lots of activities. Plus it was close to the beach, a prerequisite to attract our four daughters to visit. And it was just an eight-hour trip to where our girls were living in Northern Virginia. So I retired in February 2006 and we moved to Sun City in the spring of 2006.

Jim and Cheryl at home

Gwyneth Schultz Saunders

Gwyneth Saunders

Gwyneth was born on October 15, 1952, in Nanticoke, Pennsylvania. Three months later, her father accepted a position as preacher at St. John's Episcopal Church in Salem, New Jersey. After graduating from Salem High School in 1970, Gwyn worked as a counselor at a summer camp and that fall enrolled in Wilmington College, in Ohio. She missed the dean's list the first semester and in the second, discovering boys and partying, made academic probation. Gwyneth's parents decided that she should come home.

Gwyn had wanted to join the Navy since the 6th grade. She and her classmates watched President John F. Kennedy's funeral procession on TV, after his assassination, and it made an everlasting patriotic impression on her. In high school she had good grades, but struggled with algebra, and chose a college—her parents insisted that she obtain a degree—that didn't require algebra to graduate. Returning after her second semester, she asked her parents again, "Now can I join the Navy?" They finally granted her wish. Gwyn was envious of a male classmate who was in the Naval Academy, but at that time women were not accepted.

In her own words

I enlisted in the Navy at the recruiting station in Bridgeton, New Jersey and was ordered to report to Bainbridge, Maryland for boot camp, one of the last recruiting classes in Bainbridge because they were moving everything down to Pensacola, Florida. In January 1972 I was assigned to Recruit Training Command Women (RTCW) for 10 weeks of training. After completing several tests I was qualified to do just about anything, and picked photography as my first choice and journalism second. I had some advanced English in high school and college and the Navy gave me preference over others—in fact there were only two WAVES (Women Accepted for Volunteer Emergency Service) in my 10-week journalism class at Fort Benjamin Harrison, Indianapolis.

It was a joint services school—all branches of the military attended. There were two WAVES, two women Marines, three WACs and three WAFs and the rest were guys. The base was nicknamed "Uncle Ben's Rest Home"—many retirement ceremonies took place there. In class we had to type 30 words a minute, but I had never touched a typewriter. So there I worked at my desk with an old-fashioned manual Royal typewriter. I have since wrecked a few computer keyboards, transitioning from manual typewriters, because I pounded so hard on the sensitive keyboards. In addition to journalism classes, we had classes in photography, broadcasting and newspaper layout. Four weeks in, students selected either journalism or broadcasting as a career path. I opted for writing and ended up on the newspaper side. I loved it! I spent the next 26 years doing it in the Navy!

My first duty station after journalism school was Commandant First Naval District, in a big brick building at 495 Summer Street in Boston. There were no barracks or quarters; I found a studio apartment. My rank was journalist 3rd class petty officer (E-4/one chevron). Because I was near the top of the class the Navy offered me accelerated advancement if I extended my enlistment, originally for four years. I thought, "What's two more years?"

Guantanamo Bay

In 1973 I went to my next assignment, at Naval Station Guantanamo Bay, Cuba, where I started out in the TV studio as a broadcaster. I took my job very seriously but some of my senior colleagues thought it would be fun to make the on-air, on-camera people laugh. I didn't take that very well, and resented their attempt to make me look unprofessional on-air. They fired me from broadcasting and transferred me to the newspaper—which at the end of the day was much better for me. It seems funny and rather silly looking back at it now because there were times when I did have fun on- and off-camera. But when you are very young and new at a job you want to be serious and professional. It was one of the few times I ever took my rating—or specialty—so seriously. I was always serious about the military side, but my profession was and is too much fun. I'm rarely serious about much in my life. Life's too short.

I ended up on the newspaper with my "hunt-and-peck" typing skills, learned to type faster and eventually became editor. Soon I could figure out—to the period—how much copy would fill a specific amount of space in our newspaper. I had two junior WAVES working for me, and enjoyed the job; it was challenging and fulfilling. My only early requirement for people who worked for me in the Navy was: *"I don't care what you do, as long as you do your job well. I don't care when you do it; I don't care how you do it—meet the deadline and meet the specifications and you're fine by me."*

As I gained more experience as a supervisor, I came to care very much what my people did on liberty because sometimes their behavior endangered themselves and others. For the most part, though, do your job, represent the Navy well and life is good for everyone.

My tour at Guantanamo Bay was for one year. Though it was isolated duty I loved it. I enjoyed watching huge land crabs walk across the roads and if you ran over them you knew you were going to have new tires. We ate lots of langosta—spiny lobsters—which were plentiful as a native dish.

Next stop was in New London, Connecticut, where I worked on the newspaper attached to the Naval Submarine Base Public Affairs Office from 1975 to 1976. In the middle of a six-year commitment, my rank was 2nd class petty officer. I also served as media escort on a few submarines (such as the Daniel Webster, SSBN-626) as they went out into the Thames River. My next assignment was at Naval Recruiting District, Milwaukee, Wisconsin in 1977.

Q & A

Arnold: At what point did you decide to make the Navy a 20-year commitment?

Gwyneth: In boot camp. I signed for 20 when I walked into the gate, but they didn't let me. It turns out that was a good thing. Over the drill hall in Bainbridge was a sign that read, *"Through these portals pass the women of the greatest Navy in the world."* I wanted that and I wanted it for as long as I could breathe. There was never any question that I was going to go for 20.

Arnold: What were some of your other assignments?

Gwyneth: From Milwaukee I went to Commander Fleet Activities Yokosuka, Japan, from 1979 to 1981. Then I received a new set of orders to NATO Headquarters at Supreme Allied Commander Atlantic (SACLANT) in Norfolk, Virginia, where I was promoted to chief petty officer (E-7/three chevrons and a rocker), in 1983.

Most journalists, I found, came out of other career paths. I started and finished in journalism. My career covered broadcasting, print journalism and public affairs. Each duty station had a TV/radio studio, newspaper or a public affairs office. Some had everything. The Milwaukee assignment was mostly public relations, promoting the Navy's image to the media.

Gwyneth at Naval Recruiting District, Milwaukee, 1978

I was sent to Souda Bay, Crete, Greece (a one-year isolated tour) in the eastern Mediterranean. I loved it! We had an eight-room chief's barracks there. There were 12 of us and four lived out "in town." I was the only female CPO there and the senior female for most of the tour. From Greece, I went to Washington, D.C., to Commander Naval District Washington at the Washington Navy Yard, where I served from 1986 to 1991—a 4 ½-year tour—in the public affairs office promoting such programs as the Navy Summer Pageant while being editor of the base paper, which served the entire National Capitol Region. My next assignment was at Commander Naval Support Force Antarctica at the Seabee base in Port Hueneme, California. Every year, for three years, we deployed to Antarctica to McMurdo Station for a period of three to four months.

Author's note: McMurdo Station is a U.S. research center located on the southern tip of Ross Island on the shore of McMurdo Sound, 2,200 miles due south of New Zealand. It is operated through the United States Antarctic Program, a branch of the National Science Foundation. The station is the largest community in Antarctica, capable of supporting up to 1,258 residents, and serves as America's Antarctic science facility, and the logistics base for half the continent. All personnel and cargo going to or coming from Amundsen-Scott South Pole Station first pass through McMurdo.

Gwyneth (left) at Ross Island, Antarctica

We usually flew by way of Hawaii, ending up in Christ Church, New Zealand. It was an absolute great assignment! After I entered the Navy, I read an article in our *All Hands* magazine about Antarctica. It sounded fascinating, but there were no journalists there. It was all Seabees. Ten years later they had journalists and other ratings but it was all men. I never gave it another thought.

Getting to Antarctica

The Navy assigns each person to their duty stations through a detailer. He/she or someone in that "seat" helps and counsels you throughout your career. They try to get you the assignments you want and at the same time—they try to fill a spot where the Navy needs personnel. Detailers are hard to reach. Their phones are always busy, even if they're not in their offices. I had a power lunch with a good friend of mine whom I call my career counselor. We came to the conclusion that I would either be going to get a "hot assignment" or I was going to retire—at the time I had served 20 years in the Navy. I called my detailer, Master Chief Jimmy Bell, who happened to be in his office and answered the phone, and he said, "Chief Schultz (my maiden name), I was just thinking of you. I have just the set of orders for you—Naval Support Force Antarctica, Port Hueneme, California."

I nearly fell out of my chair. I said, "You are out of your mind! Hold on; let me speak to my boss, (Lt. Cmdr.) Rob Donovan." I said, "Boss, he wants me to go to Antarctica! What do you think?" He said, "Take it!" I told my detailer, "I'll take it!" He replied, "You're in!" "Okay!" I said, and hung up. I couldn't believe what I had just done. I'd waited my entire career for this set of orders, forgotten I wanted them and now I was going to get them. I walked around for the next 10 months and people would say to me, "Why do you have a grin on your face? You're going to Antarctica. It's cold there." And I told them, "Yeah, but I always wanted to go!"

In the meantime my dad died that Christmas. The day of his funeral his best friend came down from Pennsylvania and we were sitting in the kitchen in my family's home in New Jersey. He said, "Your dad was real proud of you. He was really impressed that you got this set of orders. He said to me, 'But I wish that girl would settle down.'" My parents were proud of me—Dad was a hawk and I was Daddy's girl so I grew up a hawk, too. That's also why the military appealed to me.

I did my three years in Antarctica and in the second year I earned the Aviation Warfare Medal, which really means that I know a little more about Naval aviation than the average "squid"—a mildly pejorative term for a sailor in the Navy. I also made senior chief while there. When the news of my promotion came down, most of the command knew about it about 10 minutes before I did; that was from a cross-country phone call from a good friend. I called my detailer to tell him I now had to think about the next set of orders and he said, "I never 'make' anyone get promoted, but I offered you those orders after others had turned them down. I knew you'd take them and I knew you'd get promoted!"

My next assignment after Antarctica was a three-year tour at the Naval Media Center in Anacostia, Washington, D.C. Prior to reporting to this assignment I was selected to attend a 10-week senior enlisted program in Newport, Rhode Island, where 69 over-achieving senior chief petty officers lived, ate, slept and studied in the same building. It was 10 very difficult weeks of studies in current affairs, public speaking, naval correspondence, evaluations and leadership. It was one of my greatest learning experiences in the Navy. I was fortunate to be among people who were eager and motivated as I was to learn and to keep up with the new methods and technologies in their chosen career.

One of the first things a lot of military people do when they meet others in uniform is to look at whatever ribbons are pinned over their heart. I saw a wide array of senior chiefs who achieved impressive credentials as they advanced in rank and status. I was impressed to be in the same company with them. It's a little humbling when you think that there were 69 of us in this building and I was part of the best and the brightest. After the course I arrived at the Navy Broadcasting facility and what turned out to be my last tour.

Impressions of service

As a job, like every other job, there are moments when you are going to hate it, but like my father told me: "*If all you do is get through boot camp, it will be so much better for you to get out in the world, and see and meet people who are different from you with different backgrounds and culture.*" I spent 26 years in the Navy not because I hated it. I spent 26 years because I loved it. It was the camaraderie of the people I worked with that made it more than just a paycheck. It was adventure! I saw things and met fascinating people—I met the first Navy female admiral, Rear Adm. Alene B. Duerk, who was the head of the Navy Nurse Corps. I met Adm. Elmo Zumwalt.

My job involved meeting interesting people and writing about them in our publications. At the same time, I tried to convey the best image as an "ambassador" for the Navy and to let the people in the Navy know how policies would affect them.

Life after the Navy

I retired in 1998, at the Navy Broadcasting facility where I was the detachment liaison for 300-plus broadcasters around the world. I spent my last nine months at the Pentagon in the Navy's Chief of the Information Office as bureau chief of the Navy Wire Service. I retired with the rank of senior chief petty officer, and my pension, medical and other retiree benefits.

I lived in Waldorf, Maryland the last three years of my Navy career. While exploring job possibilities, one day, en route to a Christmas party, I walked into a newspaper in Upper Marlboro in Prince Georges County to drop off my resume. I certainly was not dressed in any of the $200 interview ensembles I had hanging in my closet. When I handed the resume to the receptionist at the desk, she asked me, "Do you want to talk to him? He's in." Okay, I said—and there I was in a Christmas sweatshirt, green trousers and a ball cap. I thought sarcastically, "This is going to make a great impression!" Twenty minutes later I walked out and the next Monday morning I had the job. I spent the next 10 years working as a reporter and editor for the same company, the last six years as the editor of a weekly entertainment section called *Southern Maryland Weekend,* which appeared in three local county papers.

I met Tony Saunders in 1984 at NATO headquarters in Norfolk. He was in the Royal Navy and served as a public affairs officer while I was the enlisted chief in charge of our Public Affairs Office. Romance was in the air but navies, duties and distance kept intervening. For the next 18 years we kept in contact and finally managed to live on the same ocean, albeit on opposite sides. We finally got serious and married in 2002.

Five years ago we vacationed in Hilton Head and last year we decided to look for a home in the Lowcountry. We liked the area but we knew that Hilton Head was beyond our budget. We liked golf, and we liked the warm weather. We looked at Sun City and while there on one occasion, walked into a real estate office to inquire about a resale future home. We wanted to downsize from the home we were living in Waldorf and were eager to move away from the pressure of living near D.C. We came down in September 2007 and spent the day looking at houses. We found a particularly nice home with the size and design that suited our needs. We moved in on May 15, 2008.

I belong to Sunscribers, the community theatre, the chorus, the Vets Association and attend All Saints Episcopal Church, singing in the choir. I also enjoy golf and am a member of the Women's Nine-Hole Golf Club. I'm having a great time here and I think the people are wonderful and the opportunities are abundant to keep busy with enjoyable activities.

Gwyneth at home in Sun City, 2009

Richard Tesman

Richard Tesman

Dick was born on November 11, 1944 in Newburgh, New York. His father was a farmer and a machinist and did a couple of tours in the Merchant Marine, sailing down to Valparaiso, Chile and through the Panama Canal. Dick graduated from Cornwall High School in 1962 and went right into New York State Maritime College, a four-year school located at historic Fort Schuyler in Throgs Neck, New York.

New York State Maritime College sign

In his own words

When I attended the college it was a total military school. Students would have three options upon graduating: (1) an ensign's commission in the Navy, (2) a degree (mine happened to be in meteorology and oceanography) or (3) a 3rd mate's license as a Merchant Marine. Unlike the United States Marine Military Academy at Kings Point, Long Island, students didn't necessarily have a commitment to serve in the military. We could go into the Navy or as I did, sail in the Merchant Marines.

I graduated in 1966 and received a commission as an ensign and was later promoted to a lieutenant. My license in the Merchant Marine was a 3rd mate's license and I sailed oceans for a while and then I was assigned coastwise as a captain of a tanker in New York Harbor and Connecticut.

I sailed with the Military Sea Transportation Service out of Brooklyn, New York.

(The Military Sea Transportation Service [MSTS] was formed in 1949 "to provide, under one authority, control, operation and administration of ocean transportation . . . for all agencies or departments of the National Military Establishment." Some 320 ships were transferred to the new command from the old Navy Transportation Service and the U.S. Army. The organization's name was changed to Military Sealift Command [MSC] in 1970.)

On my first trip in 1966, we picked up the ship in the Brooklyn Navy Yard dry dock and went up to Thule, Greenland with PX supplies. That is where I got my "Order of the Top of the World" awarded to seamen who traverse the Arctic Circle. We only sailed during the summer because of the ice flow during the winter. My roommate from college and I sailed as 3rd mates. I would stand an 8 to 12 watch and he would stand a 12 to 4. Once we got above the Arctic Circle, we met up with an icebreaker because even in June you had to go in behind an icebreaker. That was quite an experience! We locked in a set speed behind the icebreaker, which would be a half mile in front of us, and as long as it was hitting normal ice it was fine. However, when it hit heavy ice the icebreaker had to slow down, back down and ram the iceberg again to break it up. It became nerve-racking, adjusting our speed frequently to maintain the correct distance behind the breaker.

As we sailed up the Arctic Circle the view was spectacular. We saw icebergs of all sizes. Some the size of a house didn't show on radar and others the size of a car would show up on radar because they had some earth and metal in them.

Q & A

Arnold: So basically you carried supplies and cargo but no passengers?
Dick: No passengers.
Arnold: How many in a crew?
Dick: We had about 30.
Arnold: How were your sleeping quarters?
Dick: We each had a cabin (we were officers).
Arnold: And the food?
Dick: The food was great!
Arnold: You didn't carry armament, did you?
Dick: No. I made several trips up to Goose Bay, Labrador that summer. I sailed there for about six or eight months.

Arnold: What was your commitment of service?

Dick: In the Merchant Marine there is really no commitment like other branches of the service. You sign on for the duration of the voyage. You are not locked into any long-term military commitment. Actually it's just like a normal job except you are making a commitment to go. When you return home and complete a voyage you have the option to sign on to that ship again or are free to wait for another voyage with a different ship. But in reality, if most guys like the crew they are working with and they like the destination of their next voyage, they will sign on again.

Arnold: Where else did you sail in the Merchant Marine?

Dick: After my MSTS ocean voyages I worked coastwise, on a tanker that ran in New York Harbor and up into Connecticut and out onto Long Island and down into New Jersey.

Arnold: What did you carry on the tanker?

Dick: We carried jet fuel, car gas and solvents. We sailed into Jamaica Bay. We went to the airports and did some ship refueling.

Retirement

I sailed from June 1966 until April 1969. My rank was a lieutenant in the Navy Reserve and 3rd mate as captain of a coastwise tanker. I was living in Staten Island, New York at that time. But during my career we lived in many areas of the country.

I married Diana Morse, of Highland, New York while I was serving in the Merchant Marine, where you made decent money. I had college debts and we were just getting started in married life. Diana was able to put up with the long hours and days of separation despite being at home with our first child because the money was good. What made me stop sailing was the anticipation of expecting our second child and I wanted to use my degree as opposed to sailing around the world for the rest of my life.

After leaving the Merchant Marine, I worked for General Electric in one of their training programs and remained with GE for 31 years. It came to be my primary job throughout my career. When I retired my job title was service manager for one of the GE Transportation Services Divisions for North and South America.

Sun City—and final impressions

Because we had lived all over the country, we knew where we didn't want to be. We had been coming down to Hilton Head with time-shares for a number of years. We liked this area and found it an ideal place to retire. We moved to Sun City in April 2003.

Going to Fort Schuyler and being in the Merchant Marine basically made my life. It gave me the educational start and the educational discipline that I needed as a young guy. It gave our family a financial boost to start our life.

Richard Tesman, 2009

Arnold Rosen in Korea, 1953

Arnold Rosen retired in 1995 as a professor emeritus at Nassau Community College in Garden City, New York. He received a BS degree in business administration from Ohio State University and an MS degree in business education from Hunter College. Arnold is the author of numerous journal articles on office automation and computer systems, 20 college textbooks, *Sea Gate Remembered* and *Keeping Memories Alive: Our Aging Veterans Tell Their Story.*

He served in the United States Air Force during the Korean War, attached to the 75th Air Depot Wing, Chinhae, Korea and the 543rd Ammo Supply Squadron, Ulsan, Korea. He lives in Sun City—Hilton Head, South Carolina.

Arnold Rosen in Sun City, 2009

Edwards Brothers Malloy
Thorofare, NJ USA
June 27, 2013